The Art
of Public Prayer

NOT FOR CLERGY ONLY

Lawrence A. Hoffman

THE PASTORAL PRESS
Washington, D.C.

Library of Congress Cataloging-in-Publication Data

Hoffman, Lawrence A., 1942-
　　The art of public prayer : not for clergy only / Lawrence A.
　　Hoffman.
　　　　p.　　cm.
　　Bibliography: p.
　　ISBN 0-912405-55-4 : $19.95
　　1. United States—Religious life and customs. 2. Public worship.
　　3. Public worship—Judaism.　I. Title.
　　BL2525.H64　1989
　　291.3'8—dc19　　　　　　　　　　　　　　　　　　　88-37116
　　　　　　　　　　　　　　　　　　　　　　　　　　　　CIP

ISBN 0-912405-55-4

The Pastoral Press
225 Sheridan Street, NW
Washington, DC 20011
(202) 723-1254

The Pastoral Press is the publications division of the National
Association of Pastoral Musicians, a membership organization of
musicians and clergy dedicated to fostering the art of musical
liturgy.

Printed in the United States of America.

For Shira and Daniel

who discovered

dialogue

a long time ago

Contents

Introduction

I can see it now as plainly as I saw it thirty years ago, every day I was at Banaras, for two years. Young and old go down to the water's edge at dawn and stand there, each alone in his inner self, but all together as one greater Self. One by one, as they feel ready, they walk out into the water until they stand waist-deep. Some stand there for half an hour. It is their time of *mantra*. Then as the sun rises above the green fields on the far side of the Ganga, its first rays reaching across and touching with warmth the ancient palaces and temples of Banaras, thousands of pairs of hands, cupped together like begging bowls, raise the water to the sky, and thousands of voices recite the sacred *gayatri mantra* so silently, you feel it rather than hear it. As they let the water trickle back into the holy river the sun catches it, and a million sunlit drops add their beauty to the beauty of the sound of the temple bells and the voices of devotees singing *kirtan* all in one single greeting to another day of life. . . . Is that ecstasy enough at the beginning of every day of youth, every day of adulthood, and every day of old age? And what might we have been if we had been taught such an art as this?

Colin M. Turnbull,
The Human Cycle

JUST PICTURE THE EARLY MORNING GATHERING at the river, but with ourselves among the loyal thousands gathered there. Would any of us ever presume to doubt the efficacy of the rite? Who wouldn't gladly drop a hundred years of socialized sophistication in exchange for simpler times, in order to stand by a sacred stream with the meaning of life shining through a million sacred droplets glittering in the morning sun?

Or, if you don't like Turnbull's example—it is a rather romanticized account, after all—choose from the thousands of others that anthropologists have collected for over a century and more of painstaking research. The Banaras bathing sight is certainly not alone in the annals of field literature purporting to describe successful ritual in religions that really impress their adherents with the unmistakable conviction that worship matters.

By contrast, the worship we Jews and Christians know best in our North American sanctuaries seems like a pale imitation of the real thing. Not too long ago Catholics still practiced the preconciliar liturgical forms that seemed convincingly authentic enough; even Reform Jews, who dissociated themselves from western European "medievalism" over a century ago, at least prayed in "worshipful" King James English, making stylized sentences in equally stylized ways that could never be confused with anything but religious pomp and ceremony. But even as we kept the forms, it became clear to us that the forms were all we had, unless, of course, you belonged to the few bastions of traditionalism (or of reclaimed traditionalism) that held out valiantly against the dampening effects of modernity on the life of the spirit.

This is a book for people who know the damp chill of disbelief on the efficacy of old forms, who find they cannot go home again to stand at whatever the particular Banaras of their youth happened to be, but who want still to be able to pray. It is for Jews and Christians, Protestants and Catholics, for all who find themselves by habit or by inclination in church or synagogue on holy days at least, and who wonder afterwards, given the utter failure of the proceedings to speak convincingly to their lives, why they bothered.

If you are happily engaged in daily, or even weekly, communal worship, you are among the blessed few in this land, where the masses get up at the crack of dawn only to jog, never to pray. The officially "churched" and those who claim adherence to synagogues make up only a small minority of our citizens. Only a minority of that minority actually live religious lives according to the dictates of the faith they espouse, and not all of those people go regularly to Sabbath prayer. This book differs from some others on the subject, in that it does not blame them. Indeed, it tries not to blame anyone. It admits from the outset that most religious ritual in modern-day America is banal, poorly conceived, barely understood (even by those who direct it), and bordering on irrelevancy. This judgment will come as no surprise to most Americans and Canadians who stay away from regular worship in droves. It may shock the regulars—those who attend with commendable regularity—and even some of the professionals who are there out of necessity, habit, and love, but whose very calling can easily blind them to the true state of affairs. Still I suspect that even they know the truth. Surely they must wonder why the closest thing we have to the mass ritual of the Banaras bathing is the Super Bowl or (locally) high school homecoming weekend. I have been to clergy conventions where the clergy gathered there failed to attend their own worship! And I, like every reader of this book, have found myself on too many occasions in dutiful attendance at worship services where my predominant thought was how slowly the time ticked by, as the proceedings threatened never to come to a merciful conclusion.

The book is divided into two parts, both being dedicated to the self-evident (I think) proposition that regardless of the theological finesse that may once have said otherwise, in our time and place prayer takes place only if the various would-be worshipers gathered together actually pray; prayer for us is a personal act; nobody prays "for us." Both Christianity and Judaism have known the opposite—the phenomenon of liturgical expression by the elite on behalf of the many: the monastic mass, for example, on the Christian side, and the *sheliakh tsibbur* or prayer leader known as the "agent of the congregation" in the Jewish camp. But with our modernized forms of the last several decades have come equally modernized conceptions of prayer, among which is the nearly universally accepted perspective that emphasizes prayer as belonging to the people who assemble for worship. Without consulting with one another, Protestants, Catholics, and Jews have revised their liturgies to involve the masses, who are expected to sing, chant, speak, and even direct and organize their own liturgies, rather than allow a privileged clerical class to do so on their behalf. So above all, I am addressing the challenge to involve people in their own worship, to "own it" as the popular saying goes—and hence the title, *The Art of Public Prayer: Not for Clergy Only*.

I spend the first part of the book describing the sorry state of worship that I find all around us, and asking why that is so. Lots of answers come to mind, and I do not include them all. I try to demonstrate, however, that ritual in general is alive and well in modern life; that only religious ritual is in trouble. I then carefully avoid blaming anyone for that sorry fact. My position is generally culled from a systems approach to phenomena, wherein the best way to right a wrong is to see it as arising from a badly functioning system and to summon all the members of the system to work together to achieve change. Unproductive workers on an assembly line may be responding to anything from poor lighting to distant marketing conditions so that attempts to increase productivity will usefully involve careful study of the whole industry, not just the obvious sign of trouble, the workers themselves. Mentally ill children may require family counseling, not just personal psychotherapy. Yelling at people to drive safer, eat healthier, work harder, dress neater, or act fairer doesn't usually get us as far as analyzing the whole context in which the so-called unhealthy behavior emerges. Similarly, then, rather than yelling at worshipers to pray harder, I have preferred analyzing the system we call worship in modern America, asking why it malfunctions as it does.

The first five chapters, then, outline the system as we know it. By and large, religious ritual does not work for us. Why not? What is a useful way of becoming self-conscious of our own worship patterns, so that we can improve them? How do symbols function in prayer? What elementary understanding of communications do we need if we are to alter hardened worship patterns that stand in the way of spirituality? Above all, in the absence of easy answers that fit every particular case, how can any given church or synagogue face up to its own worship problems without the fear that any member of the analysis team will be blamed for what is actually a problem that goes well beyond the negative input of any single contributor?

In the second half of the book I turn to the general notion that worship is its own art form. The "worship care teams" doing intensive self-analysis are asked to consider how their worship fulfills certain artistic demands, not those that only a Picasso or a Bach could master, but elementary understandings that we all use to fashion satisfying life experiences. My remarks here are addressed primarily to those charged with directing worship, the people who have to make decisions on music, text, or space, for example, but who have no guidelines for deciding. How should we redesign our worship spaces, if we have a chance to do so? How can we use the spaces we have to our best advantage? What is the role of music in modern prayer? Is there such a thing as "sacred music," and how do we recognize it if it does exist? Should people believe in the literal truth of prayers, or does worship language have other nonliteral functions that justify it and help us select good prayers from bad ones?

Against the truisms of orthodox analysis, I believe that theology arises out of successful prayer; it does not precede it. In general I favor liturgical reforms; I do not look wistfully back at halcyon days of yesteryear with romantic pleas for the restoration of the old-time religion. I note also that I have assembled here exactly what the title suggests: a manual, not a scholarly treatment complete with footnotes. The appendix cites my sources so as to facilitate further study among masters who have instructed me. This book should make easy reading for those as-yet-imaginary worship care committees that I see functioning in every church and synagogue intent on finding out why they persist in self-defeating ritual that fails, rather than bettering their spiritual state. The descriptions of dysfunctional worship in Part One ought to evoke smiles (and tears) of recognition, since they are composite cases drawn from the experience of Everyman and Everywoman. The Interlude—as I have entitled Chapter Six—justifies a practical analysis of what makes worship work. Part Two explores the art of worship as the perspective that will yield the best result. My goal, then, is to put a practical manual in the hands of those who care for prayer, in the hope that they may better arrange communal worship for themselves and for others.

On the other hand, with every word I typed, I became more and more aware of the fact that my analysis does not do justice to many in North America whose worship comes very close to the Banaras bathing rite of India's faithful. I have in mind the Orthodox Jewish services I attended as a child, growing up in a small Jewish community in southern Ontario. For many years I attended Sabbath worship in a traditionalistic milieu where the same group of men—though never women—met to go through their traditional prayer text with anything but attention to the matters I cite as necessary. With the exception of the rabbi, they understood little, if anything, of a Hebrew text which they rattled through in breakneck speed from beginning to end; they read the Torah, but again, comprehended nothing of its tale, and by and large whiled away the time while the scroll was being read, in congregational cross-talk. They paid no heed whatever to the role of music, preferring as a matter of rote the old-time melodies chanted rather than sung, and poorly at that, by a self-proclaimed cantor with little vocal skill, who was joined here and there by a few straggling voices not necessarily in the same key. They had never heard of sacred space, and, in fact, in a cabinet under the ark they kept the very unholy whiskey bottles from which they liked to imbibe after services. At almost exactly at the same time that the congregation rose facing the Torah scrolls to sing the final hymn of God's ultimate reign (not that anyone knew that was what the hymn was about) one old man charged with the task of preparing the liquid refreshment was bending over the cabinet below the very ark we faced, collecting the whiskey. It must have looked to an outsider as if we were praying to him!

By every standard of western worship, their rite was a failure. Except for one thing: they are still doing it; if it is a failure, they certainly don't know it! What can they learn from my book? Perhaps nothing. They are like the Armenian churchgoers I visited the last time I was in Jerusalem. There, behind the walls that set the ancient sect apart in their sustained antiquity, one finds daily worship in which old priests and child acolytes go through motions, words, and melodies hallowed by age—in fearless disregard of what we moderns think they ought to do. I make no claim to speak to or for them. They need a book on worship no more than the Hindu morning bathers and the Orthodox Jews of Ontario do. In that regard at least, they are the lucky ones. So too, I suppose, are "born-agains" of any religious stamp—Jews call them *ba'alei teshuvah*, "penitents who return"—who manage somehow to rediscover verities that command their allegiance despite their dissonance with modern life.

I mean no disrespect to any of these people when I say as a simple matter of observable fact that the majority of would-be religious Canadians and Americans are not like them. We are more like the young Moslem student from Morocco described by the anthropologist Clifford Geertz:

[He is] on an airplane bound for New York, his first trip away from home, where he will study at an American university. Frightened, as well he might be, by the experience of flying (as well as the thought of what awaits him when he lands), he passes the entire trip with the Koran gripped in one hand and a glass of scotch in the other.

Like him, most of us have discovered not literal bottled spirits perhaps, but the elixir of modernity in some guise at least, which we cannot easily let slip from our grasp, even as we hold equally fast to the texts and forms of our premodern youth. As they say, "You can't go home again."

I understand why the Jerusalem Armenians, the southern Ontario Jewish Orthodox, the born-agains and the *ba'alei teshuvah* can do without this book. In our case, worship must define an alternative universe of reality for people adrift in an unrelenting secular stream of consciousness. It must enforce a suspension of the disbelief we carry over from that secular sphere to the religious stories and patterns that our grandparents once believed without question. Ours is the context in which "worship as art" makes sense, for art is the means by which alternative universes of being have been forged since time began. But the traditionalists cited here as counter-examples manage to live in only one world to start with, and it is the world of those grandparents where it is the secular rites and symbols that seem strange, not the other way around. They need no self-conscious artistry to effect the illusion of alternative visions of their world. There is only one vision for them, and it is fused beyond all possibility of separation with the forms of traditional prayer, the dictates of which they go through without having to question their relevance, let alone the world of reality to which they point. It was inconceivable for the old men in my home town not to come to pray every Saturday morning, and where they kept the liquor for the midday "schnapps" was an irrelevant detail, incapable of marring the spiritual vision provided by their ritual script. By contrast, if most of us want to internalize a religious vision of the world, we must do so against the grain of secularity and irreligion. So we keep the whiskey out of sight, as if, in the moment of prayer at least, secular appetites do not exist.

So to those who find their age-old traditions of worship totally satisfying, I have little to say. But those who are not so blessed should not make the mistake of blaming themselves for life's complexity. They have done no wrong in accepting the compelling message of history's march into the twentieth (almost the twenty-first) century. The good old days may have been old, but they weren't always as good as we like to imagine. There is something to be said for the ethical stance that admits the possibility, at least, of being mistaken, even if that carries with it a challenge to the unquestioned world of phenomena presupposed by the act of praying yesterday's prayers. To all those who, like myself, hold modernity in one hand and tradition in the other; who cannot return to the univocal certainties of yesterday; who refuse to part with their intellectual curiosity but want also to retain the spirituality of prayer, I dedicate this book. May it help bring about the care for worship that alone will transform the tired forms that plague us into the beauty of holiness.

THE SYSTEM IN TROUBLE

1

Structuring Time

NOT ALL MOMENTS OF OUR LIVES are the same. All may be equally lasting, but some mean more than others. When we say we are "killing time" or "time flies" we recognize the qualitative distinction between some moments and others. There really are such things as *momentous* decisions, *momentary* lapses; affairs of the *moment*, and the *moments* of truth.

Our understanding of time suffers from at least two major misconceptions. The first is that we imagine time to be a straight line moving from "the beginning" to "the end." The line is stretched taut so that each point or moment on it is the same as any other. That may be so for the scientific world where laboratory experiments must be replicable regardless of whether today is Tuesday or Thursday. But it is most definitely not true for the everyday world of ordinary people, for whom Tuesday may be magnificent and Thursday disastrous.

So we would do better to chart our graph of time as if it were a curve moving up and down the page over and over again, like the diagram of a sound wave. Time has high points and low points; as we sometimes say, "I was on a high," or "I felt low." Drug users speak of "uppers" and "downers," depending on the direction their time will take as a result of their medication. Most of our days, most of our hours, are spent building up to some high point or hurtling downward to the low point on the graph. Some people allow the extremities of high and low to move so far away from each other that, perched as they are on one or the other, they cannot function; and we label these unfortunates "manic-depressives." But manic-depressives differ only in degree. All of us experience a qualitative difference in life's moments. We learn to recognize our "lows" and to bear with them until the graph swings upward again. And we work at creating those moments of exhilaration that make life exciting, challenging, and humanly significant.

Our second misconception is that we think time should be measured by the span of our lives. To be sure, that makes sense from the perspective of our being born, living so long, and then dying; and to that extent such customs as counting birthdays and remembering things by how old we were at the time are sensible. Not every culture, though, has been so individualistically oriented; many would have laughed at making individuals the measure of time. And even in our culture, it is generally people in their middle age and upward, people, that is, who are aware of their mortality, who carry the American message of considering one's lifetime as a discrete block of time that must be planned. Groups not fully in the mainstream of the American work ethic may see things differently. They may live for today as if it had no relation to tomorrow, blowing all their savings on a momentary whim, for example, instead of salting it away for the future. They earn the scorn and wrath of most people who fail to comprehend how anyone could be so foolish as to waste the promise of future achievement by indulging in transitory pleasures.

The truth is, however, that only in retrospect do the combined moments of a lifetime take on a character of their own. The entirety of life turns out to be too much for any of us to handle all at once. Though we may maintain a general notion of working toward some ultimate goal, we live day by day, or even hour by hour, breaking up our four-score years and ten into much smaller and manageable units, each with its own rules and its own graph of highs and lows.

Take something as simple as a lunch break for workers in the office. If people there have become accustomed to going out to lunch every day, they soon develop habitual ways of spending their lunch time. A few people discover friends in the neighborhood and meet daily, at a certain table, at a certain time. Each gets to know what the others order, so that when one of them alters the usual order, the others look on, astonished. Soon this lunch becomes a unit of time unto itself, a social setting where other units of time (such as the board meeting or dinner with the family) are put aside, dismissed from consciousness.

As a unit of time in and of itself, it can be graphed upward and downward, and, to the extent that the script is fixed, the high and low points can be predicted. Thus, for example, if the people meet at their table every day and immediately greet each other profusely while ordering cocktails and celebrating their togetherness, we might consider that the high point. Serious conversation may deliberately, though not officially, be delayed until all the people get there. During that waiting time, expectations build—the graph is on its way up—but with the arrival of the last person, cocktails are ordered, greetings are shared, glasses are clinked; the high moment is reached.

Not everyone spends lunch this way, but clearly some people do. In doing so, they are adding meaning to moments. Each moment in the hour-long lunch break is tied to the moment before and the moment after. A rather loose script defines behavior—who comes to lunch, who sits where, who orders what, who pays, what is talked about, what are the latest jokes, and so on. We can say that these people have forced time into a frame of meaning by ritualizing it, defining what is to be done and said for each moment of it, and then repeating the script with but minor variations each and every day.

A ritual, then, is the way we humans play out a given script of behavior during a specific duration of time. Since the play is repeated regularly, we prepare ourselves for the high and low points of the script, and could, if need be, graph them. Without ritual there would be no meaningful use of time, except for accidental events that force us to laugh or cry. Through ritual, we minimize our dependence on chance, arranging our life-time into smaller packages of moments, each package programmed to behave in such and such ways. If the ritual is successful, the high point of its graph will be reached. The luncheon partners will finally get together after much waiting and anticipating, order their usual round of drinks, and drink to each other's health, forgetting the fight with the boss, or the sick kids at home, or whatever else might otherwise have forced its way to consciousness, had those moments not been ritualistically reserved for their special part in the script. At the moment of mutual satisfaction, the cocktail glasses clinking—if that is the high point this ritual has developed—we speak of the climax to the ritual; or using the description of the ritual as our point of reference, this being a lunch ritual, we can call that high point the "Lunch Moment."

Lunch may seem too trivial an event to be characterized as ritualistic or to be given a set of titles at all. But it is not. Lunch is an hour a day, let us say, when we have the possibility of writing a ritualistic script together and playing it out to great mutual satisfaction. It is but one example of many.

A mother nursing her child is another. She goes about her task in a regular routine, saying certain favorite things while preparing the baby, looking for certain responses from the infant, finding the "proper" chair, and finally nursing her child. Is her act any different from the people going to lunch at the same time every day? Certainly not. Both nursing and lunching have become ritualized so that one act invariably follows another. Anticipation of what is to come builds to the climax of the ritual script. As the child takes the nipple and the mother feels the crying infant being soothed, or when the nursing is over and the baby falls asleep at the mother's breast—whichever has become the high point in the mother's definition of the graph of moments that make up the nursing time—we find the "Nursing Moment."

Unfortunately the word "ritual" has taken on a negative connotation. "Ritualism" is equated with the hocus-pocus magic of some presumed backward tribes practicing voodoo. This attitude is seen in popular literature where an author describes an old-fashioned stereotypical chairman of the board going through the "empty ritual" of lighting the cigar before calling the meeting to order. This evaluation misses the whole point: lighting the cigar is a ritual but not an empty one. It is indeed ritualistic in that it precedes the formal call to order, but it serves in this very way as a readily recognizable means of setting the stage, cuing the players in this particular ritual, and keying them up to the expectations demanded of them. So outsiders are wrong to speak of either the "witch doctor" or the board chairman as performing "mere" rituals. Real rituals are never "mere"!

Of course once-real rituals can degenerate into sterility. Let us call such "empty" rituals ritualizations. The script is played out by one and all, but the actors do not put their hearts into it. Their minds are elsewhere. The lunch partners may have seen half their group retire, and the old restaurant changes hands so that the familiar table isn't there anymore. New people may have joined the group, bringing new behavior, new personal relationships, and, thus, a changed script. It is hard to reproduce the same Lunch Moment now. Similarly, the mother nursing her baby may be tired of it after some time. Sleepless nights, visions of a career thwarted, loneliness as her husband leaves early and comes home late—any one of a number of things may make it difficult for her to achieve the psychological satisfaction she once enjoyed in nursing her flesh and blood. For her, now, there is no Nursing Moment. The graph just never goes very high since, despite her efforts to do the same things in the same way, she finds her mind wandering and her patience wearing thin; she cannot wait for this block of nursing time to go. She will then move happily to another time block that may still be a meaningful ritual: perhaps meeting other mothers of similar temperament in the park.

So whether the chairman who lights a cigar is going through a meaningful ritual or an empty ritualization depends on the psychological expectations of the ritual's participants and the degree to which they are able to recognize and to enjoy the ritualistic high point, in this case, the Board Meeting Moment. Let us assume it is the reading of the "bottom line" on the quarterly economic statement and the mutual awarding of kudos to all present. When the company first started, only a few people made up the board. When they got together for its meetings, they brought unusually high personal involvement in the company that, together as a group, they all expected to nurture and build. So successful were they, that years later the company has become a gigantic corporation, a multimillion-dollar enterprise, and, of the original founders, only the president remains. He still begins by lighting his cigar, and the meeting still concludes with reading the statement and congratulating the department heads. But the latter are all new now, and the sense of personal involvement is gone. The executives attend out of corporate responsibility and cannot wait for the ritualistic sign that they may leave. There is no high point on the graph any more, no Moment toward which the script can move and the actors aspire. Ritual has become ritualization.

So there are empty rituals—ritualizations we now call them—to be sure. And they are what we think they are—boring, meaningless, seemingly silly in the way the participants do a multitude of things with no inherent pragmatic connection to the job at hand. One might say that the symbolism of the acts that make up the ritual is no longer grasped, so that ritualistic cues, once pregnant with meaning, now appear like vacant words, empty gestures, vacuous activity. But there are also rituals, real rituals, where the opposite is the case, and on these we depend to convert structure-less time and necessary tasks into meaningful and satisfying experiences. For each such ritual, whether it be as simple as eating lunch with some friends or as serious as getting married, we fashion a script (or as in the latter example, follow one already fashioned for us) and build to a high point, the "Moment," which we share together because we have been taught to recognize the symbolic behavior of the script as a series of connected signposts along the way. What is necessary in each case is the common acceptance of the script; the common decision to see symbolic significance in behavior that would otherwise appear secondary or even irrelevant and foolish; and the consensus to invest oneself psychologically in the whole drama, waiting for what everyone accepts as the high point in the ritual's curve, the moment that makes it all worth while.

Our days are filled with rituals, one following on the heels of another, as we carve up time and compartmentalize it around events that involve us. Ritualizations are indeed empty, but real rituals are not. Ritualism is neither good nor bad, advanced nor primitive, but human.

I began by discussing such mundane matters as going to lunch or lighting a cigar before a board meeting. By taking the event around which the ritual has been built, we can classify the ritual itself as a Lunch Ritual, a Board Meeting Ritual or a Nursing Ritual. And by noting that the ritualistic flow of events does move in a graph-like direction toward a culminating moment, we can call that moment the Ritual Moment, further classifying it as the Lunch Moment, the Board Meeting Moment, or the Nursing Moment.

Once we concede that even such apparently mundane and daily tasks as these are played out in ritual ways, we should have no trouble at all imagining more "serious" public pursuits as being of like character. Thus public schools open each day with a ritual that may include the pledge of allegiance. This was part of what was once a more extended script of considerable import for

as novel an institution as a "public" school that owed its very existence to state support and that functioned primarily as a means of
socializing tides of immigrants into American values. Today the
pledge may be empty (a ritualization) or full (a ritual). Congress,
too, opens each seating with a ritual, and the President of the
United States is sworn in ritually, just as the Queen or King of
England is ritually crowned. These latter displays of public pomp
and circumstance have great meaning and are certainly not empty
to most people who watch them on television or even travel half-
way across the world to catch a glimpse of the event from among a
throng of thousands.

An excellent example of this public pageantry is a nationally
televised Republican or Democratic convention where the roll call
of states is ritualistically performed. Sometimes everyone knows
in advance who the presidential candidate will be, but just as on
Broadway, the show must go on. State by state the count is given;
once in a while one "great state" yields to another. Slowly, inex-
orably, tension mounts and muted cheers are silenced by a
pounding gavel and a call for order. Finally the count reaches the
magic number; someone is over the mark; the band breaks into
"Happy Days Are Here Again . . . " Pent-up emotion explodes at
once as carefully choreographed "spontaneous demonstrations"
erupt all over the floor; television personnel scurry back and forth
interviewing the winner's key supporters who respond to predictable questions with equally predictable answers. By now the
climax of the ritual is over, and the interviews are merely dénoue-
ment, a winding down from the Moment, in this case, the Political
Moment. The graph is moving down now toward the neutral
horizontal axis whence it began. Still, there was a moment of in-
tense excitation, a crescendo toward which the whole evening
built. Everyone knew in advance what it was, and what would
happen once it occurred. At each stage along the way a political
"pro" could read the signs of the script as they were being played
out and estimate how close one was to the ultimate goal of the
evening. The rules were clear to every single state delegation, and
each one performed with the polish and verve expected of it.
These symbolic gestures necessary to the Political Ritual were
sent and received, until at last the Political Moment was at hand.

Examples could be multiplied. From the world of sports one
could consider the annual grudge match between the University

of Michigan Wolverines and the Ohio State Buckeyes; or the Super Bowl madness that sweeps the country every year; or the homecoming pep rally at the local high school. Can anyone doubt the ritual nature of these events? And they are certainly not "empty" rituals, not for the thousands upon thousands of fans who know the ritual's language inside out, who see the signs and follow the symbols as they occur, who recognize the actors and their roles, and who explode together at the attainment of the Sports Moment, no less than political loyalists at the Political Moment.

The last few examples, those from the worlds of politics and sports, have culminating moments of cathartic outbursts of emotion. At some soccer games, for example, the emotional exuberance may even spill over the normal bounds of the Moment and turn into pitched battle, violence, and injury. But ecstatic joy, aggressive shouting, and loud singing are not necessary components of the Ritual Moment. These occur only when called for by the particular ritual script being enacted. The cases in question happen to be characterized by raucous public demonstrations that mark The Moment. Once written into the script they are enacted clearly for all to see. These particular Ritual Moments, therefore, exhibit characteristics that make them the most obvious examples of the crescendo that is possible in ritualized time. We must be careful, however, not to assume that such obviously emotive display is necessarily typical of all Ritual Moments.

Consider for a moment another ritual that no one will dispute, one that seems at first glance to move climactically downward to a "low" point on the graph rather than to a "high" one, in that the Ritual Moment is the outpouring of grief, not joy: a funeral. Here, too, we have an unmistakably American ritual, altered somewhat by religious preference, but in general an American cultural phenomenon. The parts or roles are clear enough: the mourners, the mortician, the clergy, the friends and relatives who can be arranged, theoretically, in concentric circles of closeness to the mourners, and who behave in ways befitting the circle they inhabit. The members of the closest circle are practically mourners themselves; they play the role of confidants, aides, helpers, mainstays. Those of the outermost circle, on the other hand, merely take time off from work to attend the funeral ceremonies, adding only their physical presence to the event, thus indicating

10

its significance. From the moment of death to the time when the bereaved are expected to resume normal activities, a lengthy ritual unfolds. Within that ritual, there are subrituals: the funeral itself, for example, or the negotiations at the funeral parlor regarding the details of the burial. At one point though, usually at the funeral ceremony, the climax begins to mount. For the first and only time, all the actors in the ritual are present under one roof: mourners, intimate friends, distant acquaintances, professionals. Now the ritual roles are enacted according to the script. The widowed spouse cries and is supported by the helpers, those within the first circle of friends and relatives. But the crying is kept in check to some extent, and the other real-life actors enter the scene. People offer consolation. The crowd gathers. The casket is closed and readied for burial. Religious services are read. The eulogy is given. At last, at the graveside, the coffin descends into the bowels of the earth, and the Moment occurs. Now even the professionals, the clergy and the mortician's staff, may be moved, whether or not they knew the deceased. The funeral ritual has culminated in the Funeral Moment.

The notion of culminating moments was introduced many years ago by the psychologist, Abraham Maslow, who named such experiences "Peak Moments." His interest was not religious worship or even ritual, but human psychology as it applies to religious experience in general. Writing in the '60s, when all institutions, churches and synagogues included, were under attack by a younger generation who considered them sterile, Maslow tried to replace organized religion with a sort of humanistic "personalism," in the sense that he denied the need for any institutionalized format to bring out the religious impulse within us. Instead he felt that every single human being has the potential for religious experience, since religion is an intrinsic element in the human psychological configuration. Nevertheless some people tend toward religious realization more than others, in the sense that they are innate "peakers," while their opposites find "peaking" distinctly foreign to them. Maslow made no attempt to hide his own positive bias in favor of people who can "peak," so he maintained that true spirituality is demonstrated in the attitude toward the world that enables peaking to occur. The mystics, prophets, and seers of religious history are famous "peakers"; the bureaucrats who run true religion into the ground by the encumbrances of organized church life, he thought, are positively ruinous for religious identity.

Later Maslow was led to emend his theory somewhat. Surely there are many spiritually sensitive people who never reach peak moments. Not everyone is an Elijah-like miracle worker, a striver after speaking in tongues, or even a seeker after emotional highs—such as the decade of the '60s featured. So he altered his expectations of true religion, explaining that sometimes, instead of "peak" experiences, one might legitimately expect only "plateau" experiences: not a genuine momentary "high," that is, but a longer-lasting sensation of more moderate satisfaction.

Despite surface similarities, the position I am outlining here is very different from Maslow's. I have borrowed his basic realization that people do not experience every moment in time exactly the same way; we do have highs, and most of us have recollections of times when the exhilaration we felt was similar to what Maslow must have meant by peaking. But Maslow was wrong to think that the goal of life is always to attain a high, and he was correct to scale down that unreal expectation until he recognized the validity of a plateau experience as well. Moreover, I recognize equal validity in low points in human emotion, the satisfying sigh of the Funeral Moment, for example. Not that we live for the days when we can attend funerals, certainly! But sadness is no less inherent to human life than happiness. We learn from both, and we develop a mature balanced character from integrating them both into our repertoire of recognized states through which we pass in the normal course of our life's progress.

Religion is the category of life's pursuits that integrates them best, and religious ritual is the means we use to structure sad and happy moments so that they occur within a framework that we understand and appreciate. Other institutional rituals work in similar fashion to structure personal experience in socially desirable ways. My second deviation from Maslow, then, is my insistence that psychological states are really far more dependent on the groups with which we identify than on some inherent psychological ability or other. Individuals die, but churches structure funerals and tell us when and how to cry. Individuals seek out glory, but political parties organize their search into a political process with the opportunity to rejoice in one's success. Even individual mothers nursing their babies learned how to do it from their mothers and their peers, who follow rules laid down by culture, class, and ethnic group patterns of which they may be only dimly aware. Who among us would give up life in society to live on a desert island, as if there alone we might find unfettered opportunity to follow an inner drive to experiential peaks and plateaus? We all know how much we need others to reach those moments.

This book, then, is about the *communal* base of individual life, and in particular, the ways we depend on *religious community* to make us what we can be. Like Maslow, I am highly critical of that bureaucratic, spiritless approach to religion that stymies attempts at successful communal prayer; but unlike Maslow, I believe that leaving organized religion in favor of some imagined state of total individualism is not a real option. Rituals are group-based, no question about that, and without rituals, we would find our inner yearnings to respond to life truncated at the elemental and elementary levels of emotional frustration that we associate with infants.

We need ritual, then, and for ritual to happen, we need ritual-reference groups. But rituals can be divided in various ways, and here Maslow was not all wrong. They may be empty (ritualizations) or full (actual rituals). If the latter, they may culminate in Moments of joy or of sadness—or of any other emotional state that characterizes human existence. And this culminating emotive state may or may not be publicly demonstrated. The Moment may be punctuated by eruptive violence or by subtle sighs; and instead of a single Peak Moment the ritual may be scripted to provide a plateau-like array of ritualized words and actions that, all together, elicit and sustain a quieter kind of contentment. The participants may have developed the script entirely on their own over a course of years, or they may be bound by the limitations of a script composed far before their time, to which they must generally comply. The full ritual, full in the sense of having implications for those enacting it, absorbs every bit of psychic energy the actors are capable of generating. At the moment of the ritual's beginning, the participants begin closing out all other activities from their minds. They follow the symbolic signposts telling them that the graph is rising and moving closer and closer to the climactic Moment. And when the Moment arrives, it is there for all to see.

I do not think that most people would dispute the existence of such rituals. We've all been to weddings and funerals, certainly. We've watched enough college football and political demonstrations to know that ritual can occur, and that people can get very excited about it. I do not think, moreover, that most people will question the fact that we readily break up our time into discrete time blocks grouped around specific events like lunch or baby nursing; and that we then pattern the time allotted to these events into a repeatable, and ultimately a predictable, order of actions, some of which are irrelevant or unnecessary to the successful accomplishment of the bare physical task itself—the nursing mother does not really need to find her "special" chair, for example. When we consider how we go about daily chores involving others, most of us will recognize something of the ritualistic in what we do. And despite all the times when ritual fails—the kids won't keep quiet during mealtime grace for example—surely we all remember many occasions when the ritual ran its course. If the participants knew their roles and were willing to play them out so that the ritual drama unfolded scene by scene, act by act, then the possibility for the Ritual Moment existed. Weddings, funerals, Thanksgiving dinners; anniversaries when couples revisit the restaurant in which they met and order what they ordered then; meetings in singles' bars where men and women go through the ritual of getting to know each other and sizing each other up to determine what further ritual, if any, is called for; couples in suburbia doing the same thing at a cocktail party (what I call dating behavior of couples), trying to decide who their friends are and what ritualistic games can be played with whom—who gets invited to your next party? with whom do you go to the theatre? whom do you see with no other couples present, but who is included in large group gatherings where conversation can be avoided? PTA meetings; Little League opening; putting the kids to bed; making love—everything from the most ridiculous to the most sublime can be programmed as a ritual in which what each participant does is determined by a script, and all present are the actors. We play out our roles hoping for the Moment that signals success, now in a supreme shout for joy, now in a quiet kiss good night, now in a satisfied nod. The Ritual Moment is a real thing that we have experienced regularly. So most people would not, I think, question the general scheme I have provided.

But oddly enough, they often do question the application of that scheme to religion. They recognize the Ritual Moment when the object of activity is real and physically present—the deceased being buried, or the bride and groom being married, for example. They came to take part in a funeral or a wedding, and that is what they got. But, they argue, why mistake that for religion? Religious ritual, they hold, is Sabbath worship, or Holy Day pomp and prayer. That such events are ritualistic no one denies. But now critics revert to considering ritual as primitive or magical nonsense. Imagine the priest holding his hands just like that! Why is the choir dressed so formally? Why spend hours reciting empty words or observing religious fasts? These are conceded to be ritual, but empty, dead ritual. No one gets married and no one gets buried. Why bother with it?

To this question, "Why bother?", every religion has its own answers. Theologians do just that: They work out a consistent and congruent position that answers such informed, or even uninformed, queries. And needless to say, people who accept the theological justification then know why they should "bother." The problem is that theologians don't always get through to the real doubters who may not be prepared to hear their theological rationales. The theologian experiences God; so—to take a simple example—the theologian argues that the ritual makes sense, given the existence of God who, by definition, wants the ritual to occur. If the doubters had experienced God, however, they would have had no plaguing doubt to begin with. They ask of the theologians the impossibility of justifying a ritual on the basis of religious verities, when, in fact, it is the religious verities themselves that are in dispute.

The problem is that such doubters lack the experience necessary to make sense out of any theological retort; and confusing ritual for ritualization, they cannot see the ritual as anything but empty words and gestures, going nowhere, including nothing but outmoded vestiges of a piety that once may have characterized medievals, but surely deserves to be uprooted from the space age. These critics may still display remnants of religiosity from time to time. They rarely have the courage of their convictions sufficient to deny any and all religious upbringing to their children. They usually prefer religious celebrations of life cycle ceremonies. They may even attend church or synagogue, at least on really important days, say Easter Sunday or Yom Kippur. But even when they do

15

come to worship, they look at it as an anachronistic empty ritual. And to make matters worse, they judge their predecessors, assuming either that the ritual made equally little sense for them or that times have changed so that the kind of sense it made is irrelevant to conditions today.

This last point deserves closer attention. Most people wonder casually how it is that a given prayer came into existence. And if we extend our imagination, picturing a community of individuals in a given time and place praying that prayer, we might even inquire what they were thinking about while they were praying. Put another way, one object of curiosity is how worship rituals developed, and what people saw in them before they lost their fullness of significance. The answer to the first question is often available to us from scholarly sources bequeathed to us by posterity. Scholars are a highly honed force of experts trained to disprove each other's claims, so that details of this or that ritual may be rearranged by different researchers who emerge from their study with somewhat different theories; but as often as not a certain degree of consensus exists, according to which we can say— for example—that a particular ritual under discussion emerged in France, say, in the eleventh century; that it was practiced by urban Jews of the upper middle class; and that it formed part of their daily activity each and every morning.

The second question is the really challenging one. When this hypothetical group of Jewish merchants sang their song, or read their prayer, or did whatever the ritual called for, what did they see in it? It seems patently ridiculous to say that they saw nothing in it, so thoughtful doubters must come up with a rationale that makes sense for the initial ritual celebrants but not for modern skeptics. There are two kinds of answers that satisfy this requirement, and both have had their day in court. They can be encountered regularly in both scholarly and popular accounts of religious rituals.

The first response assumes that people were really religious once upon a time, but those halcyon day were put to rest by the age of science. Though one may bemoan this loss of naiveté, innocence once abandoned cannot be retrieved. Thus our forebears are "exposed" as simple-minded but well-meaning folk who did the best they could to tackle a difficult existence, and what they could do included simplistic religious faith and accompanying ritualistic practice. Not so we, concludes the argument. Having tasted of the Tree of Knowledge, we can't go home again. Nor, for that matter, do most of us want to.

The second response stops short of impugning the wisdom and maturity of ages past. Plato, after all, believed in ritual, though he was hardly a mental pygmy. Some of the greatest champions of religious observance turn out to be rather brilliant philosophers and theoreticians, as a matter of fact. So it must be argued either that they were motivated by extraneous reasoning having nothing to do with appreciating religious ritual as a religious reality; or that they were mystics, whatever that means, and therefore, by definition, somewhat of a spiritual anomaly from whom we ordinary souls can learn nothing. So it is argued that rituals come about because religious leaders wanted to polemicize against heretics, or that they urged people to intone a certain scriptural verse every day, because that very verse was the doctrine upon which the religious leaders based their power and authority. To be sure, such an explanation is in the realm of possibility, but the evidence for it is usually slim or nonexistent. Its truth or falsity, however, is less significant than its function in maintaining the fiction that our forebears were wise and good, yet they could participate in religious ritual without, in fact, being religious.

Sometimes that reductionist explanation fails, however, and we are left with actual evidence of a highly esteemed religious leader, a man or a woman of monumental intelligence, taking part in a ritual and attaining what I have called the Ritual Moment. Now the other prong of the attack is launched. Such an individual is labeled a "mystic" and assumed to be beyond the pale of rationality and ordinary behavior. Once again we are saved. Now it is admitted that our forebears appreciated religious ritual, but only because they were uniquely gifted, *sui generis*, which is a scholarly way of charging them with being somewhat demented.

Now it must be admitted that if people today say that religious ritual is empty, then for them it is certainly empty. But it does not follow that it was empty for ages past. Nor is there any evidence whatever for assuming a lower evolutionary level in the intelligence quotient of Greek philosophers or medieval scholastics; or a sort of Machiavellian mind burrowing in the background of religious history, converting politics into ritual; or for writing off the clear evidence of mentally competent religious people as lunatics. The truth is that whatever people once saw or now see in religious ritual must be attuned to what people see in ritual in general. We ritualize our activities to express their significance; we do so religiously to express religious significance. Rituals, like dramas, are structured to be played out to their ultimate climactic Moments, in which the significance is in some way manifest to all and affirmed by those present. Religious rituals too are dramatically composed so that a Religious Moment is reached wherein religious significance is manifest and affirmed.

If religious ritual is empty, if the words sound hollow, and the actions seem comic, many possible causes come to mind. But none of them casts aspersion on religious ritual *per se*. The problem, if there is one, lies in the complex conditions of modern existence, which, for whatever reason, make religious ritual harder to play out, and the Religious Moment harder to recognize and affirm than is the case with rituals in politics, sports, and other areas of activity.

This book is about religious rituals and Religious Moments. It is dedicated to the principle that religious ritual can still speak to people. Religious Moments are as vital now as they have ever been.

2

Lost Symbols

THE MOST IMPORTANT CHARACTERISTIC of ritualized time is that the participants in the ritual give such time its meaning. The people we mentioned who go out for lunch every day know when things happen according to schedule and when they do not. No one else in the restaurant knows or even cares what this group does. So the participants need to develop their own signals that let everyone know what stage of the ritual they have reached and what to do next. Individual moments of time now cease being equal in importance. They are accompanied by cues to mark them in terms of their human significance. Some of these cues are signs and others are symbols.

Symbolism has been studied by philosophers, logicians, and social scientists of all bents. By and large they agree on the existence of symbols, but on no single definition of what a symbol is or how it functions. For our purposes, however, we can adopt the psychological understanding of C. G. Jung, whose perspective has been taken over, with modifications, by scholars in other disciplines. We can accept his definition, with its important distinction between "symbol" and "sign," without taking a stand on his psychological system as a whole.

The Jungian concept of symbol is easily grasped. It is a word, object, or any act of behavior whatsoever that automatically suggests to those who participate in it some further level of meaning. Jung thought that symbols refer to basic human complexes called archetypes; the immediacy of the symbolic suggestion is due to the fact that every human being shares an innate awareness of the archetypes and recognizes them unconsciously when they are pointed to. Other social scientists, loathe to accept this explanation, emphasize alternative dimensions of human society to account for a symbol's effects, such as the fact that a given society's members may share certain values or experiences and see them automatically reflected in a symbol.

In any event, a true symbol has the following qualities:

1) *It must evoke its response automatically.* If people feel constrained to explain what a thing symbolizes, that thing is not a symbol at all, but a sign.

2) *Verbal description of a symbol's significance is by definition both superfluous and inadequate.* When, for example, Reform Jews say (in their Friday night liturgy), "Light is the symbol of the divine," or "Light is the symbol of Israel's mission," they use the word "symbol" loosely. If light really symbolized either entity, we would not have to say so, and to the extent that "the Divine" and "Israel's Mission" are part of what "light" suggests, they do not exhaust its symbolic content.

3) *In a ritual that deals with group experience, the symbol's significance must be shared by the members of the group.* In fact a prime indication that various individuals really do constitute a group is their ability to respond similarly to a common symbol. They do not have to agree on the symbol's content, however, since symbolic content is always greater than what people are able to verbalize about it (see #2 above).

4) *True symbols, being immediately apprehended, seem self-evident, so people frequently hold to them with considerable emotional tenacity.* They may readily agree to disagree about a symbol's verbalized meaning, but they will not readily give up their emotional response to it.

Thus, in sum, a group's ritual symbol is an item that directs its participants immediately and with absolutely no commentary or explanation to an awareness of an experience or value that they hold in common, and to which they are attracted or from which they are repelled strongly, even though they cannot explain or even agree on the reason why. But once people adopt symbols they feel constrained, if possible, to justify their strong feelings by developing explanations in terms of sign values. This can happen in two ways.

(a) If the objects to which they have become symbolically attached are part of the official religious repertoire of their faith, we can say that they have adopted official, or *public*, signs in a symbolic way, with the result that they will quickly internalize the *public meaning* offered by their theology to "explain" the item's symbolic appeal. People will take the public sign of the cross, for example, as their favorite symbol, explaining their choice by the public meaning that "Jesus died on it"; or they will adopt the public sign of a Torah scroll, saying that it best symbolizes their faith, since (to cite another available public meaning), "The Torah was given at Sinai." On the other hand,

(b) Sometimes we become attached to chance things that just happen to be in the vicinity while we are in the midst of a deeply felt emotional experience. In such cases, the "symbolic objects" have no public theological association at all; they are merely *incidental* symbols, that is, things that were there that one time, by accident, and came thereby to be associated with the event in question. Incidental symbols are often held by individuals, but not usually by groups, since groups are public entities that prefer publicly available systems of meaning which can be handed down from generation to generation. But to individuals who hold them, incidental symbols are as real as the public ones that they learn about from their groups. They work the same way—carrying associations with the events and experiences we hold dear. The only difference is that they attract no public, or theological, interpretations. Thus, for example, I have an old elementary-school sculpture sitting on my desk at work. It means a lot to me, not because it has any official religious meaning, but because my daughter made it, and I recall the love that passed between us the day she gave it to me.

Symbols can be positive or negative. A prime example of a negative symbol for Jews is the swastika, which automatically

21

evokes recollection of the six million Jews slain by the Nazis. Jews never feel compelled to explain the swastika. They would not be able to verbalize what it conjures up in the mind and heart, precisely because what it denotes is truly symbolic in nature. So the swastika fulfills our criteria: response to it is automatic; verbal description is superfluous; it is shared by the whole community; and Jews react emotionally just looking at it. Scholars may explain that it was used by ancient cultures for purposes entirely remote from the Nazi context. But such logic is irrelevant to a Jewish community for whom the swastika has become symbolic of that which mere words cannot begin to approach.

Rituals are full of symbolic items whose symbolism is by definition never fully explained, since as soon as we feel we have fully captured their meaning in words, we can be sure they are no longer symbols. The only means of identifying whether a term has symbolic force is to scrutinize how ritual participants react to it.

If explored in depth, any number of things may be revealed as true symbols. But without such exploration we are usually aware only of the strong feelings we have about the matter in question. So debates over symbols usually revert to irrational arguments, with neither party to the debate understanding the depth of the other's emotional commitment.

But what is it, exactly, that symbols symbolize? Also, why do we find it so hard to express that meaning to others? For the first question, we might begin consulting a popular account of religious symbolism and see what it says. I read, for example, that there are different types of crosses, each with its own significance in Christian worship. The usual cross one sees is a Latin Cross. An alternative shape is the Ansate Cross, in which the top of the cross forms a loop. This, we are told, is an ancient Egyptian symbol denoting life. It was taken over into Christianity and used on Christmas to denote life made possible with the birth of Jesus. Shall we say, then, that the Ansate Cross is a symbol of life, such that Christians arriving at Church for Christmas see the pertinent cross in their worship surroundings and immediately comprehend the cue that sets the stage for the particular ritual of Christmas worship?

Alternatively I read that particular flowers have their own separate and specific symbolic significance. The myrtle, for example, symbolizes peace and love and is used, therefore, in designing wedding bouquets. Does that mean that the people attending a wedding ceremony see the myrtle and, recognizing its symbolism, begin patterning their behavior after the model called for by the wedding "script"?

Or to take a more common example, consider the holly, so pervasive in homes at Christmas. Since people hang it up as a Christmas decoration, we would imagine that the holly symbolizes Christmas in some way or other. Actually though, our handbook on Christian symbolism tells us that the holly, being thorny and prickly, represents Christ's Passion, because it is a specific reminder of the crown of thorns. The red berries, moreover, relate to Christ's blood shed on the cross. Is holly, therefore, a symbol of Jesus' birth or his death? Since most Christians use it at Christmas, are we not to "correct their error" and have them hang holly at Easter? Do we let them continue their practice and theologize that, for example, Christmas and Easter are so closely related that a symbol of Christ's resurrection is permissible or even desirable at the feast celebrating his birth? Or should we decide that, regardless of its prickly shape and red berries, holly symbolizes Christmas, simply because people use it then? Our book on Christian symbols may define accurately how holly is used in Christian art, or what church authorities have seen fit to find in holly. But in terms of a behavioral cue in ordering a ritual and achieving the Ritual Moment, holly is linked to Christmas and has nothing whatever to do with the scholarly or artistic use of the plant.

Finally, to take an example from Jewish symbolism, I recall being asked once what the six-pointed star of David (the *magen david*) symbolizes. Having just finished reading a scholarly monograph on that very subject, I launched a copious explanation in terms of when Jews first started using the star in question, how they used it, and so on. But the lady who asked the question shrugged off everything I had to say. "Rabbi," she retorted, "the star of David symbolizes the Jewish people. It has six points, you see, so no matter how you stand it up, it will always have two points on which to balance. From such a firm base it cannot be toppled. Just so, the Jewish people are firmly entrenched, no matter what history brings us." Who was right, the woman or the scholar?

Recalling the distinction between symbol and sign, we should ask first if the cross, myrtle, holly, and star of David are really symbols at all, or perhaps just signs. Secondly, if they are symbols, what do they symbolize? Since by definition a symbol eludes our attempts at defining clearly what it symbolizes, words being poor imitations of the emotive content we invest in the symbols of our lives, it follows that, to the extent that the verbal definition of each symbol's meaning is accurate and all-inclusive, none of the entities is really a symbol. They are, however, *signs* of an elite group of experts who have agreed to recognize a common public meaning in the myrtle (to take but one of our examples) whenever it occurs in art and literature, past and present. When most of us look at a painting from the twelfth century, say, we can barely tell the difference between the various plants and animals displayed there. The expert, though, recognizes each one as the particular entity chosen by the painter to represent a further value or state. Thus holly is depicted so as to bring to mind the Passion, or the myrtle to evoke thoughts of love. But these are not necessarily symbols, since the link between holly, on the one hand, and blood and thorns, on the other, is merely an arbitrary convention passed on culturally from one generation to the next and learned as a matter of rote by a minority of the faithful. Having read the handbook of symbols, I too can now spot holly in medieval art or even in contemporary homes, and even though my aesthetic sensitivity and appreciation of the artist's handiwork are thereby increased, I feel no sense of personal significance such as we stipulated must accompany symbol-recognition. I don't care very much what holly is supposed to represent. At best I am now able to say what other people say it stands for and to repeat what I have learned, if asked to do so. And I really do not care whether others agree or disagree with me.

Imagine, however, a Christian for whom Christ's Passion is of such constant importance that it informs every moment of his life. Having learned as a youth what holly stands for, this pious man never sees holly without being reminded of the central religious mystery that guides his every step. No one dares disagree with him! For such a man holly is indeed a symbol, and he speaks the truth when he tells us that holly symbolizes the Passion.

He tells us only part of the truth, however. Not that he is hiding anything; he tells us everything he knows, that is to say, that holly is really symbolic to him of the Passion of Christ.

But suppose this pious soul comes across another Christian, equally serious about her faith, but with a different background. Born in America, this second person is a woman who has faithfully kept Christmas and Easter—as well as other holy days— according to the customs prevalent in her family's history. Never having read that holly is connected with Easter, she, like her parents before her, has faithfully decorated her home with holly for Christmas. Typically pragmatic American that she is, she has probably never given any thought to the rationale behind the selection of holly as a decoration, even though she never fails to see the plant without warm memories of Christmas flooding her mind; and, conversely, Christmas without holly on her door is unthinkable.

Our two hypothetical Christians now meet at Christmas, and the saintly old man inquires of the woman why she hangs holly at Christmas. As the conversation develops, the woman discovers that holly stands for the Passion and belongs, correctly speaking, to Easter, not Christmas. She trusts the old man before her, whose wisdom is considerable. He can quote chapter and verse to prove his point, while the woman knows only what her parents used to do, and that she continues in their footsteps. That her parents might be wrong is a theoretical possibility, but irrelevant. If the old man does not insist that the woman remove the holly, the discussion may well end on amicable terms—we are trained, after all, to avoid outright fights. But if he demands that the holly be removed until Easter, he will end by forcing the woman into an untenable position. Rationally she admits that her opponent is correct. But she cannot bring herself to act on that knowledge. For her the psychologically real knowledge is that Christmas goes with holly, regardless of doctrine, theory, and catechism. As she sees things, the old man is right in terms of *sign*; her parents are right about *symbol*. The *significance* of the holly may well be what the old man tells her. But nobody changes behavior because of *significance*! And what is symbol to one person (the old man) is sign to another (the woman).

These two points need considerable elaboration. First, it is of the utmost importance to see that no one changes behavior because of a "mere" sign. Every advertising executive knows this. For the purposes of marketing, a sign is the surface content of what appears on billboards. But we all recognize by now that telling everyone how cigarette smoking causes cancer does not by itself lead people to stop smoking. The surgeon-general who wants to get this point across will have to hire an advertising agency, which will say the same thing, ostensibly, but will connect the message with something deeper and more immediate to people's motivation. That is, the message will be associated with something symbolic. Then, and only then, will we change our habit.

Ritual Moments are akin to changing habits. People enter the ritual environment without necessarily divesting themselves of the patterns of behavior appropriate for the everyday world. Presenting them with signs will never open them to an appreciation of the ritual's potential; only symbols will do that. Participants who enter the ritual field and find only signs, things which theoretically ought to mean a lot, but in fact mean nothing, will be as unlikely to exchange their mundane set of behavioral expectations for those demanded by the specialized ritualistic arena, as smokers are likely to stop smoking just because a sign tells them that theoretically they should. Yet religious leaders constantly confront problems in religion as if they were problems in signs. Why don't people come to church? They would, it is said, if only they knew that to avoid celebrating the Mass is to court sin! So we tell them this, and they still don't come. Why don't Christians practice Christian charity? They would, we argue, if they only knew the importance of clothing the poor and feeding the hungry. So we preach to them of the importance of such acts, but they don't practice them. Why don't Jews come every Shabbat evening to pray? It is a *mitzvah* (a divine commandment) after all! So we explain all this, but the sanctuary remains half-empty week after week. Why do children graduate from synagogue religious school with little commitment to religious practice, values, and survival? There must be something wrong with our curriculum, we argue. So we move Jewish history from sixth to eighth grade and create a course on symbols (by which we mean signs) that will tell ninth graders the significance of prayers, synagogue objects, and Jewish art. But children aren't fooled by the mere reshuffling of signs. Signs multiplied (more school hours), signs altered (more relevance), and signs redistributed (new curricular order) are still just signs. *And nobody changes behavior because of signs.*

The only exception to this general rule is when signs are accompanied by relatively immediate threats of punishment. We do in fact obey even irrelevant traffic signs if a police car is in sight. And if frightened sufficiently, we may even stop smoking for a while rather than contract cancer. But as the police car fades into the horizon, or as the threat of cancer becomes more distant, we speed up to a dangerous level or pick up a cigarette again. In the past, religious societies could count on enforcing their signs with the threat of punishment. People used to follow religious signs then, "Go to Church" being functionally equivalent to "Speed Limit 30." No longer is that the case, at least not in America. We need to rediscover the power of *symbols*, not signs, for they alone have the power to lead people to change their habits; only under the influence of symbols will they want to. People do not need to know more signs that presumably elicit pious behavior. These they may heed or not, depending on the degree of social pressure they feel at the time. (Parents of *bar-* and *bat mitzvah* or confirmation children will generally do what they are told, lest the family rite of passage be denied them, but they may never return to worship again.) People need to develop the art of recognizing symbols that punctuate the passage of sacred time and make Religious Moments possible.

So we return to the second moral of our story about the hypothetical conversation between the old man and the woman over the meaning of holly. What was symbol to one person (the old man) was mere sign to the other (the woman).

If asked what something symbolizes, most people will bow to the authority of the expert. They assume that symbolism, like most other things in our technological society, is the realm of specialists. There ought to be experts in symbols as there are experts in law (lawyers) or experts in medicine (doctors). Laypeople, that is, the non-experts, know not to question the experts. If we now take the same people, shift the conversation away from symbols to medicine or law, and ask them what the doctor's or the lawyer's expertise consists of, we will probably be told that there is a distinct body of knowledge that each expert has mastered. Doctors know some mysterious body of facts called medicine, for example, the difference between a virus and a bacterium. And lawyers know whether you can sue your landlord to recover damages from a flood. So the expert in symbols knows whether holly symbolizes the Passion or Christmas.

We need yet one more instance of expertise before we can compare these examples and see how it is that symbols legitimately mean different things to different people, and why people usually assume that whatever they think a symbol is must be wrong if the expert says it is something else. That further example is the expert in how books are catalogued, the librarian.

You go to the library and request a rare volume. You fill out the right card, and the librarian appears with the book. In a small library that interchange does not appear strange. In a massive university library or the New York Public Library, with its endless halls and departments, one can truly appreciate the incredible fact that with all those books, someone can find just the one you are looking for. Like the doctor, the attorney, and the symbol specialist, librarians are experts at something. They have mastered a set of data regarding filing, storing, ordering, and distributing books.

Now let us consider all these experts and decide what they have really mastered. In each case they have learned more than a set of objectively existent data, facts that presumably would exist whether anyone learned them or not. In each case they are experts not because of *what* they know, but because of *how* they are able to manipulate that knowledge. The clearest case is the librarian. Suppose the librarian cannot locate a given book, even though it is listed in the card catalogue. To argue that it is in the catalogue, so, theoretically, it must be on the shelf, is beside the point. To use the excuse that someone walked off with the book is likewise irrelevant. The only criterion for judging librarians is whether or not they have mastered the complex task of running a library efficiently. The expert librarian who knows theoretically where books are, and who publishes what, is no expert at all if books get lost, orders aren't made, displays aren't organized and call slips aren't processed. Expertise, then, has little to do with objective facts. It has everything to do with pragmatic results.

This is eminently clear from the case of doctors who are experts in cancer or other terminal diseases. These doctors unquestionably know more about the causes and treatment of the disease than anyone else. But their patients almost always die. They can hardly be blamed for their patients' demise, but unless they can internalize their own alternative practical criterion for success, they may suffer from the annoying feeling that they are not experts at all, else why do their patients die? They may even discover that they spend more time in the laboratory or visiting patients whose benign condition promises better results, while unconsciously avoiding those likely to die. Similarly lawyers who know the law codes and prior judicial precedent extremely well, but who cannot organize their knowledge effectively, will be considered failures compared to practitioners who can marshal legal data to the client's benefit. In all three cases then—library science, medicine, and law—there is some sort of data which is mastered, but that mastery is ultimately tested by concrete results. We must differentiate between a system of knowledge and the application of that system.

Regarding symbols, we want to know two things. First, what is the system of knowledge with which the expert deals? and secondly, what application thereof will be considered proper evidence that expertise over that data is established?

Neither question is easy to answer, but the first is probably the more difficult of the two. It is the first, at any rate, that has received the most attention over the years. Indeed so many people have said so much on the subject that it is more than a little difficult to avoid going off on a tangent summarizing theories of symbolism held by one great thinker or another. But summarizing other people's theories may not necessarily help us find what we want. And the theories are readily available elsewhere for those who want to consult them.

By and large, the debate over symbols has boiled down to arguments regarding what a given symbol symbolizes. Is holly a symbol for Easter or Christmas, for example? What is the symbolism of Lady Macbeth washing her hands from the crime? Or what does the number three symbolize, or the color red? The next step in the debate is the determination of *how* we can tell what something symbolizes; what criteria will we use to determine which of two experts is right? At this point the debate becomes very complicated because one is never sure how to organize a set of answers to that question. An appeal to the foremost authority on Shakespeare will not solve the Macbeth problem because the other party can always find another authority. So we push the problem of who is right farther back without even handling the question of how one decides. The issue usually becomes one of defining the nature of that which is symbolized and the nature of the symbol doing the symbolizing. We want to know if there is any necessary connection between the symbol and what it symbolizes, such that when confronted with the symbol (holly) and two or more possible items being symbolized (Christmas or Easter), we can see that only one of the two (Christmas or Easter) is correct. If enough such rules are established, we could theoretically have a whole set of rules governing symbolization, and we would have no difficulty discovering what things symbolize.

So modern culture is replete with such theories of symbolization. None of them, however, is self-evidently correct or even so convincing that it makes regular converts out of adherents of rival theories. When all is said and done, we know at most some distinguishing features of some symbols. There are those, for example, that seem to share a physical quality of that for which they stand, as red is more apt to symbolize blood, white to symbolize milk, or (in the celebrated Freudian example) the cigar to symbolize a phallus. Others seem to be arbitrary, as, for instance, the swastika stood for Nazi supremacy in the thirties, or as the donkey and the elephant represent Democrats and Republicans, respectively. On the other hand, the swastika was an old Aryan sign, so even arbitrary symbols may not be so arbitrary. That is the position of Jung, who believed that symbols arise out of the depths of a collective unconscious; what seems arbitrary to the outsider has careful logic behind it from the psyche's perspective. Is the human mind programmed with the predilection to see the world in certain ways, to dichotomize existence into opposites, for example? And are symbols related to the mind's activities so that they represent either the portrayal of one of the opposites or the unification of them both? Do things have their own inherent symbols, or do we determine symbols arbitrarily, even haphazardly? These are the sorts of questions that have filled pages of discussions on symbolism for over a century now. Unfortunately I see no way of solving any of them, so I find myself returning again and again to the realization that what counts is not a thorough understanding of the nature of the system of knowledge mastered, but the application of that mastery. After we understand how expertise in symbolism is applied, we may be able to return to the knotty question of what symbolism really is.

How then is it applied?

Try the following experiment. Invite a dozen people to a discussion on symbols, telling them that they are each to bring something symbolic from home. Let us imagine the setting is a synagogue, and the things that people bring will be items they identify as Jewish symbols. When the people arrive, each puts his or her symbol on the table, and you now go around the room asking each participant, "What did you bring and why?"

I have conducted this experiment on numerous occasions, and the results don't vary much. The items are normal household ritual objects, like Sabbath candlesticks or the tray used for a Passover Seder. A few people bring nothing, saying either that they forgot, or that they didn't know what to choose, or that the only thing they might have selected is immovable or unavailable, but that they will describe it. Some people bring items that one could never have predicted.

The conversation almost always begins on the level of sign. "I brought these candlesticks," says one woman "because they symbolize the Divine. Isn't that what we say each Friday night in services?" A neighbor who also brought candlesticks responds, "I thought light symbolized creation." The two people now discuss the relative merits of light's presumed symbolism, but neither really cares what the "right" answer is. Their discussion is purely academic. I now ask the first woman who brought the candlesticks, "If light symbolized creation rather the Divine, would you still have brought candlesticks?" Her reply invariably is affirmative. Her argument about light's meaning (as well as her neighbor's) was rooted in the fact that they just happened to have learned, somewhere in their education, to parrot back different explanations of light that existed round about them as readily available public *meanings;* neither person had ever stopped to consider whether the learned response was really correct. And now each is perfectly willing to entertain the notion that another symbolic value is the correct one. If, at the end of the discussion, the first woman has been convinced that light symbolizes creation, not the Divine (as she first thought), she will still bring her candlesticks as her favorite symbol. The reason is that she has not given up their *symbolic* importance at all. She has simply substituted one *sign* for another—"creation" for "the Divine"—and predictably, she does not change behavior (bringing candlesticks) because of new signs.

Apparently the candlesticks were brought regardless of whether they stood for the Divine, because the woman says she would have brought them even if they stood for something else. So we ask again, "Why did you bring them?" Eventually the woman answers in personal terms. Her mother gave them to her. Or she recalls, fondly, sitting as a child around the Sabbath table with the candles glowing. Or she was a war orphan, and she came to America with nothing that belonged to her parents but this single set of candlesticks, which she swore to cherish. The point is that *symbolism always evokes personal memories of something.* It is precisely because symbols are so personally relevant that we insist on asking what they mean, as if anything that evokes such emotion from us must have some grand religious or cosmic meaning beyond ourselves. The candlestick must *mean* something, it seems to us, so when by chance we read one night in the liturgy that light is the symbol of the Divine, we readily accept that interpretation as the true meaning of our symbol. "So that's what it symbolizes," we say to ourselves. "That explains its attraction." There is, however, nothing inherent in light that makes it a necessary symbol for the Divine. It may remind us of God, but only if we work at making that connection.

In sum: symbol generally comes before sign; sign is the intellectual excuse for symbol.

In fact, that is how symbols work in all of our dramatic Moments. Every ritual has them. One of the lunch people who participated in the Lunch Moment may keep an old ashtray or menu at home. Originally he may just have borrowed it or accidentally taken it home. But as years went by, the souvenir of old times spent together at the corner table every noon hour took on personal meaning. If asked why he keeps an old ashtray around the house, he will smile and explain, in his own words, of course, all about the Lunch Moment.

But a major difference between Lunch and Religion is that lunch make no claims of absolute significance: it develops no sacred narratives and no theologians. Merely an accidental symbol, the ashtray will not be singled out by later interpreters and given meaning in terms of sign. No one will think to call it a symbol—meaning sign—*of* "the Divine," or *of* "creation," or *of* "salvation," or *of* anything at all. It remains just an item of accidental symbolic significance to the few members of the Lunch group, and serves as a reminder of their good times together.

Now we can see how symbolism works, how, that is, the body of knowledge that we call symbols is applied in real life. People develop meaningful relationships with other people and play out these relationships in ritualized blocks of time, punctuated by verbal or nonverbal, animate or inanimate cues for behavior. These otherwise meaningless entities that punctuate ritual space—the menu at lunch, the holly over the fireplace, the candlesticks at Sabbath eve—become personally significant and come to be reminiscent of the ritual Moment around which the ritual revolved.

In truth, *the verb "to symbolize" is actually intransitive, because the symbols we choose in this way do not symbolize anything. They just symbolize; the verb "symbolize" takes no object.* Only our insistence on linking everything up with signs, as if symbols must always refer to something ritually significant—creation, the Divine, the Passion, love, and so on—only that foible prevents us from seeing symbols as they really are. <u>*Symbols are otherwise meaningless words, gestures, or things endowed with great personal significance because they have accompanied Ritual Moments that are important to us.*</u> In the case of the Lunch Group, the symbols will remain just that. In the case of organized religion, or, for that matter, any other institution that has developed its notions of specialized items (the gavel for debating societies, or trophies for athletic clubs), symbolic objects will be invested also with *sig*nificance, that is, with sign importance. Children first exposed to the ritual will probably select a tried and true ritual object as their symbol and will be told its sign importance. But they may not. One man brought some gold cuff links as his symbol of Judaism, explaining that his grandfather had given them to him at his *bar mitzvah*. Since cufflinks have no a priori religious sign importance, he was never told that the cufflinks meant anything other than what they are, a gift from a treasured grandfather at an emotional occasion. Had he chosen a ritual object that already had sign importance in the Jewish cultural repertoire—a prayer book, say—people would have told him what that sign importance was, and he would have grown up thinking "prayer books symbolize talking to God," instead of the much truer explanation, "Prayer books symbolize, that is, they awaken in me the fond memory of a Ritual Moment. In terms of its sign value—that is, its *significance*—however, prayer books *signify* talking to God." This truer axiom could then produce the following corollary: "Even if I stop believing in talking to God; even if, that is, the sign value loses importance for me; the symbolic value of prayer books will still remain the same."

We are now in a position to understand why people cannot explain their depth of emotion regarding symbols. When they are asked for an explanation, they revert to a discussion of signs. Suppose this man who loved prayer books remains convinced that prayer books do mean talking to God. He then meets a woman who merely meditates, and who suggests that worship services be altered to exclude the prayer book entirely, as meditation is far more successful in that nothing gets in the way. The man will react with predictable hostility at the prospect of his prayer book being taken away from him. When challenged, the two debaters discuss the altogether irrelevant issue of whether prayer should consist principally of talking to God or whether it should just be the opportunity for free-flowing meditation and the presumed connection between those two "rival" activities and a prayer book. They are like the old man and the woman who met and discussed holly. They too differed on the symbolism of an object but could come to no agreement as long as they limited their discussion to sign values, Christmas vs. Easter. It would have been much better if the woman had just announced that, having grown up with holly in her house every Christmas, she was unable to bear the thought of doing without it then; and let the prayer book lover say that he recalls the joy of holding his own prayer book during his consecration. That kind of argument cannot be lost, since no one can deny another's experience. But let the lady be drawn into an argument over the sign value of holly, and the scholar will prove she is wrong; just as the meditation expert may demonstrate with eminent clarity that prayer books just get in the way these days. But the woman will not change her holly, and the man will not let go of his prayer book. They cannot explain their stubbornness, since apparently they are being unreasonable, having lost the argument of signs. Let them know, however, that the sign value was never the issue. The sign value or *significance* is only the prop for the symbol value or symbolism, and it is symbolism that we humans cannot allow to come crashing down. Once symbolism goes, all our recollections of Ritual Moments go too; and without Ritual Moments all time is leveled to meaninglessness. That we cannot bear.

Finally, then, let us try to understand what symbolism is. Given how a set of knowledge is applied, we said, we should be able to describe what that set of knowledge actually is. We now see that the problem underlying most symbol theories is that their proponents insist on asking, "What does a symbol symbolize?", to which they expect an answer, to the effect that it symbolizes A, or B, or C. Convinced that "to symbolize" is a transitive verb requiring an object, they look for necessary relationships between the symbol and the object. But there is no object! The answer to the question, "What does a symbol symbolize?", is simply, "It symbolizes." It evokes memories of Moments.

A certain commonalty of symbols selected by people in similar cultural backgrounds is to be expected. Since most Christians enjoy the family togetherness of Christmas day, Christmas trees will probably be symbolic to many. But—to consult my handbook on symbols again—its symbolism has nothing to do with its greenness, which presumably stands for life and eternity, or with any other sign value superimposed on the tree by theologians or artists.

Now we have already seen that behavior is dependent on symbols but not on signs. It follows that our most critical challenge is helping people relate to sacred objects in a symbolic way. That is, people must come into contact with these objects in situations that we have characterized as emotionally charged ritualized dramas leading to Ritual Moments. Moreover, those Ritual Moments must be memorable. If they are marked by sheer boredom, we can be sure that people will grow up disdainfully indifferent to what religious traditions hold dear. In extreme instances of negative associations, items may even become negative symbols, evoking only bad memories. We have already seen the ultimate example (for Jews) of the swastika, and others can readily supply their own equivalents: burning crosses and white hoods for Blacks, for example. A less extreme example is the man or woman in rebellion against an overly severe childhood, who therefore becomes a confirmed atheist but then adopts that atheism with such "religious fervor" that he or she never tires of pointing out failures of the church; or grown adults who don't go that far, but who nonetheless feel distinctly uncomfortable in churches or synagogues, because they are reminded subconsciously of unsatisfactory experiences as children. The task for those who wish to facilitate Religious Moments is to be sure that children in their formative years identify positively with their religious experiences and to see to it that positive experiences occur in religious environments.

Alas, that almost never happens today. Religious schools in most churches and synagogues are failures that deal, at best, in signs. Children generally forget signs anyway, but even if they learn them, they rarely invest emotional significance in them. The signs do not become symbols. How can they become symbols as long as we isolate the learning experience from symbol-producing Ritual Moments. To take but one example: If we consistently separate little children from their parents at times of prayer—as I see some churches and synagogues do—the children may learn by rote the rules of how to function as worshipers, but they will never achieve the warmth that comes from being with their parents at sacred times. If their highest emotional peaks are reached while watching a football game with Mom and Dad, or riding on a bike with the kids, football and bike riding will become symbols of Ritual Moments—as the menu was to the lunch crowd. Our task at the very outset then is to reshape religious education so as to deal with symbols, not signs.

A second challenge is the lost generation of adults who have been raised on sign curricula and know better than to become personally involved in mere signs. On the other hand, they have had symbolic experiences elsewhere. So they specialize in taking part in Ritual Moments outside the sphere of religion. Jogging with friends, watching the ball game, celebrating New Year's Eve, going bowling, attending cocktail parties, joining committees, psychotherapy—any or all of these may be ritually programmed with endless care to provide symbolic depth and the experience of Ritual Moments.

If we want religion to compete, we must provide emotionally satisfying experiences within religious environments. Only then will religious, rather than secular, symbols become part of people's lives, so that they return to religious rituals for the satisfaction that comes from Ritual Moments; and only then will they really want to know the accepted religious sign value (if there is one) of their symbols, and thus discover also what intellectual depth religion carries.

In sum, symbols do not symbolize anything; they just symbol-ize. They remind us of Ritual Moments in which we have invested great emotion at one time or another. Though we share symbols, we may differ on the sign value attached to them, without doubting the supreme importance of their common symbolic significance for us all. Using these common symbols, we can take time—which is utterly meaningless in itself—and program its flow on the ritual graph until the Ritual Moment is attained. Without common symbols we can do no more than force or embarrass people to go through the motions, explaining all the while what each symbol is—that is, giving its sign value—and how to use it. The result is depressing, as most clergy can tell you. Most worship services assemble people who share no symbols—though they may have been taught some signs—and have no emotional invest- ment in what transpires. What the symbolically aware see as being supremely important, the average worshiper finds boring. Like a child watching Shakespeare and having to ask at every line what is happening, so the average worshiper leaves the church or syn-agogue without comprehending in the least that, for some, a Religious Moment has passed. How sad!

3

Worship Systems

I KNOW OF A LAW FIRM that has just fired its second secretary in eight months. A history of the firm indicates that this year is typical of others. Though the firm is old, established, reputable, and competent, it finds that for some reason secretaries are hard to keep. The partners don't know how to explain their constant search for able secretarial help; the pay is adequate, benefits are substantial, and no undue demands seem to be placed on the holders of the position. Yet letters do not get written, legal briefs are often late, and, in general, no one is satisfied with the clerical department. So they conclude that their difficulty must have something to do with the sorry state of the working force these days.

The firm's problem is not very different from a synagogue that complains how hard it is to find good teachers to teach Hebrew to children in a course that meets for one-and-one-half hours every Sunday. Every year the pattern is the same. Lots of people apply, and on paper, at least, many seem qualified. But when the course gets under way, and the kids finally get to class, not very many weeks elapse before both parents and children discover a noticeable absence of learning. By May or June members of the Sunday School Committee find themselves agreeing that once again the teacher who was hired did not get the job done to everyone's satisfaction; a subcommittee will spend the summer advertising for a new teacher. Dossiers of prospective candidates will arrive, and the annual Hebrew hunt will be under way. Strangely enough, no one on the committee stops to ponder the significance of the fact that those of them who grew up in this congregation never learned Hebrew here either. The problem is so old, it is entering its second generation. Yet no one on the committee considers the notion that perhaps the problem lies not with the teacher but with the synagogue. No one wonders whether it may not be rather strange that after twenty years or more of hiring and firing teachers, the "right" teacher has yet to come along.

The experience of perennial problems that somehow never get solved is familiar to everyone. Normally competent people somehow find themselves embroiled in seemingly insoluble difficulties that just will not go away. Public schools, for example, take their educational pulse every so often and decry the fact that "Janie and Johnnie can't read." So they change the textbooks, or the teaching method, or the audiovisual aids, or even the teaching staff, only to discover five years later that the new Janies and Johnnies in the system still can't read. Universities bemoan their graduates who are abysmally ignorant of basic skills and knowledge. So they alter curricula, fire deans, publish new catalogues, and get (alternatively) tough or soft, again to find out that the illiterates still get through school, and that the kind of education everyone wants never quite becomes the norm in most classrooms.

What goes wrong? Why can't the law firm get its clerical work done? Why can't the synagogue school teach Hebrew? Why do public schools and universities fail to live up to their own expectations?

More important than the question, "What goes wrong?", is the observation, "Look how the problem is attacked." In each case the institution finds itself unable to solve recurrent problems and resorts to equally recurrent solutions that have failed before and will surely fail again. That is, they blame the problem on someone or something. Secretaries are no good; Hebrew teachers can't teach; the reading textbook is outdated; the curriculum is too strict (or too lenient). Those in charge then exchange the designated culprit for another secretary, teacher, book, or curriculum. And when that fails (as of course it always does), they go through the same exercise of identifying a villain and replacing it all over again.

The process of finding someone or something to blame is called *scapegoating*. Though scapegoating never solves the problem, it does play a major role in institutional life. It allows the people who make up the institution to avoid locating the real problem, which is usually so pervasive and so deeply rooted in the institution's life that trying to apply a real solution would prove very painful. It might mean rethinking basic institutional assumptions, or reshuffling essential departmental relations. So it is much easier to imagine that some one single entity in the organization is at fault: the secretaries, the teachers, the textbooks, or the curriculum. Perhaps everyone's favorite scapegoat is "the times." People aren't as responsible "these days." Kids are too spoiled "nowadays." By deciding that the times are the problem, people can avoid working on the painful source of ineffectiveness, yet still not have to fire anyone, or go through busywork like redesigning curricula, or doing whatever else the scapegoating of a particular object calls for.

Now it may seem as if we have strayed very far afield from the subject of ritual, but we haven't. As we saw in the last chapter, ritual, too, is often perceived as ineffective and failing. But rather than truly try to solve the problem of the failing ritual, people generally scapegoat someone or something. The alternative, after all, is to re-evaluate the very essence of religious life and the very institutional substructure on which religions are built.

Let me take a simple case in point: congregational singing in Reform Jewish congregations. Reform Judaism was born as a sort of Jewish Reformation in the nineteenth century. For many Jews in western Europe, the dawn of modernity opened up the opportunity to achieve civil rights and to enjoy the normal amenities of citizenship that hitherto had been denied them. Though full equality was not nearly as close as they imagined, these Jews did learn the modes of behavior that normally marked the non-Jewish world, including its religious ritual life. They instituted the reform of traditional rituals, many of which seemed medieval in quality, systematically reworking old ceremonies to fit modern sensitivities. That process continued into the middle of the nineteenth century when Jews migrated to America. On these shores also, they attempted to alter age-old rituals so as to fit contemporary notions of aesthetics and religiosity.

One change in ritual that seemed called for was the institution of congregational singing. In traditional worship modes congregational singing had not been unknown; far from it. But that singing differed substantially from the characteristic singing practices that we associate with modern houses of worship, in that the old style had been marked by the spontaneous singing of folk melodies, entirely in Hebrew (which few understood), and without benefit of musical scores or sophisticated musical settings and modern trained choirs. So by the end of the nineteenth century American Reform rabbis were anxious to encourage *modern* congregational singing. And since that seemed tantamount to hymns, they began writing hymnals, collecting modern scores, training choirs, and introducing aesthetically acceptable but singable music into the worship ritual.

The parties to the long and agonizing process are two clergy organizations in Reform Judaism: The Central Conference of American Rabbis and the Cantors' Association of America (later renamed The American Conference of Cantors). Both were in their infancy in the 1890s, and as part of their agenda of fostering the success of American Judaism, they felt compelled to encourage modern religious music in the synagogue.

At their annual convention in 1892, the rabbis held an extended debate on the topic. Among other things it was noted that "the Jewish synagogue is indeed sadly in need of Jewish music." In its absence those congregations using hymns had adopted Christian songs, particularly those borrowed from the Methodists. Many rabbis had already composed their own hymnals containing those offerings they liked best, but no single uniform book was available for all congregations to buy. The discussion ended on a note of urgency, as the member rabbis were moved to recommend to the Cantors' Association that as soon as possible they compose music for a variety of Jewish prayer texts, which individual rabbis would submit; these new hymns were then to be bound as an official Jewish hymnal. The "fault," in other words, was declared to be in (a) the non-Jewish music and (b) the lack of uniformity in the extant books.

The cantors, however, were loathe to accept the invitation. There was no guarantee that the lyrics forwarded by the individual rabbis would ultimately be accepted by the rabbinic body. Without such a guarantee in advance, the cantors were unwilling to proceed with the arduous task of musical composition. But the next year, tired of waiting, the rabbis voted to collect whatever music they could find and to issue that as an interim hymnal. This step prodded the reluctant cantors into composing some new tunes, however, and a hymnal was finally produced. An introductory volume appeared in 1893 and a definitive hymnal was published in 1897. Reform congregations should now have been able to sing hymns.

Indeed, if sales are any indication of success, success was guaranteed. Even the 1893 volume, which its editors declared to have been so hastily produced as to contain "little of permanent value," was (to everyone's surprise) received enthusiastically. By 1911 the official book was practically a best seller, given the limited market available at the time. But also to everyone's surprise, even though most congregants had a copy, almost no one made any use of it.

So the next year yet another discussion was scheduled for the rabbis' convention. A speaker addressed the problem of "The Reintroduction of Congregational Singing." He reviewed the long history of Jewish congregational singing and concluded that it was "rather strange" that, in spite of the publication of the hymnal, "in few, if any, of our large congregations do even a minority of those assembled on Sabbaths or Holidays really sing the hymns."

He was right. A survey taken the following November revealed "the most surprising result . . . that the hymnal is even less generally used than had been assumed."

This sorry pattern was to be repeated time and time again. In 1930, for example, the rabbis met to figure out how to stimulate congregational singing. In 1932, and again in 1960, new hymnals were produced, but the "full-volumed joyful noise" called for back in 1912 never materialized. Again people blamed the hymnal, or the kind of music, or the cantors, or the choirs, or anyone and anything around who could conveniently be scapegoated.

As recently as 1977 all the old hymnals were deemed outmoded, and plans for a new one were instituted. That year an interim edition with a flashy, inviting cover was published. To my knowledge almost no one ever uses the interim book. Though a few cantors or musical directors may resort to it at times to find a musical setting for a prayer, the individual congregational members neither own the hymnal nor have a copy of it in the pews; ninety per cent of them probably do not even know the book exists. So the interim hymnal managed once again to do absolutely nothing to encourage communal singing. Undaunted by evidence that 1979 is no different than 1892 in that, then as now, new hymnals do not communal singers make, the editorial board that year proceeded on the final edition. In November 1987 the book finally saw the light of day. Its publication was heralded at the biennial convention of Reform synagogue leaders meeting in Chicago. Every single one of the 4,000 delegates was given a free copy to take back home, in the hope that the gift would promote mass sales around the country. It is too soon to say whether the 1987 hymnal will be more successful than the 1897 one. But it seems abundantly clear (to me, at least) that no book, no matter how well conceived, will *by itself* solve the problem of getting people to sing their prayers.

At least no new book *alone* will solve the problem. When we simply declare the hymnal the culprit and change it every so often, we scapegoat the song book; and scapegoating the song book is no different than scapegoating anything else. It ignores the basic underlying problem.

In all these instances, we would be better off stopping our futile search for an imaginary culprit responsible for undermining our efforts. No amount of scapegoating will successfully correct what is essentially a much deeper defect going beyond, for example, what particular hymnal is in use or what particular Hebrew teacher or secretary is now being employed. The underlying fault does not lie in any one single entity in the prayer service, the law firm, or the Sunday school. In each case the culprit is the institution as a whole. Put another way, we can identify the problem as inhering in the very system of things of which it is a part. The problem, then, is systemic.

The notion of a systemic problem has been around for so long now that it is amazing to see how long it has taken us to apply it to the area of ritual. All that is required is a rather elementary understanding of systems.

We all know what a system is, and we regularly act with that understanding in mind. Imagine your son sitting at one end of a teeter-totter. On the other end is a much lighter child, so that your son finds himself sitting permanently on the ground with no way to divest himself of enough weight to get his end of the teeter-totter to swing in the air. After trying in vain to push himself up, he calls you to help. Now you could (but you don't) reason that the problem lies with your overweight son, who must be pushed up; this diagnosis would lead you to go to his side of the seesaw and lift it up, thus forcing the other end down. But only a fool would do that, because it is much harder to lean down and pull up than it is to reach out and push down. So the normal correction of the weight inequity is to go to the other side (the one where the light child sits perched on high) to push that end down, and as the consequence to let your son ride his end up.

The reason we can and do act that way is that we know instinctively that the teeter-totter is a system. We recognize intuitively that any problem with one of the elements in the teeter-totter (in this case, one of the riders) is really a problem in the relationship between the system's constituent parts (in this case between the light child, the heavy one, and the relative position of the fulcrum that distributes force). So a malfunction that surfaces in one of the parts can be solved without ever going near that part. We adjust a completely separate part and thus redistribute the relationship between the parts, eventually reaping the reward in the part perceived as "The Problem."

Our choice of where exactly to apply the corrective measure in the system depends first on how the parts are related. We would never think to push down on the middle, or fulcrum, for example, since that wouldn't change the relationship between the ends. We must also know what part within the system is available for us to tackle. Thus, we could have pulled up the fat child, but that would have been harder—that is, less available to our efforts. The problem, in any case, is the way the parts of the system relate to each other; the problem is with the teeter-totter and its two inhabitants (seen as a whole), not with the single rider who happens to sit on one of the ends.

Of course the seesaw is a mechanical instrument, and the relationship between its parts is easier to recognize than in those systems that involve people only. But there are people-systems, where the relationship between the parts (the people) is mediated not by a mechanical observable entity, but by less tangible relationships. A case in point is an imaginary renowned physicist whose son enters college bent on emulating his father. To everyone's surprise, the son, who did so well in high school, simply cannot master college science. The anxious father virtually drives himself crazy trying to help his faltering son, but in vain. Finally, deciding that the son must suffer from some emotional

45

block, the father schedules the young man for some psychiatric counseling. But the psychiatrist insists on talking to the father, too, and eventually convinces the father to leave the son alone, not even to inquire how he is doing or what he is studying. Amazingly, nothing whatever is prescribed for the perceived problem, the son. Yet, lo and behold, two things happen. First, the father discovers he can live quite well without having to bear the burden of his son's successful completion of college. Second, the son, freed from the anxious parent who obviously shone in the very area the boy wants to master, discovers he is able to complete his assignments, and he begins to do as well as his aptitudes had indicated he should.

This, too, is a system, involving an apparent "sick part," the son; other parts presumed to be "healthy," like the father; and connecting links of a variety of emotional ties. The psychiatrist recognizes the relationship between the parts and knows that, even though the "sick" part is not available for corrective measures, a remedy can still be applied to the other part (the father) so that the benefits extend back to the son. Without recognizing the system, the psychiatrist might well have scapegoated the son, and induced the boy to spend years in therapy trying to make him better, by which time he would have failed school.

So let us take a look at rituals from the perspective of systems. For simplicity's sake we will limit our description to communal worship, that is to say, to a particular type of religious ritual, rather than trying to encompass all rituals ranging from football rallies to people going out to lunch, or even just all rituals dealing with religion, from baptism to ordination of clergy. We shall call our system "The Worship System."

At the outset, we have to recognize that each system is really part of a network of subsystems within a larger system, yet each can be broken down into its own smaller subsystems. Recall the boy on the teeter-totter, for example. The teeter-totter system, if we can call it that, was part of a larger "playground system." The problem of the inequity in weight could have been solved by having recourse to other things in the playground. For example, the light child could have been given a large rock to hold, thus equalizing the weight of the two children. We would then have solved the problem by adjusting the boundary between the system under analysis (the teeter-totter and its riders) and the larger system of which it is a part (the playground). Seen from this perspective, the system under discussion is always a subsystem of some other larger system, which, to continue the imaginary progression, is itself subsumed under a higher-order system, and so on.

By the same token, working in the other direction, the teeter-totter, which is a subsystem of the playground, can be arbitrarily broken down into its own subsystems. The heavy child, for example, may himself be considered as such a subsystem, as can the mechanical parts that make up the teeter-totter. Perhaps, focusing on the latter, we might notice that the fulcrum is really movable, and that we can rearrange the forces exerted by the two riders by moving the fulcrum from the center toward one of the ends.

Our worship system, then, is a part of a larger system, which we can call the Church or Synagogue System. (See Diagram 3:1 for details.)

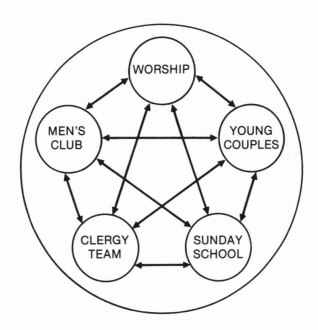

Church or Synagogue
System

[Diagram 3:1]

Worship is one of several subsystems of this larger whole, the others being such systems as The Young Couples Club, the Men's Club, the Sunday School, the Clergy Team, and so on. Frequently rituals that go wrong in the worship system can best be handled by doing something to one of these other subsystems of the "parent" Church or Synagogue System. (Let's call them first-generation systems). There is a sort of input from one system to the other, so that by changing the Sunday School system in certain prescribed ways, we would alter the way children perceive worship, and rituals within the worship context might be more successful. Similarly, to revert to a problem mentioned earlier, the synagogue that couldn't teach Hebrew might find greater success if it were to alter the worship system, regularly singing certain Hebrew prayers, for example, and making it clear that participation in the attractive ritual involving group singing demanded precisely the Hebrew knowledge that could be gleaned from the educational system. In this case, we would be adjusting the boundary of two first-generation systems (worship and education) changing the worship system in such a way as to adjust the input to the educational system, and thus solving what was originally perceived as solely an educational problem without directly altering the educational system at all.

But suppose we look at the worship system without consideration for its other, parallel, first-generation systems. Like the simple teeter-totter, it turns out to have subsystems of its own—we'll call them second-generation systems—though these are by no means as clearly visible as the first-generation system, worship, of which they are components. In fact, the very division of the worship system into its constituent subsystems may be quite arbitrary, depending in large part on what will prove helpful in the end, in terms of our long range goal: understanding how ritual works and converting empty ritualization into full rituals, complete with shared Moments.

We begin with the individuals who make up the system, the people who have come to pray. Each person is an individual with his or her own personality, character, aptitudes, moods, and so on. Moreover, each participant in prayer has come from other personally engrossing systems: their particular families, for example, or their jobs, or neighborhoods. Each of these will have had an effect on what is expected from prayer, and consequently, on how much knowledge or emotional commitment each person can or will invest in the ritual about to occur. The extent of concentration, the appreciation of the music or sermon, the very ability to recognize what the ritual is about and to participate in it—all these critical items are affected by the various systems out of which our worshipers have emerged and in which they participate at other times, perhaps that very day. Each individual, then, can be isolated as a system in and of him- or herself. So as not to bias our arbitrary breaking down of the worship system inadvertently by using emotionally charged labels, let us call each individual an A system. The individual worshiper, then, is the first of three worship subsystems—or second-generation systems—worth enumerating.

Before we move on to the second subsystem, however, we must recall the nature of the particular first-generation system of which the A system is a part. It is worship. Hence, though we could be interested in anything that makes up the complex individual we are calling A, the focus of our interest in A is not how A functions at work or in leisure time, for example, but how A relates to the act of worship. We don't have to define right now what worship is. That will come later. All we need to say is that by definition we have isolated a system called worship, and either our title is without any meaning, or there must be some entity called worship. Too many people have spent their lives at empty rituals and concluded that they or the people they know are necessarily negatively disposed to worship. They don't believe in it, they will say; though they come to prayers, they come not to pray but to hear the sermon, or to enjoy the company of friends, or to respond to an invitation of a family celebrating their child's confirmation. So their experience leads them to deny that within themselves they have any need or desire to worship. If they are correct, they are really not part of a worship system, and we would be better off naming the system represented by their gathering by some other name that better expresses what they are doing there.

But there is no reason to assume they are correct. When they say they personally do not need to pray, they are unknowingly "scapegoating" themselves, mistakenly (though understandably) blaming themselves for a system failure. To be sure, their past experience in a worship system that too often has broken down into empty ritualization without Ritual Moments cannot and should not be denied. But it does not follow that these people are congenitally incapable of experiencing ritual in a smoothly functioning Ritual System any more than it follows that people who have never gone to a good art gallery would not be able to appreciate art if they were given the chance to see it. Of course if they have been led to think that what they have seen are art galleries, they will surely claim that art is of no interest to them. But here, too, they would be scapegoating themselves. The problem lies not with them but with the "Art System," which has led them to identify "non-art" as "art."

The situation with people who say they cannot pray is identical. Substitute "church or synagogue" for "art gallery," and we find people who have experienced empty ritualization (= non-art) instead of ritual (= art). Mistaking ritualization for ritual, they conclude that religious ritual is meaningless. Since, however, they hear that other people appreciate religion (as in the above case it was known that some people enjoy art), they blame their incapacity to respond to prayer on themselves.

But if the word "worship" is to have any semantic reality at all, it must correspond to some genuine human experience, and there is no reason to assume that the ability to pray cannot be as general a human aspiration as the desire to eat, talk, or play. We therefore posit a need to worship as making up part of everyone's A system, though we grant that this need may rarely or even never have been met.

Moreover, to be absolutely clear about what we mean by worship, we have to say something about God. We need not to get bogged down in theological debates, but it seems pretty clear that when Jews and Christians speak of worship, they have in mind some kind of communication with or apprehension of God. When we say that the individual worshiper (or A system) has a need to worship, we mean that a man or woman in prayer must be able to (1) actually encounter God; (2) recognize the divine encounter for what it is; and (3) learn to express that encounter in communication, verbal or otherwise. Later we shall see that one of the causes for the breakdown of the worship system is a misunderstanding regarding the appropriate metaphor to express the divine-human encounter in our time, and a consequent failure to recognize that encounter, even when it occurs. Rather than fumble for the right words now, let it just be said that I have no intention of avoiding what most people consider the real issue of worship: the presence of God. A later chapter will be devoted to it.

There are other A-needs, too, certainly: the need to socialize, or to receive communal recognition, for example; and they, too, may be met in the worship setting. But they may also be met elsewhere. What we are interested in is what makes prayer different from football rallies, study groups, and family reunions. Worship enables people to encounter God. So for the worship system to be a worship system, the A-need requiring discussion is precisely what the title of the system says: worship.

Now consider all the individuals, all of the A's, who come together in prayer. They are transformed from individuals into a worshiping assembly with its own unique rules and regulations of behavior that can arbitrarily be isolated as another second-generation system, which we can label "B." If the A system is the domain of the psychologist, the B system is the realm of the sociologist. Of course the worshiping group, or B system, exists only because of the individual A's; if the A's didn't come, there would be no B. But precisely because the individuals (the A's) depend on the group (B) to meet whatever A-needs they have, there arise certain group needs, too. If, for example, the group possesses no common language, so that individuals within it cannot communicate, or no structure, so that people don't know what they should or should not be doing, then the group will not satisfy the needs of its members; the people will stop coming, and the group will disband. These group needs we can call B-needs.

Now when we were talking about the A-needs of individuals, we were careful to differentiate worship from other activities that people enjoy. This led us to identify the recognition of a divine-human encounter as the particular A-need that is most pertinent to worship. Here, too, as we discuss our worship group, we should ask how a group meeting for worship differs from a group meeting to play bridge or to hear a concert. What special B-needs does the worship group have if it is really to be a congregation at prayer?

Before answering that question, we have to step back for just a moment and consider how religious groups differ from non-religious ones. Imagine the following conversation. The scene is the conclusion of a church social.

51

Allan: As your organizer for this wonderful evening, I have a request of you all. Please help us take all the dirty dishes into the kitchen and move all the tables to the side. Thank you. (At this point everyone begins helping except George).

George: Why should I help, Allan?

Allan: Because the Sunday School needs this room tomorrow morning at 9:00 A.M., and it doesn't seem fair to ask the maintenance staff to do all the work cleaning it up.

George: Why not? That is their job.

Allan: True, but it's only right to help out when we can.

George: Why?

Allan: Well that's what Christianity is all about, isn't it? Haven't you ever heard of Christian charity?

What makes the conversation interesting is that George keeps receiving different answers to what sounds like the same question ("Why should I help?"). At first Allan gives him the practical answer, "Because we need the room tomorrow morning." That fact is undeniable. But George doesn't see what it has to do with whether he should help or not, so Allan "ups the ante," so to speak, and reverts to an ethical answer, "Because it's not right to make the maintenance people do all the work." Ethical advice is deniable, however, so George now argues that it is right to let the maintenance people do the work for which they contracted. Now Allan feels the need to justify his own ethical judgment by recourse to a religious notion that both he and George must surely share as members of the same church. This final answer, "Christian Charity," is unarguable. You either believe it or you don't.

Arguments regularly "progress" through these three stages: from (1) disagreement over *facts*, which are empirically demonstrable; to (2) disagreement over *logical deduction* from those facts, which is rationally arguable; to (3) disagreement over *first principles*, which are assumed to be self-evident.

The problem with identifying a group as "religious" is the cultural bias that we Jews and Christians bring to the word "religion." We would like to say that a religion ought at least to have a belief in God, and, in fact, we have actually done just that in so far as we have identified a particular A-need that we called the divine-human encounter. This book is addressed to Christians and Jews in whose tradition that encounter is real. But what do we do about such great religions as classical Confucianism or Buddhism, which do not have a concept of God in the same sense that our western faiths do? Yet there are Confucian and Buddhist religious rituals, which function the way our own worship does. Similarly, closer to home, American religion contains such groups as Ethical Culture Societies and branches of the Universalist Church where a belief in a God who hears prayer, anyway, would be denied; yet these faith communities have religious services.

Two consequences flow from the recognition that there are world religions with rituals equivalent to what we call worship, but without the concept of a personal God. The first is that their rituals are indeed worship, as long as they have their own definition of worship's goal that is functionally equivalent to what we call the divine-human encounter. Later I shall call this encounter by a more inclusive title, allowing for the possibility that other faiths, too, can—as we would say—be in communication with the Ultimate Power of the Universe, but still be unwilling to describe that communication in the same personalistic terms that characterize the traditional Jewish and Christian language of prayer. But secondly, the realization that groups identify God differently allows us to look not at God, but at the groups themselves, in the hope that we can find some common feature to their structure or function that is independent of the particular God-concept that they espouse. If we can thereby avoid limiting our analysis to traditionally theistic Jews and Christians, we can hope to say something useful about the worship (or the worship equivalent) of *all* groups in all religions that satisfy the human need to be in touch with the Ultimate Power we call God. Even here among us, we might otherwise wonder what, for example, Reform Jews, Mennonites, the Society of Friends, and Orthodox Jews have in common. Obviously, it is useful to work with a generic identification of all such groups, so as to be able to make comparisons among them.

There will be two B-needs, or characteristics of worshiping groups, therefore. The first will be the nature of the group experience itself. The second will be the way in which it connects members of the group with the Divine. We have to phrase both of them in terms that are free of the bias associated with this or that church or doctrine.

Let us begin with the nature of the group experience and the attempt to define what makes a group religious. Based on what we saw regarding the ultimate basis of arguments in first principles and the common need for people to have a group that provides those principles, we can say that a group functions religiously to the extent that it governs itself and its members by what it and they consider a set of ultimate principles, which are used to justify behavior on the highest possible level, that is, on a level that is beyond argument. You either accept them or you don't. Since we all have to justify what we do, we all have such ultimate concepts, and are thus, all of us, part of one religion or another, though we may not recognize it.

To the extent that any group has such ultimates, it functions religiously in the lives of its members. If, for example, a business were to hold firmly to a final principle like, "The bottom line is the annual profit statement," it would have to be considered religious, even though the Jewish or Christian ethic would hardly applaud its religion. If a member of the board were to object to the profit/loss calculus as the final word, citing biblical ethics as justification for the objection, other board members might respond that "Business is business," meaning, actually, "You can't mix religions." If the board member persisted, he or she might be forced to resign for holding principles incompatible with the business charter, or, as religionists would put the same thing in their own traditional context, for the sin of heresy. Heretics are banned because their objection goes beyond the two elementary stages of fact and logic. They question first principles, which by definition are beyond question for anyone who wants to stay in the group.

We can go even further and reproduce the above imaginary conversation as part of a supper meeting of a chapter of the Communist Party, somewhere in Moscow.

Comrade Alexei: Before going home, please help us clear the room.

Comrade Georgei: Why should I help, Alexei?

Alexei: Because the Lenin Study Group needs this room tomorrow at 9:00 A.M., and it doesn't seem fair to ask the maintenance staff to do all the work cleaning it up.

Georgei: Why not? That is their job.

Alexei: True, but it's only right to help out when we can.

Georgei: Why?

Alexei: What kind of Communist are you? Haven't you read anything Lenin has to say about helping each other in a classless society?

Though Comrade Alexei would be the first to deny it, he is giving a religious answer to a religious question. Why help others? Because, ultimately, that is the right thing to do. How do you know it is right? Because Lenin said so. The difference between Allan the Christian and Alexei the Communist is the set of ultimate reasons selected. The former believes in God, so he quotes Christian doctrine. The latter is an atheist, so he cites Communist dogma. Both rely on ultimate sources of authority of one sort or another to justify their behavior.

Technically speaking, both men belong to religions. Allan will probably call Alexei a godless Communist, this being our modern linguistic equivalent of such older labels as heretic, pagan, heathen, and idolater. Jews and Christians will surely agree that Comrade Alexei's ultimate source of authority is unacceptable; even though it is used in this case to justify perfectly legitimate Jewish or Christian behavior, there are other cases where Communism diverges enough from Judaism and Christianity that it must be considered by them as misguided. Still it cannot be denied that from a purely formal point of view, both Allan and Alexei belong to groups that claim to know ultimate truths and to justify ways of life on a level of final principle, where further argument is not possible. So I have to call both systems religious, even though I, personally, deny the truth of the Communist "religion."

Is it possible then that even Communists worship? Yes and no.

Insofar as we define worship as implying the presence of God, obviously Communists don't worship. On the other hand they have some notion of something ultimate, perhaps party solidarity or the memory of Lenin; and they have rituals, too, a May Day parade and celebration, for instance. To the extent that they provide rituals that invoke these ultimates, they participate in "religious" rituals (which we might consider "idolatrous") designed to satisfy the A-need of Communists (whom we might call "idolaters") by setting up a group ritual in which their particular ultimates (which we might call "idols") are confronted.

Any group, then, that provides ultimate answers is by definition a religion. Every such group provides religious rituals that satisfy the individual member's need to confront the ultimate. We call our rituals of this kind, worship, and our ultimate, God.

We are ready now to return to the question of the group needs, or B-needs, that is, the needs of the B-system. We have already said that, like every other group, worship groups require all the things that make groups viable vehicles for the fulfillment of its members' needs. But these are A-needs. What more can we say about the two specific B-needs that we mentioned—needs, that is, for the group as a group?

We can answer that question on the basis of our definition of religious groups. Since religious groups provide ultimate values that guarantee personal worth, the worship group must be cohesive enough to be able to foster a sense of the members' shared affirmation of each other as ultimately valuable from a religious perspective. Worship then does more than evoke the presence of God. It provides religious identification, declares what is right and what is wrong, and explains why being a Christian or a Jew is ultimately valuable. Worship defines a world of values that group members share; it both mirrors and directs the social order in which the group lives. In Part Two, we shall call this the creation of an alternative world of experience that individuals internalize from their rituals and then enforce on their further perception of life's circumstances as they go forth from their rituals into the world at large. As the worship ritual is played out, individual members of the group give and receive messages that support their decision to affiliate with their religion and allow them to return home with their religious identity enhanced. If one A-need is to perceive God's presence, another is to see in the worship service a reflection of the religious community's identity: its goals, its values, its judgments, its concerns; so that people leave with a sense of their own value reinforced and their own identity within the amorphous mass of humanity clearly established. The B-need is whatever it takes for the worshiping community to function effectively at achieving these ends. We shall see later that the key here is successful communication.

A second diagram (3:2) will illustrate what we have been describing. First we draw an oval, representing a group at prayer. At various points on it we draw "A"s, representing each individual (or A-system), who together constitute the group (or B-system); the boundary that constitutes the oval passes through each A and represents the fact that the individual A's are united in the unique constellation that we call B.

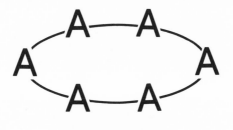

B—System

[Diagram 3:2]

Now let us recall the two individual (or A) needs that we noted. The first was an actual sense that God was somehow present, that worship really is worship, not just socializing or working together. Since people usually picture God as being "up there," so to speak, we can diagram this need by adding a vertical arrow from the group upward (Diagram 3:3). This vertical axis represents the generic equivalent of the divine-human encounter. In Jewish and Christian parlance, it is the sense we have, when we leave worship, that we have indeed prayed. For the time being we can call the vertical axis "The Transcendent" (represented by the letter T), allowing a variety of religious experiences through which worshipers are prepared to say that they have transcended themselves and encountered the Divine. The second worshiping group's need, then, is to bond the worshipers together in such a way that their sense of their ultimate identity is linked somehow to the Ultimate Power we call God.

The two needs are intertwined. We saw that when we pray together we provide a mirror image of ourselves, sending and receiving messages about the nature of reality, the values and aspirations that we hold in common; and we bind ourselves together as an actual group rather than as sole individuals, united in our commitment to ultimate purposes, respectful and affirmative about each other's worth. In contrast to the vertical axis by which we relate to God "above," this need can be represented as a horizontal arrow running through the oval, connecting the A's together. The horizontal axis is the process of group identity, the means by which individuals define and affirm who they are and what they stand for.

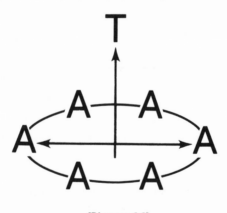

[Diagram 3:3]

One more element must be added to our diagram before it is complete. Group identity has both a positive and a negative aspect. When we say who we are, we also say who we are not. Imagine, for example, a world in which there were only men but no women. In such a universe we would have no word "man," since "man" and "human being" would be synonymous. The word "man" is necessary only because we want sometimes to say "man" = "not a woman." Similarly "human being" means "not an animal or a vegetable"; "animal" means "not a human being or a vegetable"; and so on. So every positive definitive term implies other things that are ruled out.

Moreover the items ruled out are not just things chosen at random. "Man," for example, does not imply "not a desk." "Man" means only "not those things that might conceivably make sense in context," which must consequently be overruled, e.g., "man" = "not a woman," since human beings may be either men or women (though not desks).

Hence the horizontal axis of group definition states who we are, but does so in precise ways that also state who we are not. Who we are not is not chosen randomly, but with care, to select out of the infinite range of possibilities only those alternative groups that conceivably we might be. So we must add to the diagram two heavy vertical lines representing the boundary of the worshiping group. And on the other side we draw other ovals to stand for the range of possible alternative group identities that our group deliberately sets bounds against. These we label arbitrarily as W, X, Y, and Z. (See Diagram 3:4.)

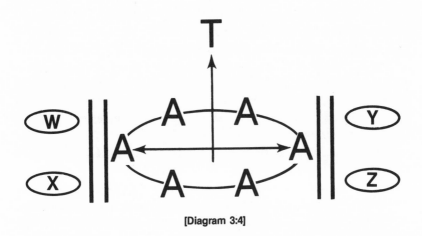

[Diagram 3:4]

Liturgies are full of examples of prayers intended to reinforce positive identification with one's own group by demarcating clearly the difference between this and other competing groups. The Nicene Creed, for example, reflects the Orthodox definition of God the Father and God the Son as separate but equal entities, according to a decision reached in the Council of Nicaea in 325. It was adopted in 473 in the city of Antioch as a boundary against a Christian group known as Monophysites. And in 589 it was similarly recited as a mark of distinction between Orthodoxy and the Aryans, another conceivable alternative Christian identity that the Orthodox Church saw as heretical.

In Judaism a blessing against a variety of alternatives, including Christianity, was added round the end of the first century, the very time when some Jews might have identified with Christianity. The blessing announced in effect that one could not be both Christian and Jew. It thereby relegated Christianity as an option beyond the double boundary line, making it one of the W-X-Y-Z network beyond the pale.

I could go on at length, indicating the many prayers now in worship services that began as subtle or outright denials of alternative group identities, but the examples given should suffice to illustrate the point. Though the groups that compose W,X,Y, or Z change with time, the process of defining our religious community against some alternative or other is constant. Old prayers (or for that matter, actions—consider how the way people baptize indicates the church to which they belong) may or may not remain, once the alternative against which they set boundaries is no longer a reality. But new prayers or actions will in any case be added as boundary markers against new alternatives. The horizontal axis of group identity cannot be understood without comprehending at the same time who the reasonable alternatives across the boundary are.

It will come as no surprise by now to see that I call the final subsystem of the worship system the "C-system." It consists of all the technical props for worship: the prayer books, pews, cups, crosses, flowers, incense, special clothing (robes), and so on. Obviously the entities that compose the C-system are not people and can have no needs in the sense that human beings do. But even an inanimate system is a system that either functions or does not, and therefore has "needs" or conditions that must be met for it to work. To take an obvious example, the cup must have wine in it and be available to those who are supposed to drink it.

The C-system here is not unlike the teeter-totter seen independently of the people riding it. Both are subsystems of a larger whole; each is a mechanism for achieving its own appropriate ends. The teeter-totter is a simple device that even little children can figure out and manipulate successfully to give them the desired ride. The worship C-system, on the other hand, is very complex, composed of hundreds of items with no necessary, built-in, mechanical rules governing the way they are to be manipulated in the worship ritual. Clergy spend considerable time memorizing the rules and practicing the art of using the C-system. They know that proper handling of the C-system items enhances the possibility of achieving both A-needs and B-needs. In other words, proper use of the objects of worship fosters a sense of God's presence and builds a firm sense of group identity.

The most important thing to recognize about the C-system is that the worship props making it up must be congruent with the nature of the congregation using them. People raised in a high church tradition are taught to identify religion with the replete regalia that goes into worship, and they may be most distressed in a Quaker meeting house. They may say that they have trouble finding God there or that they find the group of Christians around them somewhat foreign. Jews may be unable to pray effectively in a room containing a cross, since the cross is a C-system item immediately identifiable with Christianity, and therefore, in most Jews' minds, incompatible with Judaism. They will say, "This just doesn't feel like a synagogue," by which they mean, "We cannot achieve Jewish group consciousness here." Ideally, then, the C-system consists of items with which the worshipers identify, and (to revert to our previous discussion on symbolism) their identification should be on the emotive level of symbol. The use of these props according to the right rules reminds us of who we are, tells us that our group and its values are supremely important, and suggests the possibility of God's presence among us.

When a group finds its self-image changing, the first thing it generally does is change the C-system, which it identifies as "just things" and easier to tamper with than the members themselves. Sometimes they are right. The church architecture may be too barren, the seating too impersonal, the ritual objects meaningless. A more proper explanation of the problem is not that the C-system has changed, but that they, the worshipers, have. The C-system no longer suggests what the group's newly formed identity has become. We shall see that much of our problem with worship today is that the C-system is not compatible with the emerging group identity of the B-system. It is unable to suggest either personal significance or the presence of the divine, thus thwarting the A-system. When people say they cannot pray, one way to help them discover that they can may be to change the C-system. Exactly how it should be changed will concern us later when we know more about today's religious identity.

In sum we have identified all phenomena as systems that must be treated as wholes. Seeing the worship system this way, we have divided it into three convenient subsystems labeled according to the first three letters of the alphabet. The individuals are each A-systems; the totality of such individuals coming together as a praying group constitutes the B-system. And the props they use during prayer—everything from the layout of the space to the design of the books—make up the C-system. The C-system, too, has needs if it is to function smoothly: carpets need cleaning and hymnals require storage space, for example. But props serve people, so our focus is still the individual worshipers who need to achieve a sense of God's presence (the vertical axis) and a feeling that they belong to a group with an inherent right to express their ultimate values (the horizontal axis). These two goals of worship are the two axes on which successful worship rests. Horizontally speaking, members of the worship system identify with each other and draw moral guidance as well as human sustenance. Vertically, they relate to God in a way they call prayer.

The most common reason why these two eminently desirable goals are not always achieved is the next subject to concern us.

4

Sending Messages

SUCCESSFUL RITUAL REQUIRES SUCCESSFUL COMMUNICATION. Participants in the Lunch Ritual, for example, were able to celebrate the Lunch Moment because they shared the capacity to send and receive messages that all could understand. The Democratic or Republican national convention works because people recognize the cues telling them when to applaud, when to stop, and so on. The mother about to nurse her child knows how to respond to a certain kind of cry, which she has learned to recognize and to interpret as the hungry cry, and she prepares both her baby and herself in the familiar ways that tell the child food is on the way. In worship, too, people have the satisfaction of successfully completing the ritual only if communication amenable to the experience of worship is successfully sent and received.

Communication is the script in action, so to speak, telling each participant what to do, when to do it, and how to respond to the others; it is the "energy" that makes the ritual system run. Despite the obvious differences, a machine that requires an uninterrupted energy circuit, too, will serve as a very nice analogy.

Most of us have thermostats in our homes; these simple gadgets are outfitted with a metallic strip designed to bend according to the temperature of the room. At a given point this metal piece bends enough to make contact with another, and an electric circuit is activated. The circuit in turn starts the furnace. Put another way, we can say that the thermostat tells the furnace to start, or that communication amenable to successful heating occurs.

The thermostat can break down in a number of ways. But what makes it so simple is that its repertoire of communication is limited to the binary function of telling the furnace either to heat or to shut down. So, for example, the metallic strip may break off, in which case the message to heat will not get across. The system has stopped communicating. Alternatively, the dial on which the temperature is written may not reflect the correct point at which contact is made; though we set the dial to sixty-eight degrees, contact does not occur until the temperature in the house dips to sixty degrees. In this instance we freeze through eight degrees because, even though the system is communicating, the message to heat or not is getting through at the wrong time. In these cases of breakdown, a problem results from the faulty execution of a simple communication. The simple message of "Heat (yes)!" or "Heat (no)!" either does not get through at all or does not get through when it should. Never do we get the case of a message regarding heating being converted into a message about something else. That is, the thermostat never tells the furnace to light up with colors, or to dance, or to turn on the faucet in the bathroom, because the message repertoire of the thermostat and the furnace is unidimensional. Thermostats send and furnaces receive messages about heating, but nothing else.

The communication repertoire of more complex machines, on the other hand, is multidimensional. The dashboard of my car hides an intricate wiring system that connects buttons and dials to lights, windshield wipers, a cigarette lighter, a defroster, and a radio. Under normal conditions, when I push the right button, the circuit controlling the appropriate function is activated. But it is conceivable that once in a while a malicious mechanic might switch them, so that when I activate the dial for the lights, the windshield wipers go on, and vice versa. In such a case the message being sent does get through, but it is diverted along the way and converted into "meaning" something other than what was intended.

Rituals are more like the automobile dashboard than the thermostat-furnace, though they share something with both examples. What they share is the fact that successful completion of the ritual "circuit" depends on the proper message "script" being both sent and received according to schedule. But rituals, like the dashboard, have multidimensional message repertoires. And the usual problem with rituals that don't work is not that the messages fail to get through, but that the dimension on which they are sent differs from that on which they are received.

We can picture these different "dimensions" of message sending as if they were alternative wave frequencies or channels on a multimedia communication machine, like television. A television receiver must tune in to the right reception channel, or even the most painstaking and sophisticated message will not get through. There is this difference, however, between the television analogy and the system we are describing. On television many senders broadcast simultaneously, each on its own assigned frequency, and we receive whichever of them we wish just by tuning our dial to the channel corresponding to the frequency in question. In most normal human communication systems only a single sender broadcasts at a time, but it is as if that single message is immediately scattered onto many parallel frequencies (or channels), each with a different scrambling code, so that the same message emerges differently, depending on the channel we are tuned to receive. Some idea of this process lies behind the popular idiom we use to describe people who hear us but somehow miss the point of what they hear: "They were not on our wave length," we say, or, still more precisely, "They weren't tuned in to what we were saying." They may insist, however, that they were, because they did hear us say something. But we will be equally adamant that what they heard was not what we meant. Communication requires listening to more than just our words, for it is as if the same words are scattered across many competing channels the minute we send them. Our listeners must be tuned to the right channel, or they will get the words, but miss the point.

A good case study of what I mean is the ritual we normally employ when meeting someone we know. You bump into your friend on the street and say, "Hello, how are you?" The proper response is, "Fine, thanks, how are you?" The point is that your casual friend is supposed to answer "Fine thanks" even if she is not so fine. If she responds instead by telling you all her woes—how her kids have chicken pox, how she has begun to disappoint her clients, how she fights with her husband, or how she has started drinking too much—she may find that (unless you are very close friends) you quickly extricate yourself from an embarrassing situation. The communication wires got crossed. You sent a simple Ritual Greeting Message, "Hello, how are you?". But your friend was on the channel where words are decoded literally; the message was thus removed from the dimension we call "Greeting" and interpreted as if it were on the dimension of serious intimate conversation. Communication got through, but the message was routed onto the wrong channel along the way, where it was decoded inappropriately. We might say that communication amenable to greeting was sent but not received. The result was dissatisfaction by both partners. You were denied the conclusion of the Greeting Ritual, while your friend didn't get the sympathy or the help that her troubles deserved. Both people ended up embarrassed, which is to say, neither knew how to complete the ritual script properly.

The most prevalent problem with rituals, then, is not that communication does not get through, but that it is routed onto a different human frequency, so to speak, and decoded improperly by its receivers. Ritual systems are composed not of mechanical parts, after all, but of people, who are blessed with a multidimensional communication repertoire of immense capacity. So the human receiver can usually make *some* sense of the messages received. Unlike the television set, which cannot change channels to adapt to a message that seems incorrect on the frequency to which it is tuned, people generally enter a conversation alert to many possible channels of meaning and then adjust their reception capacity to the one that makes most sense. The problem with faulty ritual is that the messages sent are received, but on a channel—or dimension of meaning—other than what the sender intended. In such a case we say that the completed message was not amenable to the particular ritual experience that the ritual script ostensibly called for.

So when people say of religious ritual, particularly worship, that they have no use for it, or that they do not experience it, or that it doesn't work, they mean that the experience we call worship isn't happening, even though they sit through the ritual in which it is supposed to occur. And a common cause for their complaint is that the worship system is somehow scrambling the communications so that the completed message is not amenable to prayer.

To be sure, the normal response to a system breakdown is to scapegoat the person at the other end of the communication.

Parishioners will be quick to indicate their dislike for long-winded sermons that the minister insists on preaching, while at the next ministers' convention the pastor will grumble about the rampant irreligiosity and dearth of spirituality in churchgoers. But scapegoating rarely solves problems. Next Sunday the minister will probably give another sermon designed to awaken dormant religiosity, and parishioners will go home once again shaking their heads at the mental incapacity of their spiritual leader.

How much better it would be if we were to:

(1) diagnose the problem as systemic,

(2) decide that the problem lies in the worship system as a whole,

(3) analyze the relation of the worship system to its other first-generation systems to see if they are getting in the way of worship,

(4) determine what might be wrong with the subsystems of the worship system, that is, the individual worshipers (A), the worshiping group (B), or the worship props (C), and then

(5) turn our attention to readjusting the system so that communication amenable to worship can be sent and received.

Keeping in mind our twofold definition of worship goals, we can see that our question about communication turns out to have two parts. Worship services actually take place, but people say worship doesn't happen there, at least not in their experience. That means that, first, the script of the worship ritual is being scrambled somehow so that even though people hear the hymns and read the prayers, they have no sense of them as the sort of thing that evokes what we call the vertical axis or the Transcendent; and second, they receive no clear definition of their religious identity as members of an ultimately meaningful group. That is to say, the level of communicative discourse is not amenable to worship, as we defined worship in the last chapter.

Seeing the worship system as interacting with other first-generation systems, we want to know whether (and if so, how) the other systems might be getting in the way, so that, for example, words of worship are perceived on the dimension of the Men's Club meetings or the Sunday School; and secondly, we want to break down the worship system itself into the three subsystems described in the last chapter to find out what might be going wrong in any one of those systems or in the place where the systems connect with each other.

In both questions we are dealing not with single systems, but with interconnections between systems. Again the thermostat provides a useful analogy for the kind of trouble that can be encountered. We spoke before of a single unidimensional message to the furnace. Suppose now, to save money on our energy bills, we buy a timer to hook up to the thermostat. The timer is an automatic device that sets the temperature on the thermostat very low all night, but raises the temperature setting an hour before we get up, so that, by the time we crawl out from under our several layers of blankets, the house has warmed up sufficiently to prevent our freezing to death before breakfast. We now have two simple unidimensional systems, each capable of sending one and only one message. The thermostat still says "Heat!" when it gets too cold, and the timer stipulates what "too cold" means at any given time of the day or night. A system breakdown may occur in either the thermostat or the timer or at the point where the thermostat and the timer come together. If the message to heat doesn't seem to be getting to the furnace, and there is nothing wrong with the thermostat, a probable source of difficulty will be the point at which the thermostat and its parallel system, the timer, come together. That meeting point or *interface* between the two systems may itself be dependent on the timer, so that, for example, if the timing mechanism is off, the information received where the thermostat interfaces with the timer will likewise be off.

So we come back to the essential principle: everything depends on everything else. Our goal is always to get the system's message through. Arbitrarily we divide the whole into systems and subsystems; we define what a proper message would be; and by looking at the various parts and their relationship to each other we attempt to correct a communications breakdown.

With that in mind we return to our worship services in which true worship as we have defined it doesn't seem to happen. We shall look first at the worship system's parallel systems and how they interface with the worship system. And then we can look at the worship system's subsystems and how they relate to each other.

Of critical importance is the recognition that, even though we have consistently used machines to illustrate our strategy, we are discussing people, not machines. The A's, B's, and C's, the interfacing of systems, and the technical talk about parallel systems and subsystems should not blind us to the fact that it is the *people* who come to pray who concern us. We should now take a closer look, therefore, at the average church or synagogue goer, and the various systems such a person participates in just by being part of that religious institution.

Synagogues I know offer their members a number of activities. These activities, moreover, tend to cluster together so that, for example, people interested in continuing religious education for adults might be inclined to attend guest lectures, but then would also be attracted to educational films or Bible study sessions. These (and similar) activities with their regular coterie of participants eventually develop organizations, like (in our case) an educational committee to plan and execute each year's study events. These events and the people involved with them are readily distinguishable from the synagogue as a whole and might be called the Study Cluster, or to use the term we are used to, the Study System. There is thus a Study System, a Youth Activity System, a Men's Club System, and so on—all subsystems of the Synagogue System as a whole, or to revert to terminology we used above, *a series of interfacing first-generation systems* paralleling each other. The Worship System is just one of these. Thus, a man or woman coming to pray is familiar not only with the Worship System, but also with several parallel systems, each providing a different dimension or channel of communication, and, therefore, a certain predetermined input to the expectations brought to worship services.

A potential problem exists in that participation in parallel systems, each on its own channel, may result in inappropriate expectations while at worship, so that the worship message or communication will be received on a channel that makes perfect sense in another system but not in prayer. Moreover, all the systems are coupled, as the timer was to the thermostat. Worship, like the thermostat, depends on all the other systems that affect it; they are like a series of timers. But the other systems may themselves have broken down, or they may interface in such a way as to prohibit even the sending of communications amenable to worship, let alone the receiving of them. Obviously we cannot consider every example of these generalizations, but a few real-life instances readily observable to any church or synagogue watcher will illustrate some ways in which worship is foiled.

David C. has belonged to his community synagogue for over ten years. He comes from a synagogue-oriented family, his parents have always belonged to a synagogue, and he was raised in a Sunday School not too much different from the one whose policy he now decides in his capacity as Sunday School Committee Chairperson. When he moved into town, he noticed that many people were not members of the synagogue, and of those who did affiliate, very few were active. But joining and working in a synagogue seem to come naturally to David. He made his presence felt quickly, and has since chaired half a dozen committees. His real interest, though, is the education of the children, since he feels personally dedicated to the transmission of his religious heritage to the next generation, just as his parents cared to bequeath it to him. In all ways, then, David is an admirable synagogue member: active, concerned, Jewishly sensitive, highly motivated. But David rarely comes to pray. In fact, if the truth be told, even when he comes to prayer services he still does not come to pray. People don't usually discuss the matter, so he has never had to confront this anomaly, but David has never taken worship seriously. He feels at home in the sanctuary and recognizes all the cues by now, so that he knows when the ritual script calls for him to sit, stand, read, sing, or listen. But emotionally speaking he is not involved in his prayers. In fact praying bores him. His mind wanders even while his lips move in mechanical recitation of the text. Occasionally the sermon or discussion makes him think a little, and sometimes he is moved by a particularly artistic cantorial rendition. But generally he passes the time looking around the room to see who else is here tonight and looking forward to the chance to talk during the coffee hour that he knows will follow Sabbath eve services; sometimes he uses the time to plan particular official presentations that he will be called upon to make during services by virtue of his role in the Sunday School Committee.

That is what David is doing now. Tonight is Scout Sabbath, a special annual Sabbath service honoring the scout movement. The pulpit is outfitted with a row of special chairs where uniformed scout leaders are sitting. Also the congregation is fuller than usual, its regular worshipers augmented by faces new to everyone, people who have come because their children who are scouts are being honored. David's job is to offer a word of greeting to the children and their parents. As the congregation rises to participate in a prayer, he has just about finished figuring out what he will say.

David doesn't know it, but he suffers from all the problems listed earlier.

To begin with, he is incapable of receiving any communication whatever on the worship channel. Unknowingly he consistently decodes such messages in a context other than worship, one where he feels more comfortable, usually the channel that we can call instruction or education.

He is the product, you see, of a religious school system that dealt only in signs, never symbols. Insofar as it was ever dealt with at all, worship was taught as a cognitive discipline with certain facts and lessons to be committed to memory and reasoned through. The educational system was modeled after the public schools, outfitted with a curriculum of subjects, and structured with grades that one passed through. But how do you "pass" prayer? In a school oriented around the mastering of skills and data, that determination can be made only on the basis of demonstrating the capacity to manipulate concepts and items *relevant to prayer*, but not prayer itself, and that is exactly what David once learned. When he was young he memorized important prayers and responses and internalized some general notions about what Jewish prayers said. As a teenager he even learned their histories, often fascinating accounts of how this or that prayer text had come about in antiquity or the middle ages. The actual expression of his own religious feeling, however, had no place in the curriculum, so even if as a child David had (by chance) ever experienced worship, he certainly never learned how to accept it and to talk about it, and therefore

he never had his sense of religiosity in worship reinforced.

We would say the educational system got the best of him.
Taught to accept only rationally provable concepts and rewarded
for critical acumen, he now reads the prayer book as if the words
there were treatises on prayer rather than prayer itself; and if occasionally moved emotionally, he explains his feelings by his
ability to appreciate aesthetics. He sits back in detached admiration of the cantor's voice or the religious poetry. He can read
about worship, judge sermons on worship, and appreciate the
poetry that is the stuff of worship; but he cannot worship.

Moreover, tonight is the Scout Sabbath. There is an entire network of new people present simply because they are involved in
scouting, so that we have two systems at work simultaneously, the
Scout System and the Worship System. And they are not coupled
very well, if at all, since most of the Scout System members never
even come to the synagogue; they can barely follow the prayer
service. Bowing to necessity, the rabbis go out of their way to tell
the newcomers what to do and to give them time to find the right
page. Unfortunately that interrupts the flow of worship communication, so that even if our mythical David C. could receive
messages amenable to worship, he would not be able to do so
tonight. To complicate matters, the normal ritual of the evening
has been altered drastically to include extraneous scout rituals like
the scouts' pledge and a color guard, activities that may mean
something to the scouts and their families, but which are wholly
out of place in the context of Sabbath worship. That is to say, a
large percentage of the messages being sent are irrelevant to the
dimension of worship to start with. By sitting through the prayer
service concentrating on what he will say to the visiting scouts,
David has actually correctly perceived that this has become more
of a Scouting Ritual than a Worship Ritual. He knows that his role
in the drama being enacted is to send a message to the scouts
validating their presence in a setting that is unfamiliar to them.

If "special Sabbaths" occurred only once or twice a year, it
might still be possible for regular attenders of worship services to
celebrate the worship ritual and to achieve the Worship Moment
at least on the other occasions. But special Sabbaths have become
the norm in this synagogue, whether or not they are advertised as
such. This is primarily because the scouting movement is not the

only outside system to vie for authority in the sanctuary. David C., after all, is typical of the synagogue leaders, and he relates to the worship service from the vantage point of other synagogue systems. Since he can receive communications on the intellectual or aesthetic channels, the ritual committee has begun to program academic and artistic displays within the worship context. Throughout the year special speakers or singers are advertised in the temple bulletin and city newspapers, and predictably, new faces, drawn by the guest personalities, continually come and go. A high proportion of the messages thus regularly focus on the intruding attraction rather than on the worship experience, and the worship service, or script, insofar as it is followed at all, will not be received as worship: not by the newcomers, certainly, who have come here tonight solely to enjoy the speaker; and not by many of the regulars either, for they have become regulars in large part only because they expect good programming by now. Ironically, anyone who really appreciates prayer has probably decided to stay home. Rival systems have so taken over the worship system that the prayer service has become an empty vessel into which a whole host of *ersatz* activities have been poured. Week after week the Men's Club, the Young Couple's Club, the new members' group, the youth group, the Interfaith Committee's annual program, or a visiting folk choir—systems all—invade the sanctuary and play out a ritual as if it were worship, when in fact it hasn't been that for many years now.

No wonder David, like most of those in attendance at services, reports that he has never experienced worship, and that he finds prayer dull or meaningless. As we said at the outset, people who say they do not appreciate religious ritual should be taken with the utmost seriousness. Religious ritual, in this case worship, is not even represented at their churches and synagogues. The systems to which it is interfaced have sabotaged it to the point where worship communication is rarely sent or received; nonreligious ritual masquerades as worship, and when religious moments are described by others, people here correctly report that they have not experienced them.

A starting point, then, to providing religious Moments, real worship, is to synchronize the connections between coupled parallel systems that prevent the worship system from functioning in the first place. Educational systems should deal with symbol, not sign; children and adults should be encouraged to recognize their own religiously rooted emotions for what they are, rather than explain them away as something else. Scouts, Men's Clubs, and all other groups irrelevant to prayer should not be allowed to intrude on the worship system, even though many regulars will start going elsewhere for their entertainment. Sermons and choir performances should take a back seat to worship communications, which should be sent without apology to the growing group of pioneer regulars who learn again to pray. Just as surely as there are Nursing Moments or Sports Moments so there are Worship Moments, if we would only let the Worship System function without trying to turn it into what it is not.

But suppose we are lucky. Suppose we have a synagogue blessed with far-sighted leaders who avoid the pitfall of splintering it into its various systems and planning for each of them as if they were totally autonomous, linked in no way with each other. Suppose, that is, the various committees that decide policy for the Men's Club, the Sunday School, and so on really consider the extent to which decisions regarding the school curriculum, for example, might affect worship. The synagogue would be seen as an enormously complex network of interacting systems, and due attention would be given to the input generated by any one system and fed into another. Under these ideal circumstances, the congregation of worshipers would meet on the Sabbath for prayer, unfettered by communication disorders such as we have described.

As our next step we could turn to the Worship System itself and guarantee that communications amenable to worship occurred, and that, consequently, the Worship Moment was achieved. This would demand our looking at each of worship's three systems (the individual, the group, and the props) to see that they are functioning adequately. And we would look, too, at the interface between each of the subsystems to ascertain that no disharmony exists at their point of meeting.

Again the theory is easily illustrated by pointing to problems that every rabbi, priest, or minister will recognize immediately. Though the following examples are drawn from Jewish experience, they are by no means uniquely Jewish. Whenever I describe them I get the same grudging nod of recognition from Christian and Jewish clergy alike.

Consider the interface between individual and group. Here the most common problem is a group that has learned to receive worship communication so that the prayer service properly presents a ritual script familiar to everyone—everyone, that is, except one individual. Whereas most individuals that compose the group know the script (their A-systems interface well with the B-system, that is) one person does not (he or she interfaces poorly). The most prevalent example that I have observed is the case of teenagers and their parents.

Over the last few decades Reform Jews have discovered the tremendous impact of summer camps on teenagers. It is generally assumed, and quite rightly so, that nothing rivals the camp in its capacity to educate children in religious values and to socialize them into a religious way of life. A simple glance at the list of applicants for the rabbinate, the cantorate, and other professions related to serving the Jewish community reveals a highly disproportionate number who have elected these callings because of their positive experience as teenagers in a summer camp.

The contrast between summer camp and religious schools back home is a vivid illustration of the difference between a curriculum of signs (school) and a curriculum of symbols (camp). At camp teenagers who may only have been marginally Jewish experiment with a religious lifestyle in a supportive community of adult role-models and an extended network of like-minded peers. This is often their first experience of Jewish symbol formation, in that daily Jewish living is correlated with a warm, caring, and supportive community. Part of the experience is prayer, usually conducted in such a way as to reflect the worshiping group. The music has a soft, folk-rock character; songs led by a guitarist are sung in unison. Creative prayers are composed and read by group members, who emphasize in what they write the underlying concerns of the teenagers present. In a myriad of ways the various subsystems dovetail and produce genuine Worship Moments. Camp graduates return home imbued with the desire to continue their experience in their local synagogues.

Unfortunately that does not usually happen. One of the reasons worship works at camp is that all the other camp systems reinforce the worship system there. At home an entirely different network of systems must be confronted. Moreover the worship script at the local synagogue differs dramatically from the camp ritual to which the teenager is so attached. So we picture our teenager (the A-system) trying to function at synagogue services back home and discovering that she is completely out of step with the worshiping group there (the B-system). There is nothing wrong with her or the group. The two systems (A and B) simply cannot interface successfully.

Problems between individual worshipers (A-systems) and the worshiping group (B-system) will invariably arise when the individual and the group have different self-identities. Worship, after all, is the playing out of a symbolically overlaid dramatic script in which the group defines what it is against the backdrop of what it understands to be ultimacy (the horizontal axis). Unless our individual, the teenager in this case, is willing to trade in her symbols and teenage camp-oriented definition of being Jewish, there is no way for her to identify with the group. Ironically, the severity of the conflict varies directly in proportion to the success of the camp. To the extent that she has related to camp Judaism on the level of symbol, she will be unable to participate in her worship services back home.

This teenager's exclusion from the adult community exemplifies a more general social phenomenon with which religions must deal. There was a time when religious communities led insulated lives, in which home, work, church, civic activity, and socializing circles reinforced each other. Worship services (on the horizontal axis) had no difficulty reflecting in the strongest possible terms the deeply felt and unambiguous identity of people who knew precisely who they were. Catholics, for example, regardless of their age or sex, shared a general consensus on Catholic virtue. One grew up in a Catholic neighborhood and went daily from a Catholic home to a Catholic school where you played with Catholic friends and learned from Catholic teachers. Practices like refraining from meat on Friday were simple givens then, part of the ancient cultural values to which all subscribed. The priest celebrating the liturgy could feel relatively certain on any given Sunday that those present constituted a genuine community in which little argument would be found regarding basic Catholic doctrine and behavior.

In such an atmosphere the priest and, for that matter, the worshipers could and did send messages that were clearly understandable to each other, even though non-Catholic strangers who might have walked through the door would have been baffled by them. The closely knit social community that once was Roman Catholicism thus developed its own shorthand communication system consisting of words and gestures that evoked the same response in everyone. Children or teenagers who did not fully comprehend everything that happened did not, on that account, presume to question the validity of the Catholic system. They assumed that though they might lack the understanding to know what a given communication meant, surely their elders or at least the sisters at school knew. The fault was in themselves, not in the Catholic community. They had been taught not to identify as members of a subcommunity with the right to take issue with the larger Catholic community of which they were a part. So worship services followed predictable patterns that reinforced the general consensus of Catholic identity. No one worried about internal dissenters from the group or about people who might not fully comprehend the elaborate tapestry of Catholic faith being played out before the eyes of the faithful.

This picture is essentially true for all religions in the United States until fairly recent times. For some it began to change around the turn of the century, when enormous immigrant groups and tides of rural families inundated our cities and faced the broadening reality of polyglot pluralism, such as they had never known back on the farm. The Great Depression only hastened the move to the cities. Serving in the army side by side with Americans who were mixed racially, culturally, ethnically, and religiously further eroded one's old loyalties. Postwar mobility—both geographic and class—brought about by massive technological breakthroughs during the war completely did away with homogeneous religious groupings where everyone took old truths for granted. By the '60s people rebelled against established virtues; and by the '70s people felt so free about denying traditional values that they stopped bothering to rebel. They just opted out.

A Catholic priest today faces a very different congregation of worshipers than those faced by his predecessors. While some parishioners have attended Catholic schools, many have not. Some do not practice birth control, and others do. Some still like to refrain from meat on Friday, while the majority eat what they want, this latter novelty even being sanctioned by a modern

77

church, which has virtually revolutionized the old Catholic world that was once so predictable.

There simply is no single homogeneous Catholic community gathered in church this Sunday. Sharing little that is familiar, they no longer communicate in that special Catholic shorthand that facilitated highly sophisticated and highly satisfying worship. Communications can no longer serve to reinforce group solidarity based on a shared identity when that identity is no longer shared.

No religion in America is composed of one single group anymore. We have amorphous communities of young and old; long-time residents as well as both victims and beneficiaries of American mobility; couples, singles, widows, divorced, and on and on and on. That means that we all can nod assent only to a very general definition of identity, nothing so specific as to alienate subgroups. So our worship services emphasize only a few religious verities, usually of obvious ethical appeal, or doctrines that everyone in the group takes for granted without thinking too much about. Above all we invest little emotion in what we do. People of diverse views are allowed to come and go without getting upset. To avoid a potential conflict among the many factions among us we draw a liturgical portrait in which differences are papered over with a thin veneer of general religiosity to which everyone can assent without very much commitment. The result is ritualization, not ritual, as everyone who has experienced real worship built on symbols, emotional involvement, and genuine concern will attest.

The problem is soluble only by granting the validity of different individuals and multiple lifestyles. Within the broad outlines of group definition, subgroups who share common concerns and identities should be encouraged to adopt their own worship script. What will emerge will be a strong statement of personal identity and the discovery of religious reality. Asking everyone always to pray with everyone else in the same standardized way at the same time and place is bound to achieve only one result: what people care about most, their own personal identity, will be shared with like-minded people anywhere except the sanctuary. To be sure, they will ritualize their lives together, but not religiously. And they will continue to report that worship—that is, what goes on in the sanctuary—is meaningless.

78

So individuals who come to worship today may have trouble identifying completely with the totality of those who compose their religious group. Technically, the interface between these individuals (A-systems) and the worshiping group as a whole (B-system) has broken down. One way this breakdown can be mended is by altering the composition of the group. If the B-systems are reduced in size and converted into homogeneous groupings of A-systems, if, that is, we allow like-minded worshipers who feel a sense of community with each other to pray together without worrying about satisfying the needs of others who will be praying separately, we can establish in microcosm the community solidarity that once existed in macrocosm before urbanization, industrialization, and mobility entered our lives.

Alternatively, and I think preferably, we have to recreate a sense of genuine community among all the special interest groups, so that when they come together for prayer, they will have something beyond their special interests to celebrate. Their worship will then be a rediscovery of a newly found communal religious focus that they did not know existed. The theme of celebrating religious community will occupy us in Part Two.

Meanwhile, however, having described the conflict between the A- and the B-system, we can turn briefly for a look at the two other interfaces in the worship system: the group (B) and the props (C); or the individual (A) and the props (C). The former case is rare, since it would imply that we had a group using props that were meaningless. One can think of hypothetical examples: a group of Moslems trying to pray in Westminster Cathedral from the Book of Common Prayer, for example. But generally groups left on their own develop their own set of religiously significant items and build their worship scripts around them.

Conflicts between individuals (A) and props (C), on the other hand, are common. Our teenager returning from camp would find a synagogue with pews, an organ, and a choir. At camp, however, she learned to sit in the round, singing along with a guitarist. Or consider the reverse: her parents visiting camp worship. The same communication that evokes the Worship Moment in her is received by them very differently. Mom and Dad dislike the music, to start with, since it sounds like the same folk-rock stuff that emanates from radio and headset, but doesn't belong (they say) in religious worship. In any case, they are not accustomed to singing themselves—certainly not to a guitar—and they consider sitting on the ground uncomfortable and inappropriate. We have individuals who, as outsiders to the group, do not share allegiance to the system of objects around which the group's worship script is built. Whenever these objects are used in the communicative process, their message is lost on the strangers. They will not know when to stand up and when to sit down. When ritual objects are presented for their attention, they will not know what to do with them. Like invitees to a formal dinner party, who do not know the etiquette of what silverware to use, they will pass their time in distinct discomfort, continually looking anxiously at the others hoping to get some clue as to what to do next.

Successful worship demands that the interface between subsystems not be in conflict. In essence that means that all present must constitute a group, able to send and to receive messages appropriate to the worship ritual. The props must be mutually significant to all. Individuals must not feel out of place. Everyone must belong. If the Worship Moment is the successful communication to each individual that this group is ultimately significant, there must be such a group present, and its members must be able to identify with its significance.

5

Mixing Messages

THE PICTURE I HAVE DRAWN SO FAR is admittedly grim; I didn't plan it that way. I originally conceived of this book as an exciting description of what might be. I have certainly experienced a Worship Moment; I know firsthand the wonder of religious ritual; and I am surely not alone. But I had to come to terms with the vast majority of Americans who call themselves unchurched or unaffiliated, as well as with those who belong, technically, to a church or synagogue but who do not take prayer on Saturday or Sunday morning as seriously as the football game on Saturday or Sunday afternoon. There was no point in scapegoating them. Then, too, there are my clergy colleagues, Jewish and Christian, whom I observe going through the motions during prayer, but whose interest clearly lies elsewhere: social action, counseling, preaching—anything, it seems, other than worship. But they are victims of the system, too, and should not be scapegoated. If they do not regularly pray with fervor it is because they, too, have never known a Worship System that showed them they could. So I returned to my studies determined to comprehend the Worship System as it generally functions around the country. And, as I say, the final picture is pretty grim. In most places worship doesn't function; it dysfunctions.

In the last chapter we saw two trends that can nullify any possibility of real worship occurring. The first was the negative intrusion of parallel systems into the sanctuary, the subtle "programming" of worship time with speakers, events, music, and happenings that lay to rest the notion that anyone really expects to pray here. The second difficulty arose from the fact that religious communities are no longer so monolithic that a single prayer service can evoke wholehearted assent from all its members. So we have used worship to paper over the differences among us, making prayer into the lowest common denominator, and inadvertently sending the message, "As long as you come once in a while, you don't have to take this too seriously."

We are sending mixed messages. On the one hand we preach the supreme importance of prayer. But when prayer comes in conflict with something else—a recognition of scouting or a display of supposed denominational unity, for example—we do not practice what we preach. And that is the other message. We all know that one is judged by what one does, not by what one says.

We need to spend one more chapter on how worship fails, before we can turn to Part Two and how we may make it succeed. The picture may become even grimmer in the interim, but one rarely heals a patient by ignoring the extent of the disease. The one thing left to explore at some length is how we send mixed messages, even within the confines of the prayer service itself.

Again, our starting point is communication, the script that governs how ritual systems work. At issue are two levels of communication: one that we call communication and another that has been called metacommunication. *Metacommunication is communication about communication.*

When I was in rabbinical school, I learned to read a most difficult literature known as Talmud. What made it so hard was that the words were written with absolutely no punctuation. That meant that even if I knew each and every word's meaning, I still had trouble combining them into sentences. And without question marks or periods, even after I knew the sentences, I was never sure whether I had a question, an answer, a declarative statement, or an emphatic conclusion. Worse still, if it was a question, let us say, I had to determine whether that question was serious, a passing jest, a sarcastic objection to what someone else had said, or mere rhetoric. If the question was serious, then the following sentence would probably be an equally serious attempt at an answer. If the question was a joke, it might receive no response at all. If the question was a bit of sarcasm, the next line might be a comparable biting remark by the other speaker. A rhetorical question, on the other hand, might elicit an answer by that very questioner, or even not be answered at all. Since the Talmud is set in a genre of debate without clearly identifying the speakers, my understanding of the argument depended on how I myself construed the words and sentences. I later learned that the Talmud does have its own form of punctuation, special words that occur in the text but are not to be translated as meaning anything; they are introduced there by the editor to instruct the reader on *how* to read the words they follow or succeed.

I thus learned two lessons: first, that words by themselves are not yet communication, and second, that when people finally do convert them into communication, they do so by providing cues as to how their words should be interpreted. In literature, these interpretive cues are called punctuation. *What punctuation is to literature, metacommunication is to communication.*

Here is an example. When my children were little, they informed me that when they asked me a favor and I said, "Maybe," I really meant, "No." I thought about that for a while and decided they were right. If I was working and they asked to play a game of Monopoly, say, rather than face the fact that I was busy with something else, I would think vaguely to myself, "Maybe I'll finish in time to play," and then I would answer, "Maybe." But really I meant "Probably not," which was equivalent to a prior judgment that I would work until it was too late (because I always have more work than I have time); and therefore, in practice, "Maybe" meant not just "Probably not" but also "No." Shortly thereafter, however, one of the kids asked if we could see the circus. For a variety of reasons I was pretty sure we could. But not being sure that we could obtain tickets, I answered, "Maybe." According to their own theory, the kids should have walked away depressed, but instead they were elated. How did they know that "Maybe" with regard to the circus meant "Probably yes," while "Maybe" with regard to most other requests meant "No"?

They knew because of metacommunication. In some subtle way, I indicated how they should understand my "Maybe." We cue our own communication all the time, so that people can "read us." Sometimes it is in the way we talk (verbal punctuation). Sometimes it is by means of body language: a smile that indicates a joke or a careless shrug of the shoulders that means we don't care. If I say of the budget deficit, "The President will balance it," I may accompany my statement with the kind of determined look that shows I mean the remark as a serious vote of confidence in the present administration. Alternatively, I may smile knowingly or even sneer, so as to leave no doubt that I mean the exact reverse of what the words themselves say.

Metacommunication determines how we respond to the communication. If I really mean that the President will balance the budget, you may reply, "I certainly hope so," or, "I don't have as much faith in him as you do," or, "What Presidential policy leads you to say that?" If I am being sarcastic you may say nothing at all (in words, that is), but nod knowingly or join me in my disdainful look, thus indicating that my sarcasm is not lost on you and that you agree with me. By replicating my metacommunicative punctuation, you make my words stand for yours, just as surely as if (in writing) you were adding a ditto mark to the conversation. In either case, *how* you know what I mean depends on the metacommunicative cue sent and received. People who do not send or receive these cues very well are in a constant state of embarrassment. They never know if others are being serious or not.

As communication, worship too depends on metacommunicative cues. I recall a particular synagogue where the organist begins playing softly before anyone arrives. The ushers, who may have been joking in the corridors until now, suddenly become serious. New arrivals are greeted by ushers wearing a reserved face. The words of greeting are the same as they were two minutes ago. But the ushers' visual cue has changed. The new people nod a curt "Hello" and proceed quietly to their seats.

On most Saturday mornings the rabbi of this congregation can be found orchestrating the ritual script of a *bar-* or *bat mitzvah,* part of which calls for him to address the young man or woman who is officially entering adulthood. The entrant is barely thirteen, however, so the rabbi usually begins his charge with a metacommunicative smile meaning, "Relax; we're friends; don't worry; this will be painless." But eventually he gets carried away—surely he should say something significant on this occasion—and at that moment his voice rises while his smile disappears. The metacommunication is clear: it means, "Joke time is over; this is a religious message that you better take seriously." Throughout the address the child responds not to the rabbi's words (which, as often as not, he or she barely comprehends) but to the metacommunicative cue accompanying them.

The actual communication in worship is generally very clear. The words from the prayer book and the accompanying instructions (e.g., "The congregation rises") are usually patently obvious, deliberately so, since the congregation on any given day is made up largely of people who would not know the rules otherwise. Many are here just for the special program of the hour, like Scout Sabbath, or because of their own personal circumstances: someone in the family just died, or they know someone being confirmed this day. So extra care is built into the ritual to tell people what they are to do. That is, knowing in advance that the ritual's "actors" will not know their lines, modern liturgies see to it that the "cue cards," so to speak, are readily visible. Some synagogues even go farther: they make use of a knowledgeable person to walk around during services, prompting individuals who have special roles in the service as to what they are to do, and when they are to do it ("Go up to the pulpit now; stand beside the rabbi; she'll nod to you when it comes time to read your prayer"). So if it were just a matter of communication, everything would proceed without a hitch.

The problem is the metacommunication, however, or to be precise, the problem occurs when the metacommunicative cue contradicts the patently obvious meaning of the communication that it punctuates.

Congregational singing is a good example. In scores of places the singing is done by paid professionals who are aspiring opera singers moonlighting in churches and synagogues. Their credentials for the job consist in their ability to sing better than the average parishioners, who otherwise would be doing the job themselves. These singers may be completely untrained in the art of leading people in congregational singing, however. Let us now imagine a case in which the parishioners have recently expressed an interest in singing, with the result that the soloists have been directed to invite the assembled worshipers to sing along. This they dutifully do, but their tone of voice, the music selected, and the key in which it is sung make it obvious to all that they really do not welcome congregational singing, at least not very loud. Predictably, only a few people sing, and they do so practically to themselves.

Another example comes from the Jewish holiday of Purim. Traditionally Purim has been an occasion for noisy fun. The biblical Book of Esther is read, and people are encouraged to boo, hiss, or make noise whenever the archvillain, Haman, is mentioned. In the nineteenth century this folk tradition was dropped, or at least modified, in some westernized Reform synagogues where the accent on decorum made noisemaking, even on Purim, seem inappropriate for a spiritual house of worship. Today, however, people are rediscovering ethnicity and folk traditions and devaluing the extreme formality of the last hundred years; so the noisemaking is returning to Purim.

In one city the rabbi has begun admitting many old practices into the service, but has balked at reintroducing the Purim custom. Some people, however, want Purim fun reinstated. So several years ago the rabbi bowed to necessity and invited everyone to bring noisemakers and have fun at Purim. When the holiday finally arrived, he explained the rules of the evening and began to read the story of Esther. But almost no one made any noise! The metacommunication was clear from the rabbi's voice, his face, and his manner of explaining the rules. He said, "Make noise"; he meant, "Keep quiet."

Now the most important point about all of this is that if the worshiping group (the B-system) really wishes to avoid congregational singing or to maintain discipline on Purim despite trends to the contrary, the discrepancy between the communication and the metacommunication is not bad. Far from causing a B-system problem, it solves one. The metacommunicative message, "We are not serious about telling you to sing and make noise," overrides the content of the communication itself. The underlying *real* purpose, which is to hold on to the status quo, will easily be accomplished. The system will function smoothly despite the lip service that is paid to the changing values, which may have been fully accepted elsewhere, but not here. Success or failure in communication depends entirely on what we define as the goal of the system fueled by that communication. If the goal of our first example is to overcome a rampant populism that "threatens" to replace the tradition of entrusting artistically excellent music to trained soloists, the system works beautifully in keeping out accessible melodies that the assembly might actually sing. By inviting participation in such a way as to underline and clarify the rule against participation, it defuses a potential challenge from those who want to convert "listeners" into "singers." We can judge the system a failure if, and only if, (a) the goal of the system is worship, and (b) worship is defined by the group in question as demanding participation. So *the success or failure of a system depends on the arbitrary definition of what the system is supposed to do in the first place.* That principle will demand further attention shortly.

In either case, however, whether judged as a success or a failure, the dissonance between communication and metacommunication causes problems for at least *some* of the individuals (A-systems) who are inclined to take the communication seriously and then are cued not to. Thus when the music director says, "Please join in the singing of . . . ," there may be people present who do not read the metacommunicative cue properly. Perhaps one man who enjoys singing doesn't come frequently enough to know the music director's views, or he may be the kind of person who takes things literally and frequently misses cues elsewhere as well. To the dismay of the majority present who do recognize the cue, and who know better than to follow the explicit instructions, this man starts singing in a booming voice. Of course systems have built-in safeguards against such miscreants. Others present give the man a dirty look. If he himself doesn't notice these sidewise glances, at least his family might, and they can be counted on to shush the old boy up. If need be, people will say, "Shhhh!" rather generally, and then escalate their warning by staring directly at the fellow. Eventually special police, who go by the innocuous title "ushers," may have to step in to enforce the rule. Things rarely go that far, but no matter what stage is reached before the would-be singer is silenced, the result in terms of his own A-system is disastrous. He is frustrated, censored out of the group, unable to affirm his own place among these worshipers, and publicly ostracized by them.

The same disappointment results for the young family who comes to make noise with their children on Purim, only to find out that the rabbi isn't serious about letting them do so. Lest I be misunderstood, let me point out that the same A-system discontent would have resulted even if the roles were reversed. I am not arguing here either for or against singing and Purim noise. I am merely making the point that it is the metacommunication, not the communication, that determines what we do; and when these are in conflict, some people will mistakenly follow the communication, only to get hurt in the process. They will probably not come back, by the way, since few people willingly get clobbered twice. Instead they will join the ranks of the multitude who say religious ritual is cold, barren, and uninspiring.

The proposition that people confronted with mutually exclusive communication and metacommunication will not return to the scene of the conflict is worth more than a casual sentence. Over fifty per cent—and in some cases almost ninety per cent—of nominal synagogue or church members do not attend weekly worship services on any regular basis. The possibility should be pondered that mixed messages have sent them scurrying off to alternative activities where the rules are clear.

Consider an analogous situation: a young man has just received his driver's license. His parents are justly proud of their son, who is blossoming into manhood before their very eyes, and they tell him so at every opportunity. On the other hand, he is the last of three children to grow up and leave the nest. Underneath their pride, the parents are haunted by some ambivalence about "losing" their last child; and the father, particularly, may have some psychological problems accepting his little boy as a man.

As everyone ever faced with this all-too-common situation can attest, this interesting family dynamic manifests itself in a hundred ways. Suppose now, for the sake of argument, the son begins asking for the family car. Certain obvious conflicts arise. Practically speaking, if he uses the car on a given Saturday night, his parents may have to stay home. Less obvious, but more serious, however, are the conflicts hidden below the surface. Let us suppose a case in which the son's driving away independently in the car to meet a date signifies, to the father, the father-son conflict. When he asks for the automobile tonight, the son will get two messages. The surface communication is "Yes," but the metacommunication, that is, the way the father says "Yes," the interrogation regarding the son's plans, and so on, indicates that the father would really like to say "No." The total message then is that the boy may take the car, but it would be better if he did not. The inevitable result will be that the boy will still opt to drive, since having a date is dependent on being mobile, but he will feel guilty about it, and whenever possible he will avoid further confrontational situations with his father.

Worshipers face the same sort of mixed messages all the time. In our two cases above, they were told simultaneously, "You should sing," (the communication) and, "We wish that you kept quiet" (the metacommunication); or, "Noise is appropriate tonight, and you need not worry about keeping your children quiet," but "To be honest, we wish you would keep them quiet anyway." Indeed the very relationship between parishioners and clergy is not unlike that of parent and child. Priests are called "Fathers," after all. Clergy often represent people to whom "backsliding children" confess. So worshipers given conflicting instructions by clergy are structurally identical to growing children told, "You may," but also, "You may not," at one and the same time.

The major difference in the car analogy is the fact that the boy needs the car to meet his date. That need takes priority over the conflict with his father, so that he has no choice but to go through the ritual of asking for the automobile (answering the usual questions, making the usual promises about being careful, and so forth), and only thereafter driving away. Worshipers, on the other hand, usually have no such overriding need. Unless they are the true and loyal cadre of believers, or people tied inextricably for other reasons to the church or synagogue, they have no compelling reason to put up with mixed messages that only embarrass them and bring out the conflicts between clergy as parents and parishioners as children. To come week after week only to be told continually both "You may" and "You may not" is a no-win situation. To follow the "You may" message means antagonizing the clergy (the parent) as well as other worshipers (the children) who have decided to play it safe and follow the "You may not" message. But to give in to the hidden "You may not" means frustration because you really want to; and—worse—it entails continual verbal abuse from the clergy who excoriate you by reminding you that "You really may, in fact you should," even though they mean, "You may not—you really shouldn't."

The analogy of the young man and the car is worth extending here. If the worshipers decide to follow the metacommunication, "You may not," they resemble the teenager who decides not to take the car. He will be frustrated because he cannot drive and meet his date. And worse, as if to add insult to injury, his parents will eventually ask him why he doesn't take the car and go out on Saturday nights like the other kids.

Everyone knows enough to avoid no-win situations like that. So our would-be worshipers will probably opt to stay clear of worship services whenever possible. They may, of course, show up whenever overriding needs present themselves, just as the boy will request the car when there is really no choice. So for life-cycle events like funerals or baptisms the family will dutifully come to do what they must; and on major holidays when prayer is sensed to be absolutely necessary, parishioners will sit uncomfortably for hours in the pews, if that is what it takes; but they won't come regularly. And when they do come, they will sit passively, preferably in the distant pews near the door, essentially removing themselves from real involvement in what transpires.

Our grim picture can now be summarized. For the variety of reasons sketched above, the Worship System has broken down in the majority of American churches and synagogues. Having been taught to scapegoat themselves, the worshipers confess, "I'm sorry, but religious ritual doesn't mean anything to me." Their admission gets us nowhere. What they say is absolutely correct, to be sure, but the blame lies elsewhere. The problem is systemic. The system has broken down, because of conflict in the interface with other first-generation systems, conflict between worship subsystems, or the faulty working of one or more particular subsystems. Communications are received on a channel of interpretation that is not amenable to worship, and sometimes worship communications are not even sent in the first place. Messages are mixed, and people stop coming. No amount of preaching at people will correct the situation. We will arrive at adequate corrective measures only if we treat breakdown systemically.

Sometimes, but only sometimes, the "fault" does indeed lie with an individual, that is, within the A-system. In such a case, the analogy is a sick cell within an organism. Though the organism as a whole is healthy enough, one single deviant cell may not be. That single cell may even grow malignantly until the entire organism is affected sufficiently to stop functioning. In the face of such a threat, we resort to radical surgery, if necessary, to save the organism. We remove the pathological cell, and the organism as a whole is saved.

The parallel for our purposes can be called *worship pathology*. That is, the B-system or worship group both sends and receives messages amenable to worship; but one single organism (or A-system) doesn't fit in with the other worshipers. Usually social pressure combined with the fact that such an individual has already been convinced that the fault is his or her own—that is, he or she has accepted the role of scapegoat—results in the pathological individual sitting passively without interfering with everyone else. There is nothing really "wrong" with such a person. Only from the viewpoint of the entire B-system, of which that individual is a part, does he or she appear to be pathological. Worshipers so afflicted eventually recognize that they are outsiders, so they sit there until they can leave, and then do not return. The system has performed surgery on a potentially malignant cell, whose pathology turns out after all to have been benign.

A problem for the system occurs only when such a person slides from the category of benign to that of malignant. Take, for example, a woman who comes to worship thinking she can sing out loud. That was what the cantor said last week. When she gets there, however, she finds that the people do not sing, for all the reasons listed above. If she simply corrects her own misconception, saying in effect, "I missed the metacommunication," and thus stops trying to sing, she is still in the category of pathological, but benign. What happens, though, if she doesn't recognize the metacommunication, so that even though no one else is singing, she does? She interferes with the mood of awesome solemnity that the B-system has collectively established, and her aggressive behavior within the B-system will have to be corrected. People will look her way, whisper for quiet, or even call the ushers to reestablish the desired mood.

Alternatively she may perceive the metacommunication clearly and distinctly, but disagree with it. Having herself a need to sing—an A-need—she may rationalize her own condition by saying, "Singing together is good for worship. This congregation must be taught to sing. I shall teach them." Again the built-in corrective measures of the B-system will be called into play, but this time the pathological A-system has already decided on a course of outright defiance of the rules, so that the conflict between her and the other worshipers of the B-system will escalate to the point where she successfully prohibits the other worshipers from accomplishing their Worship Moment.

Interestingly enough, however, successful pathological defiance is relatively rare, and when it does occur, the guilty party is rarely an average worshiper. Most worshipers are hardly brave enough to risk the social ostracism that comes from challenging the B-system's corrective mechanisms. So pathology is usually limited to its benign manifestations: people who find themselves uncomfortably out of place, but do nothing about it (except, of course, not return).

So aggressive pathological behavior almost always emanates from a certain subgroup of worshipers: those who are so comfortably established in the B-system that they feel free to tamper with the communication energy that makes it work.

Both Judaism and Christianity preach that all are equal before God. The social systems of real people are never so egalitarian, however. When a handful of people first come together to form a religious community, they may relate to each other as equals, but eventually some establish themselves as decision makers, while others become decision followers. Groups at prayer are no different, in that some people act as if they belong there and have the right to determine what the rules should be, while others carefully avoid any overt act that might challenge what people are doing. I have already referred to this phenomenon by observing that some people who come to pray are regular attenders, while some come infrequently enough to be mere observers, content to watch the proceedings from the sidelines. It is time we spent some time more exactly determining the subgroups into which any worshiping assembly can be divided. Looking out at those who come on any given Sunday morning, a pastor can distinguish four such categories of worshiper, each with its own degree of propensity for initiating action, and therefore, also, for challenging the rules in a pathological way. They can be plotted diagrammatically, as if they were four concentric circles radiating out from a center where the "liturgical action" occurs.

The circle farthest from the center is the *Watchers*. These are the people who almost never come to worship. Everyone knows, if they are here today, it must be for a special reason. They may be intimately involved in some other system that draws them here: they are the parents of the scouts on Scout Sabbath, for example, or relatives of the guest preacher, come to honor their family commitment and hear their advertised famous visitor, or people drawn to the worship services to celebrate their own life-cycle events. In the last category, for instance, the most prevalent phenomenon in synagogues is the *bar* or *bat mitzvah*. Large congregations find themselves with a different *bar* or *bat mitzvah* every Saturday morning, with a majority of the congregation composed of the celebrating family's friends and relatives, but otherwise complete strangers to the habits and social network of the host synagogue. Frequently their presence so dominates the morning's proceedings that the regular worshiping group, if there ever was one, stays home. Shabbat morning becomes not worship at all, but a programmed *bar* or *bat mitzvah*, designed to reinforce individual Family Systems; Saturday after Saturday, a different family plays the role, inviting its own systemic network of Watchers for the occasion.

As strangers, these Watchers know little or nothing about the communications of the B-system. They are probably somewhat unfamiliar with the props of the C-system too. They are handed books that they may never have seen before, hear music that is foreign to them, and generally must be told exactly what to do and when and how to do it. At services other than those in which their family role entitles them to sit near the front, they may be recognizable by the fact that they prefer seats near the back, ideally near the door as well, where they can slip in and out without drawing attention to themselves. Psychologically it is as if they are prepared to make a quick exit. They are only partly present in the first place. If they must play a role in the ritual script— say they are grandparents of the *bat mitzvah*, or the father of the bride—they are told in advance what to do, and ushers make sure they sit closer to the action, prompting them when necessary to make sure they play out their part. These Watchers are the last people to tamper willfully with the system's communication, unless, of course, they happen to be mentally ill.

The Watchers are the fourth and farthest circle from the action. Let us skip over the third circle for a moment and describe the second circle, which I call *Regulars*. At the very opposite pole from the Watchers, the Regulars are the people who come all the time, not only to worship services, but probably also to everything else in the church or synagogue. They are the lay board, the decision makers, the committee chairpeople, the organizers and the attenders of most functions, the folk you can count on to make a function work. As Regulars they have completely internalized the communications. Handling the props and sending and receiving messages are second nature for them. Unlike the Watchers who sit at the back of the room, these Regulars feel free to sit up front, and even to leave their seat and move around, within the confines of acceptability—something Watchers would never do, since they don't know what those confines are. Becoming a Regular means accepting a code of conduct that is nowhere spelled out, but is part of the rules governing the many settings in which these Regulars meet. To take but one example, a would-be member of the board has to learn how far you can go if you want to challenge established policies. Failure to accept the rules will result in being dropped from the board. Hence by the time a man or woman achieves Regular status in the Worship System, he or she has fully assimilated the communications rules, and though in a position to challenge them, rarely does so. Still, the Regulars have great latitude of action, so they can stretch the boundaries a little. And sometimes this stretching becomes aggressively pathological for the system.

In many synagogues, for example, the president of the congregation is given the right to sit on the pulpit beside the rabbi and to make the announcements regarding future synagogue activities. At a prescribed point in the service, worship ceases for a moment, and the president rises to say some ritualistic things about what is happening in the next week. Actually, it is often very hard for the assembled congregants to take in what the president is saying, since the announcements tend to sound like a long jumble of names, places, dates, and times. The remarks may even be unnecessarily redundant for the very promotional purposes they are said to serve, since a list of the activities usually already appears in bulletins, newsletters, and other far more effective organs that advertise what is going on in the community. Why then does the president insist on giving them?

One reason is that the remarks succeed at something else, the hidden agenda. For one thing, they are a presidential prerogative, a sign of the president's status. For another, they give credit to the other Regulars who have organized things, conferring social status also on them. If the Regulars listen carefully, it is not to find out what is going on, since they already know that, but to make sure the activity they are personally organizing is noted. The Watchers ignore the entire Announcement Ritual, since they have no intention of coming to anything anyway. In essence this is part of the self-definition (or horizontal axis) of the B-system, and therefore not out of place in the worship setting, even though it is not worship itself.

But a "pathological" president may decide to convert the ritual into an opportunity to give a sermon. Standing at the lectern, she may drone on and on about the importance of the events, even quoting Scripture or sacred lore gleaned as a child in some Sunday-School class long ago. People now become restless, and week after week dread the interminable delay caused by the president who has stretched the boundaries of this ritual role too far. Since the Regulars know when the president's time to speak will come, they begin looking at each other with knowing glances during the prayer preceding the announcements and even find their anger spilling over into the praying time afterward, to the extent that they cannot concentrate on prayer then. This is a case of malignant pathology. One individual (an A-system) has a certain need that takes priority over the ritual script of the B-system, altering the latter's rules of communication and making Worship Moments hard to arrive at.

Another example is a particular Regular who has attended Mass for years and never gotten used to the changes introduced after Vatican II. Preferring things as they were, he cannot comprehend why English should have replaced Latin, why the priest should have turned around to face the congregation, why involvement of laypeople should be encouraged, why new music and even dancing now find their way into worship. Here is a worshiper who has become a pathological cell in a system changing its rules, while he still finds his behavior programmed according to the old set of instructions. As long as he limits his complaints to situations outside the worship experience itself, the man is benign. But suppose, as the Regular he is, he feels obliged to grouse noisily from his seat during the celebration of the Mass. He then interferes with the reception of Worship Communication on the part of those sitting around him, and may even disrupt the entire proceeding by drawing general communal attention to himself rather than to those sending the Worship Communications.

Most Regulars will not be malignantly pathological. But some may, since they feel comfortable enough to challenge accepted practice and sometimes to institute novelty; and if they do act unilaterally, they may prove difficult to deal with, since their Regular status makes them relatively immune from the normal self-regulatory mechanism (such as ushers) built into the system. They appoint the ushers, "hire" the pastor, and are the congregation's elected leaders, they will argue. They may also be major donors and valuable workers without whom the church or synagogue would have difficulty functioning. Pathological Regulars who disturb Worship Communication are therefore a serious challenge to the system.

The third circle, which we skipped over before, can be called *Movers*. In terms of involvement, they are somewhere between the Watchers and the Regulars, but they are usually in the process of moving toward one or the other of these two extremes. They may be relative newcomers who began attending as Watchers, but who now wish to enter the inner circle of Regulars. So they attend things, get to know the Regulars, volunteer for committee assignments, get appointed to minor offices, and generally build up familiarity with the rules governing conduct in the synagogue or church subsystems. On the other hand, they may be moving in the opposite direction. As new people take over leadership positions, old people leave them. There is never a complete turnover, of course: frequently, the network of Regulars constitutes its own closed corporation, tacitly preventing anyone new from entering, as those in power simply rotate among the important positions every year or so. But there are always some people who find their psychological commitment to the church or synagogue waning and discover they are spending more time elsewhere, working for the local hospital or the Red Cross, for example. They may also be people whose movement away from the circle of Regulars was forced upon them. People moving toward Regular status will not usually display pathological symptoms, since that would work against their ultimate goal of acceptance within the Regular circle. People who have chosen to move away will also rarely disturb the status quo, since they don't care enough to bother. But people forced to abandon their membership in the circle of Regulars are almost invariably prone to becoming pathological to the system.

The reasons they may have been forced out are legion. Like the man who can't stand the change in the Mass, they may be the Old Guard bent on maintaining the old-time religion. Like the long-winded president who speaks too long, they may be Regulars who bend too many rules and anger enough other Regulars that they are removed. Whatever the reason, they will probably be the center of a cluster of other worshipers who share their attitude or who like them personally. So they are usually not loners, but representatives of rival subgroups within the B-system. They represent alternative B-system identities not so far beyond the pale that the system has already censored them out. They may advocate congregational participation in a system of traditional liturgical passivity, or they may be liturgical conservatives in a church that has been moving steadily toward liberalizing old worship procedures. Whatever the case, they embody the genuine options that challenge the system as it stands. It is this group of marginal Regulars, the people who wish they were Regulars and want to reverse their social direction, so as to move toward the center of action rather than away from it, that most often generates malignant pathological behavior. Unless the B-system can reach compromises with its several subgroups led by marginal Regulars, or so successfully define itself that these would-be Regulars give up and leave, the worship service will degenerate into an outright battle. Worship, remember, always provides a self-definition of the B-system, and if that B-system is fraught with antagonism, the portrait provided by the worship service will show it.

A final source of malignant pathology is the first circle, the one to whom the sending of most communications has been entrusted: the *Professionals*. Not all religious groups have professionals in the sense of people paid to orchestrate the service. But those that do are the majority, and by vesting people with the right to lead the Worship Ritual, we give them considerable leeway to determine what we as a worshiping community will do. Naturally, these Professionals are not completely free. Usually they can be hired and fired, or at least removed by recourse to some higher authority. Usually, too, as Professionals they have studied the boundaries governing worship, both in their religious tradition, and in this particular church or synagogue particularly. But that very learning permits them the rationalization that what they do is religiously valid and desirable. Moreover, as we saw before, religious Professionals are often viewed as parental figures who by definition can decide what to do. And finally, as good Professionals trained to know how to do things, aware of the many licit options, and anxious to create Worship Moments, these Professionals are potential sources of novelty rooted in the best possible motives. But however well intentioned, innovations can, at times, fail and become pathological.

Again the list of possibilities is endless. The music director who refuses to let people sing songs that would "symbolize" positively in the worshipers; the preacher who thinks everyone comes only to listen to the sermon, so unjustly extends the sermon, but cuts back on the prayers; the volunteer choir that sings for fifteen minutes, oblivious to the fact that the congregation is standing at this point and cannot concentrate on anything except sitting down and being relieved of listening to irrelevant pseudoartistry. In sum, Professionals, though generally trained to create Worship Moments, may nevertheless (like any other A-system) have their own A-needs to foist on the worshiping B-system, sometimes to the point of disrupting the Worship Ritual and destroying any possibility that worship will occur.

In all these cases then—Regulars who change the rules, disgruntled Movers, and Professionals who misuse their power—individual A-systems encroach on successful worship in the system. We call that kind of system breakdown *Worship Pathology*.

There is, however, a second kind of breakdown that is even more serious; it is also more pervasive. Hard to spot in the first place, it is very difficult to correct. At least in worship pathology there is a culprit, some particular person (A-system) who opposes the cooperative endeavor of the other people in the group (the B-system). In this second kind of breakdown there is no such malignant cell within the system. The system just fails to function.

The mechanical analogy is usually called *the problem of the black box*. We picture a machine encased in an opaque box; we cannot see into it. The mechanical parts are not available to us for examination. All we know is that the machine does not do what it should. If we could see inside it, we might discover some particular part that is not functioning properly, but since we cannot do that, we have to treat the box as a whole, that is, as a system, and apply corrective pressure somewhere outside the box, hoping that in some way we can get the correction to spread throughout the box until it starts behaving the way it should.

Worship systems turn out to be black boxes sometimes. As far as we can see, everyone seems to be doing everything right, but worship doesn't happen. When the problem is generalized to the system in this way, so that the worship system just doesn't seem to function, even though there is no pathological part, we have the second kind of breakdown: not Worship Pathology, but *Worship Dysfunction*.

Most of the examples given so far in this book are cases of Worship Dysfunction. In the case of Scout Sabbath, for example, there is no recognizable person at fault. The same is true of the Saturday morning *bar-* or *bat mitzvah* syndrome, in which different families take over the sanctuary each Sabbath morning in order to go through their own private family ritual that only looks like public prayer. A church service built around a famous preacher may be another such case. Here the congregation is mobbed by tourists who want to hear the great speaker, who sit through the accompanying liturgy even though no praying in the true meaning of the word is reported. The same may be true, to take a new example, of a folk-rock Mass if the folk-rock is the actual activity rather than a Mass. In each of these cases the worship system is in a state of dysfunction, since by definition, an outside observer would have to say that what happened was a celebration of scouting, or entertainment, or whatever, but not what we defined as worship.

In each case, however, the people involved may be unable to recognize that there is even a problem. They come together to honor the scouts, to hear a famous preacher, or to hear some folk-rock, and that is precisely what happens. So the concept of dysfunction must be emended slightly. The system is dysfunctional only from the viewpoint of our definition of its function.

This is very important, for it indicates the difference between mechanical black boxes and human ones. If, for example, your toaster breaks in such a way that every time you put in a piece of bread, it immediately pops up burned to a crisp, you would correctly observe that the toaster is in a state of dysfunction. We distinguish now between other people standing around outside the toaster waiting in vain for edible toast, and the mechanical parts of the toaster within the toaster itself. The people, those outside the system in question, are in unanimous agreement that the toaster is dysfunctioning. That is because they can all agree that the purpose of toasters is to make toast, not charcoal. From the hypothetical perspective of the toaster parts, though, the toaster system is functioning with admirable perfection. Every time bread goes in, out it pops, burned. As a system for burning bread, the toaster is completely reliable. It never fails. If the toaster parts could talk, they would argue that the problem lies with the people observing it, who project unreal expectations on the toaster. It is not a toaster in the first place, it would say, but a burner. As a burner, it is functional and without peer. The people would then respond that if it were a burner it should have been advertised in the store as such. No one with such a toaster would hesitate to get it fixed, that is, get it converted from a burner to a toaster. The point is that *dysfunctional systems often function very well at doing something we do not want them to do.* They are dysfunctional only from the perspective of our own arbitrary definition of what they are supposed to do.

The worship system may be functioning quite well, then, at something other than worship. The difference between it and the toaster, however, is first, that with the toaster, everyone looking on could reach agreement on what functional toasters do, whereas the people observing worship systems may differ on what proper worship is. And secondly, even if we could decide what worship is—if, for example, everyone were to agree with the definition offered here—we would still be left with a system in which the internal parts are not things like the toaster, but other people. And people, unlike mechanical parts, cannot be arbitrarily tampered with.

The example of the school system that cannot teach reading is useful here. If we define the school as a system that is supposed to teach reading, then the system is an obvious failure. No teacher or principal is walking around deliberately sabotaging the learning process, however, so we have no obvious case of pathology. This is system dysfunction. Predictably, the school board and PTA become frustrated at a general systemic problem and scapegoat something: the curriculum, perhaps, or the reading teacher. That is, they assume all breakdowns are pathological, so they work hard at finding a cell that can be blamed.

What nobody notices, however, is that the dysfunctional school system is doing other things remarkably well. The PTA raises money nicely, for example. Its members might argue that even though they funnel this money into better reading programs, Johnnie and Janie still can't read, so that in the end, despite the PTA's fund raisers, education is still a failure because of bad teachers and old curricula. From the perspective of the system as defined by its ability to educate, the PTA, too, is no success, for if it were, better education would occur, and the problem is precisely that it does not. But it does not follow that the PTA is a failure. On the contrary! Newcomers to town are socialized into the community through the PTA. Perhaps one of the real reasons for the thriving PTA is that it fulfills this important function for people. It is a place where parents can meet other parents, work together with them, and eventually make friends. It is also a place where people can spend their leisure time "constructively." Moreover, it may serve political ends, if the PTA activity is a steppingstone to running the school board, which, in turn, is a step below town office. Whatever the actual case, the PTA may be an absolute failure at bettering education, and thus be as dysfunctional as the school itself in that regard, yet it functions smoothly and effectively at the other unannounced things it does. Even if it could be proved that for over a century of trying, the PTA has not helped children read better, its members would never vote their organization out of business. They would simply say, "We have to try harder."

In sum, we can posit a law of institutions that goes like this: *Most systems are mostly efficient most of the time. If they seem to be inefficient, we are probably not looking at what they do efficiently.* Unlike toasters that become burners, human systems are made of human parts who will not easily agree to change. They usually like what they are doing efficiently.

A corollary to this rule is that *every human system has two sets of purposes. One is stated publicly. The other is not. In the actual functioning of organizations, it is the latter that takes priority.* In our case, the PTA states publicly that it exists to help children read. In fact it exists for the unstated goals tied to the town's social and political systems. Only with respect to the official goal is the PTA dysfunctional. With regard to what it actually does, it functions beautifully.

The only way to get the PTA to change is to get the leading people, those who constitute its most important "parts," to recognize that the dichotomy between the stated goal's failure and the unstated goal's success exists. The next step is to recognize that the stated goal is not working precisely because scapegoating rather than correcting dysfunctional systems is occurring. The leaders of the PTA may then discover that other school subsystems are also doing the "wrong" things right, but the "right" things wrong. Individuals in those subsystems must be won over to the cause of examining the system as whole. Eventually we would have the equivalent of the parts of our black box examining the box from within and seeing the mixed messages, the faulty communication, and so on. And slowly, very slowly, the school system might heave with change brought about from within, in which no one is scapegoated, but the relationships between the parts are readjusted until Janie and Johnnie really might be able to learn to read.

Unfortunately it is that kind of prolonged system correction that the worship system requires. There, too, even though from the perspective of worship the system is a failure, it is successfully doing other things. It, too, provides a social network for the regulars and a place to meet and greet each other. It certainly awards status to those who work hard. It recognizes scouting well enough. It just doesn't provide Worship Moments.

To make matters worse, the people in the Worship System, unlike the school, are not convinced that the stated goal of the Worship System even exists, or that it should. The ability to read is an observable phenomenon that everyone recognizes as existing in some people and desirable for all others. But worship dysfunction has been going on for so long that people are not even sure they can or should pray. So changing the Worship System so as to facilitate worship will require, first and foremost, the grudging recognition of individuals that Worship Moments are desirable, even possible. When it comes to worship, people are so culturally deprived they don't even know what to look for.

In what follows we will turn to both worship pathology and worship dysfunction. The fact that worship is rare in many North American churches and synagogues in no way detracts from the genuine human spiritual needs we posited at the outset as a description of successful worship. Presumably group prayer need not be a failure forever. But to change matters for the better, those who lead it will have to know more about what makes it work. Insofar as that knowledge corrects their own ineffective management of the rites they are appointed to lead, they will be correcting simultaneously their own ingrained habits that have become pathological in at least a benign way. By refusing to allow their errors to become further entrenched in the system and thereby avoiding further detriment to the system, they will be making sure that their pathologies never become malignant. And even after we have worked at correcting our own pathologies, we still will have the problem of systemic worship dysfunction to handle. How does a system get an unbiased look at itself, so that it can replace endless and useless scapegoating with a genuine overhaul of itself in common dedication to a new beginning? That is the question we take up in Part Two.

CORRECTING THE SYSTEM

6

Interlude: Talking About Worship

Theological Language

BEFORE SUGGESTING SOLUTIONS to the many problems plaguing successful worship in America today, we ought to stop and take stock. We have seen that there really is such a thing as prayer. We human beings are ritualizing creatures. From simple personal activities that we initiate for our own comfort, to the public spectacles we attend, we cannot do without the rhythmic punctuation of ritual in our lives. In that sense the religious rituals we call worship are no different from ritual in general. All ritual expresses the deepest human yearnings for order, meaning, and structure in what would otherwise be utter chaos. The second law of thermodynamics states that existence tends generally toward a state of absolute random disorder called entropy. Human beings by nature fear entropy. Where we find it—and we find it everywhere—we solicitously enforce its opposite: where there was wild undergrowth, we plant rooted gardens; where once our prehuman ancestors plunked themselves down just anywhere close to food and warmth, we build numbered houses on squared-off grids of streets in bounded cities. Similarly composers show us how to hear sound, not just noise, and painters demonstrate specific shapes, not mere splotches of colors. In other words human society is largely the totality of patterns we human beings manage to enforce on previously patternless emptiness. What are all these activities but the ritualization of things, the process of putting them in order and rehearsing that order whenever and wherever we come across it? We go for walks on a familiar street, hear the repeated motif in our favorite symphony, listen for familiar words from a friend, and watch time and space unfold as if there were no entropy, as if we men and women had conquered the meaninglessness of random accident and erected instead the rhythmic familiarity of predictable forms.

We have seen, however, that while people have no trouble recognizing ritual in general in their lives, they have some difficulty in seeing its value in religion. By emphasizing a systems approach to human phenomena, we have isolated two distinctly separate causes for this "worship blindness": *worship pathology,* on the one hand; and *worship dysfunction,* on the other.

Worship pathology problems are those caused by parts of the system that fail to work adequately, and they alone make up an endless list of howlers. Informal conversation at ministerial conventions regularly turns up one tale after another about things that go wrong, some of which are practically American folklore by now. I don't know if any officiating minister has even really fallen into the open grave while delivering the eulogy, but they do it on television all the time as symbolic testimony to people's general observation that religious ritual doesn't work. I do know of other equally ludicrous testimony to the ubiquity of Murphy's Law in religious services: a Watcher at a relative's *bar mitzvah* ceremony who was invited to "dress" the Torah Scroll after it had been read; she mistook the silver plate that hangs down over the Torah's cover—often called the "breastplate" of the Torah—as something she was to wear, since, I suppose, she knew she had breasts, and when asked to put the breastplate on, unfortunately she did on herself!

The list is endless and would be endlessly entertaining were it not for the fact that beneath the humor lies the grudging recognition that Americans have far less trouble identifying with these mishaps than they do with stories of genuine Worship Moments, which by and large are unknown in their actual lives in church and synagogue. In truth, the howlers are merely cartoonlike caricatures of what really goes wrong all the time in a system that often cranks to a halt: people who miss their cues, implements of worship that malfunction, seating plans from which you can't hear the preacher, unguarded wine cups that attract bees who drown in the wine, candles that won't stay lit, and, of course, the cast of characters charged with prayer who have their own needs for attention, dominance, or some other human foible that gets in the way of the activity they are supposed to facilitate.

Even worse, we said, is *worship dysfunction*, the system as a whole going askew, satisfying some other need than that for which it is named. This is the Black Box Syndrome, in which what is going wrong cannot even be seen from the outside, since no matter how closely outsiders observe the system, they will see only what it does or does not do, but will never adequately comprehend why what it does is so satisfying to people who ostensibly say they are not satisfied by it: why the cantor who complains that no one sings is actually happy to be able to sing alone; how it is that regulars can mutter about the fact that, over the years, no one new has come forward to help with Sunday morning ritual arrangements, when, in fact, they are by now their own small fellowship group anxious precisely to continue a system in which no new blood threatens the integrity of their small alliance; why the preacher who threatens fire and brimstone each Sunday really depends on the people's continual sins so that he can continue fulminating against them. (Can you imagine a story about a flock of parishioners who so loved their pastor that they took his words to heart and gave up sin? The successful pastor, having internalized no role other than that of calling people to contrition, would be threatened with early retirement. The obvious end of the tale would be a parish meeting in which the good parishioners, who loved their pastor, after all, voted to take up their previous life of sin so as to give their minister something to do again.)

Obviously worship dysfunction is the harder problem to eradicate. But there was a reason for introducing worship dysfunction only at the end of the narrative of sorrows that constituted Part One, and there is a similar reason to postpone a discussion of correcting worship dysfunction from within until after we have spent some time looking at worship pathology, the things that are easily fixable without complex systems analysis. There is no reason why candles can't stay lit, people can't sing, and worship can't provide meaningful Moments for those fortunate enough to attend services designed to allow them to happen. So before we turn to strategies for converting dysfunctional systems into functional ones, we should handle the far easier problem of suggesting ways in which already functional systems can make our worship come alive with the joyful celebration of all that God has given us. For Christians this will be an affirmation of their life in Christ; for Jews the fulfillment of the *mitzvah* of prayer, with *kavvanah*.

To begin that task we have to give some thought to how we talk about worship, and to do that I draw your attention to the end of the last paragraph, which I repeat now for analysis, this time underlining some of the words that stand out by their difference from the kind of talk that has characterized this book so far. Here is the passage:

> So before we turn to strategies for converting dysfunctional systems into functional ones, we should handle the far easier problem of suggesting ways in which already functional systems can make their worship come alive with *the joyful celebration of all that God has given us. For Christians this will be an affirmation of their life in Christ; for Jews the fulfillment of the mitzvah of prayer, with kavvanah.*

What makes the italicized part of the passage different from the rest of this book so far is the fact that it is couched in religious rhetoric idiom. The first part ("the joyful celebration of all that God has given us") is general Judeo-Christian rhetoric, tinged somewhat with a general Christian flavor—Christians write this way more than Jews do—but recognizable to members of both communities. Thereafter I've written, first, Christian, and then, Jewish language. Christians know what "an affirmation of their life in Christ" is; and Jews recognize the word *mitzvah*. But neither party identifies with the religion-specific language of the other. There is nothing wrong with rhetoric. We rarely make a point without it. But we do have to choose the kind of rhetoric we decide to use, and the problem with much of the discussion about worship reform is that it is phrased in religious language that does not necessarily lead to useful conclusions. It befuddles more than it clarifies, and it is so associated with piety that it effectively shuts out the possibility that anyone will debate it. Since much that follows avoids religious language, and since we will get nowhere in correcting what goes wrong in our worship services if we do not make a point of translating our woes out of the normal religious rhetoric that we usually use to describe them, I need to spend a few more paragraphs on the nature of language systems.

The approach I have taken suggests that religious ritual is like all other ritual, and if that is the case, then it should be approachable from the neutral perspective of a language system that describes any other human behavior in groups. To be sure, we need religious language, too, and when I say we should use neutral language to diagnose worship problems, I do not mean to imply that we can do without values that, by definition, are not neutral at all. We can use a neutral vocabulary to discuss the worship *systems* of Jews, Catholics, Mormons, and Baptists, for example, without thinking these groups are all the same in terms of their own particular religious life. The values by which people determine the *goal* of their ritualizing, and therefore the *criteria* by which they decide if those goals have been met, can be derived only from within their own religious traditions, and toward that end they will need to use their own internal theological language. But attention to making the ritual do what their theology wants it to do depends first on the willingness to look objectively at the ritual without theological presuppositions.

People therefore have to become adept at the difficult art of translating their internal language of theology into an external language that other people, too, understand. In this context it is worth re-examining what I said above: that is, that we can make our "worship come alive with *the joyful celebration of all that God has given us. For Christians, this will be an affirmation of their life in Christ; for Jews, the fulfillment of the mitzvah of prayer, with kavvanah.*" Take apart that statement for a minute, to see what I mean. There are four parts, or fragments, to it:

1. [We want] worship [to] come alive
2. with the joyful celebration of all that God has given us
3. . . . an affirmation of their life in Christ
4. . . . fulfillment of the *mitzvah* of prayer with *kavvanah.*

Sentence fragment #4 is so parochial, even many Jews will not follow it. I deliberately wrote it in highly technical theological language, not even translated out of the Hebrew. Most Jews know that a *mitzvah* is a commandment, but only a small percentage of them recognize the technical word *kavvanah* meaning "intent." It is used theologically to imply that divinely given commandments cannot be fulfilled perfunctorily; they require the proper religious attitude. The idea in this case is something to the effect that when we pray, we do so not just to fulfill the letter of the law, but with heartfelt desire to do God's will, and with care for the proper carrying out of all the details with which we are overjoyed to have been charged in the first place. This is the kind of sentence congregants get used to hearing from rabbis in their sermons. Interestingly enough, even when they don't understand it, they never question it. They know it is insiders' language that probably means something, and they are usually content with their own general idea that it has something to do with being a good Jew and living a good Jewish life. Christians, on the other hand, must read the line (or listen to it in a rabbi's remarks) with utter puzzlement—like listening to the local garage mechanic telling you there is something wrong with the "carborundum freeble" in your car.

Fragment 3 is as parochially Christian as Fragment 4 is parochially Jewish, the difference being that all the words in Fragment 3 are English, so they sound as if we ought to be able to make clear sense of them easily. But if the truth be told, its meaning is not obvious at all. As a Jew I know easily enough what it means to be "in a house," or "in a car," or even "in trouble," or "in the middle of writing this sentence." But I do not know (without being told) what constitutes a life "in Christ." I do not even know what evidence I would have to produce to constitute an "affirmation of a life in Christ." Jews are as puzzled by this Christian theological formulation as Christians are by the Jewish words of Fragment 4. I don't know how many Christians sit patiently listening to such religious language emanating from the pulpit, without knowing for sure what the preacher is talking about, but I suspect there are quite a few. Like their Jewish neighbors listening to Fragment 4 about *mitzvah* and *kavvanah*, they assume that whatever the minister is talking about, it must be right, probably some vague reference to a Christian way of life that can go unquestioned.

Fragment 2 is general religious rhetoric that a politician addressing a joint Jewish and Christian audience might use, at a civic Thanksgiving ceremony on the town square, perhaps. Intended for all Americans to understand, it is even more general than the Christian Fragment about "a life in Christ." Who can't understand "a joyful celebration of all that God has given us," after all? The answer is "lots of people." To begin with, the millions of people who make up Eastern religions would have at least some trouble with our particular Judeo-Christian concept of God; but more than that, even for good Christians and Jews, the concept of God's gifts is by no means obvious. What we have here is actually a very sophisticated idea in simplified rhetorical disguise. Even the politician-speaker probably doesn't understand how God gives gifts, but he or she has probably been to church or synagogue and heard the phrase enough to be able to use it without too much thought about what it really means. It sounds nice and elicits support as a broad-ranging call to the religious life in general. Even the word "celebration" is in fact a religious term in its essence, but the politician as well as the listeners miss that point. What comes across is the idea that we all ought to be happy about life's bounty.

Fragment 1 is the only nonreligious phrase in the sentence, but even it is rhetorical, and the idea of "coming alive" is closely related to religious language—it comes from the idea of the resurrection of the dead—even if it is not strictly religious anymore.

What has really happened in the sentence being analyzed is that I have combined neutral language that everybody understands with religious language that only some people understand; and there is enough neutral language that even if you don't understand any of the religious language, it doesn't matter! You will still get the idea that worship should "come alive" (= not be deadly, avoid being boring, be meaningful, and so on), and that it should be "a joyful celebration." What I have done successfully is speak to insiders and to outsiders at the same time. Those in the know will picture living a life in Christ or doing a *mitzvah* with *kavvanah*; the people I called Watchers, those who rarely come to religious services and know little about religious rhetoric, will at least relate positively to a "joyful celebration of all that God has given us." And even a complete outsider knows what "joyful," "celebration," and "come alive" mean.

At times we need to exercise theological critiques about what we do. Readers of this book are probably either Jews or Christians, after all, who want to be true to our respective traditions. But in this chapter I want to explain why I am writing about prayer without talking much about God or other religious concepts that you might expect to find in a book on worship. I want to insist on the equal need, at times, to be neutral in our description of what we want prayer to be.

How must we talk about worship, then, at least in part, while we try to make it "work"? The answer is "nontheologically."

The problem is that not all forms of language actually provide us with useful descriptions of things, even though they often lead us astray by looking as if they do. Religious language is often like that. It sounds nice; it satisfies; but it does not describe, not always, anyway. And when it comes to fixing anything, whether it is the toaster that burns or the service that bores, without being able to describe dispassionately what the toaster or the service actually does and what you think it ought to do, you will get nowhere in fixing it.

The following not-so-hypothetical parallel should be familiar to all parents who have teenage children.

Teenage years are marked by growing peer relationships at the expense of old family ties. Thus teenagers do a variety of things together in which they develop their own language that ostensibly describes what it is they do with each other. Their parents, however, have trouble recognizing what teenspeak means. A favorite current word—I think, though if I already know it, the odds are it is not current any more—is "awesome," which, however, has nothing whatever to do with the religious sense that the same word conveys in my vocabulary. A favorite rock star's latest hit is "awesome," for example. So is the rock star him- or herself. The best movie this week is also awesome, as is the New York Yankee first baseman who is batting .323. Yesterday, I asked my daughter to define what awesome means. "What kind of things does it describe?" I asked. She had just used it for something so ordinary that now, only twenty-four hours later, I cannot even remember what it was. "'Awesome' means 'big' or something like that," she said, "but sometimes I use it only because I am in a good mood."

In other words, despite their theoretical grammatical function that we learned in school, adjectives do not always or simply describe the things they modify so much as they tell us about the mental state of the subject doing the describing: the way in which the subject perceives the world, as much as the nature of the world that is said to be perceived. Without knowing the rules of the system, however, it is impossible for an outsider to know what the adjective is doing. And what goes for adjectives goes also for nouns, verbs, adverbs—in fact, for language in general. That is because people who see a lot of each other and who do special things together develop their own vocabulary to express what they do and/or what things mean to them as opposed to everyone else. People outside their circle rely on their ability to "translate" from their English into ours.

Suppose, now, my teenage son wants me to purchase tickets for him and his friends, who have decided to while away a Saturday or Sunday together. They had better not tell me, without commentary, simply that they want to attend something "awesome," or they may be surprised to discover that I have arranged for them to attend services in New York City's most prestigious synagogue or cathedral. We see, therefore, that specialized subgroups who want to be in communication with outsiders have to translate what they want to the experts they entrust with their fate. I call the means we use to make ourselves understood to outsiders "translation grammars." Architects talking to each other may say, "The building decisively addresses the street"; the client will be told, "Your new office building is designed to have a prominent place on this particular street." Your doctor may admit you to the hospital for a pneumonectomy; what you need to know is that you are having a lung removed. As we all know, there is "legalese" ("The rest, residue, and remainder is hereby left to the heirs, successors, and assigns . . . "); "businessese" ("Reference is made to . . . "); "TV commercialese"("available in large, super, and family size"); and "researchese"("The findings may be considered correct within an order of magnitude").

There is "religionese," too, unfortunately. Like specialists of all kinds, we religious specialists are an internally cohesive group with our own language system designed to express concepts and experiences that we know we have; we call it "theology." I don't mean complex theology, just simple sentences in which we insert theological language, like the parts of the sentence I underlined above. It is not gibberish; we talk to each other and know what we mean. But it hides a multitude of sins, allowing us to nod knowingly even when we are *not* clear about what we are about. The fact is we have to use "translation grammars" for ourselves as well, lest we end up saying sentences that sound as if they mean something, when they do not.

I have in mind the "Lewis Carroll syndrome." Carroll was an English mathematician whose father was a clergyman. He knew how to make nothing sound like something, as illustrated by his famous poem, *Jabberwocky*, which (as we all know) features a mythical beast, the Jabberwock, slain by a young child. Early in the poem our hero is warned:

> "Beware the Jabberwock, my son,
> The jaws that bite, the claws that catch!
> Beware the Jubjub bird, and shun
> The frumious Bandersnatch."

Later still the hero finds himself in the forest:

> He took his vorpal sword in hand:
> Long time the manxome foe he sought—
> So rested he by the Tumtum tree,
> And stood awhile in thought.
>
> And as in uffish thought he stood,
> The Jabberwock, with eyes of flame,
> Came whiffling through the tulgey wood,
> And burbled as it came!
>
> One two! one two! And through and through
> The vorpal blade went snicker-snack!
> He left it dead, and with its head
> He went galumphing back.
>
> "And hast thou slain the Jabberwock?
> Come to my arms, my beamish boy!
> Oh frabjous day! Callooh! Callay!"
> He chortled in his joy.

What makes Carroll's poem so fascinating is that it sounds sensible when it is not. It's hard to believe, after reading it, that there are no actual bandersnatches, jubjub birds and jabberwocks; that the woods aren't "tulgey" and the days "frabjous"; or that we don't normally "galumph," "whiffle," and "burble" (we do "chortle" nowadays, but we didn't until Carroll coined the word here and told us—somehow—what it was).

Though Carroll's father was a clergyman, Carroll wasn't; so no one confuses his gibberish with theology. But suppose he had written not just this poem, but books and books of them, all filled with the same nouns and adjectives used over and over again, like the words of Tolkein, with his imaginary Hobbits. After a while people wrote literary descriptions of the Hobbit kingdom as if it really existed, and they would do the same thing for Carroll's mythical forest of creatures who live only in "tulgey woods" and die by "vorpal" blades. You get the idea. Specialized languages may or may not correspond to actual experiences people have. From the language itself it is impossible to tell. Religionists who have experienced worship naturally describe it to others in the theological language they know best. To repeat: I am not saying that theology is gibberish, only that an outsider listening to it will have no choice but to treat it as if it were. We may even unknowingly slip at least *some* theological "gibberish" into our own deliberations, beguiling ourselves into thinking that we understand the problems, when in fact we have merely cited a theological stock phrase that elicits a closing "Amen," allowing us to go home without changing anything.

If we want to be sure we are functioning in the real world of changing systems by which human beings communicate and act, we would do well to wish along with Robert Burns:

Oh wad some power the giftie gie us,
To see oursels as others see us!
It wad frae monie a blunder free us.

To see ourselves as others see us would be a gift indeed! For it really would free us from countless blunders. If we want to overcome shortcomings of which we are not even aware, therefore, we must learn to see our worship as if we were outside observers, to describe our goals in nontheological terms, and to readjust what goes wrong by seeing it as others see it.

The Language of Art

There is still another way that people talk about worship, a nontheological way from which we learn a great deal. If theology is the insider's language, this other way is not. Think of the following descriptions of Sabbath worship heard anywhere across the country in churches and synagogues alike:

"I was moved by your message, Father."

"The prayer you offered was beautiful."

"Everything flowed so smoothly."

What is striking about all these evaluations is that they are appropriate not only to worship, but to art. The biblical authors were on to something when they advocated serving God "in the *beauty* of holiness." They sensed the similarity between aesthetics and worship. So the second, nontheological, speech code that even outsiders use to talk about religious ritual is aesthetic.

We human beings have at least three parts to our personality, three ways in which we differ from the animals below us on the evolutionary spiral. I want to look briefly at each one of them, in order to see what aesthetics is actually about.

Somewhere off in Africa, a lion attacks a gazelle. The surviving gazelle spouse hurries mournfully back to her little gazelle family, takes stock, and readjusts to life without her male gazelle mate around any more. Human widows do the same sort of thing, but where we differ is that the gazelle does not write a book, have a conversation, or even raise the question, "Why do bad things happen to good gazelles?" Animals and people suffer from injustice; only people *recognize* it as injustice. Only people question why injustices should exist. One function of religion is to answer questions about injustice, to envision society without it, and to plot a path designed to bring such a society about. We call that function of religion "ethics."

Compared to us, animals vary in intelligence, but like human beings, they do know things. In many ways their instincts are more developed than ours, so in a sense they know even more than we do about survival matters such as whether a predator is near or how to find their way home in the dark. No matter how many twists and turns a bee takes during a day, it can find its way home in a straight "bee line," whereas I cannot find my car in a parking lot ten minutes after I have parked there. On the other hand, the human brain has incredibly evolved and is incredibly involved! People have memories that go back culturally through generations; and we have developed languages that allow us to learn more, think deeper, and communicate in more complex ways, so that despite all the examples of unbelievable animal knowledge, we obviously know incomparably more than animals do. Most striking, however, is not what we know, or even how much we know, but the fact that we are able to know what we know. Only in books like Orwell's *Animal Farm* do you get animals who think, talk, and philosophize. In real life, systems of thought belong to human beings who, knowing that we know, are able to ask how it is that we know, and how we can know that what we know is really so. The realm of knowing about what we know is also religious in its essence. What is human nature? What is truth? Is there a God? What happens after we die? These are profound religious issues having to do not with ethics and action, but knowledge of ultimate truths.

There is also a third form of human uniqueness. The beaver sits methodically gnawing on a tree to fashion a plank to build a dam. Up close you can hear the rhythm of its teeth beating on the tree trunk. But the beaver's interest starts and ends with the practical task of dam building. People, on the other hand, have an interest in the pattern of the activity itself: the particular rhythm of the teeth on wood, which can be hurried, altered, inverted, repeated, and so on, until we get music; or the particular design of the dam when it is done, not its practicality alone, but just the way it looks, and how it would look if it were two colors instead of one, twice as thick as it is, or reflected by the sun in such and such a way. We call this third area of human specialization "art." Art talk is aesthetics.

At various times Christianity and Judaism have treated worship as if it were essentially an exercise in ethics, truth, or art. All three concerns have entered it in every age, of course, but the emphasis has varied, and whether we decide it is essentially one thing or the other will determine how we talk about it and what we expect of it. In the interest of being straightforward I have avoided too much historical substantiation thus far, but it is enlightening to see how people have looked to their worship to provide ethics, truth, and beauty, so I want to talk just a bit about different eras in the religious history of the west, so as to see that religion can be any or all of them—and why, for us, it should correctly be viewed as art (my point by the end of this chapter).

Start with truth. Throughout most of history religion provided men and women with what they knew. Religion was all-pervasive in society; either formally or otherwise it was charged with the definition of what knowledge was in the first place, and then with the task of passing that knowledge on to society's members. For great eras of Christian history there were no schools other than church schools; monks wrote and kept the documents defining what later generations would call history; and religious representatives alone passed judgment on what fields were appropriate to study, as well as what opinions were proper to hold within those fields.

Jewish culture, too, emanated from religious authorities of the time, "fear of God being the beginning of wisdom" (as the Bible put it), and wisdom being defined as that which was conducive to or emanated from proper fear of God. To be sure, Jews studied medicine, business, law, and a host of other subjects that we would consider areligious. Their knowledge was by no means limited to pious discussions of holy writ. But even these so-called nonreligious disciplines (as we would describe them) were religious for them, in that God had created the world and all that inhabit it, so that knowledge of anatomy or of business contracts was as religious in its essence as the study of biblical narrative or Talmudic ritual. Whether Jews subordinated their study of the natural world to official synagogue doctrine on the nature of things or whether they opened their vistas to scientifically objective observation of phenomena depended largely on what the rest of their environment did, so that in liberally oriented times like the Italian renaissance, they were more open to free discovery and nondogmatic theorizing than they were, say, in the Italian Counter Reformation period after the Council of Trent. In twelfth-century Provence (southern France), for example, where free-thinking Christian intellectuals had established philosophical bastions, an explosion of creative Jewish knowledge also occurred; and when papal writ established an early Inquisition to bring down the freethinking Christians there, Jewish authorities conspired likewise to burn Jewish books and hound their liberal-minded authors.

Liturgy then was far from what it is today. I am not even discussing now the forms, which may have differed, or the words, the music, the actions, and the participation of the laity. I mean the intent behind the public act of prayer. Worship filled a role that we now allocate to other institutions, namely, the providing of knowledge and the socializing of people into the correct ideas of the very paths their thinking mechanism should take. This is nowhere more evident than in high Gothic cathedral architecture beginning in the twelfth century. It was at that time that a certain Abbot Suger in France created a novel church structure that we call Gothic. In contrast to the prior style (called Romanesque), which was dense, dark, and somber, Gothic cathedrals expanded the inner space of the church by using a new technology of arch construction that supported more weight with fewer internal columns and made large windows (including the first dazzling round rose windows) possible. The next step was an external extension of the internal support columns, weight-bearing structures called flying buttresses that were connected by arches to the interior, but were actually built outside the church walls. Now the inner space was revealed as a vast flow of light in which huge stone ceilings were miraculously floating on air, while artistic stained glass windows broke up the sun's light into a veritable rainbow of brilliant color, directing the gaze and thoughts of all in attendance heavenward in admiration of the Creator of all. By this time, too, church music had been converted into polyphonic harmony, that is to say, not the conscious control of all voices into a single sound of praise, but the opposite: the breaking up of monophonic sound in a way that paralleled what the colored windows were doing to monochrome sunshine. The effect of the whole was a vivid display of mathematical harmony, whether in color, sound, or even geometric space, of which the church as a whole was the best evidence and witness imaginable.

All of this occurred simultaneously with a development in thought called scholasticism. Precisely at the same time that Suger was designing his cathedral, and throughout the following years when the Cathedral at Notre Dame, for example, furthered the Gothic structural revolution with its use of flying buttresses, newly built church universities were appearing, most notably in Paris, not far from the churches under discussion. There an intellectual equivalent to the artistic revolution was taking place, as thought itself was being broken down into its permutations and combinations. Scholasticism is thus known—often parodied (unfairly)—for its theoretical disputations on highly technical and often tiny distinctions. Simultaneously, as the new churches with their lighted interiors spread, a form of thought known as neoplatonism became academically more popular; it emphasized the idea of a God of light, whose will and creative potential were likened to the same emanation of light that the church architecture demonstrated visually.

We shall see later that knowledge can be considered art. But here we have the very reverse; art being knowledge. People had churches, not schools, to attend in those days, but churches became their schools, not only in the simple sense that they may have learned "reading, writing and 'rithmetic" from the itinerant monks passing through town, but in the far loftier sense that going to church regularly was an education in itself, a living, breathing experience of God's light and truth, a clear demonstration of how to think, even if not always of what the precise content of one's thought should be.

Under such a system both the content of what is said in church and the form in which the content is presented are subservient to the idea of truth. Theology has the upper hand here, determining what is permissible on the basis of whether correct opinions will be advanced or retarded. Here, then, is the first model of a liturgical system: a system that judges worship on the basis of its truth value. Not that art (and, of course, ethics) are unimportant. It was Gothic art itself, afterall, that carried religious truth, especially since by this time the liturgy itself had largely been privatized among monastic circles, so that the actual words of prayer, and even the sacrament of the eucharist were rarely or never part of the regular experience of average lay worshipers. That is, ordinary men and women attended church for its overall effect rather than to consider exactly what the words of prayer meant (they didn't understand or even hear the Latin anyway) or what their theological import was. Nevertheless, what the liturgy was supposed to achieve was the imparting of truth, the spreading of doctrine, the demonstration of correct opinion and knowledge of what the church knew to be the case.

We shall see later that one of the profound errors of our time is to believe that liturgy still functions that way. I will leave the elaboration of this point to further chapters, but for clarity let me state the idea in general right away. Whereas once art was correctly conceptualized as a means toward knowledge, we in our time have reached the conclusion that knowledge is actually a form of art. Many of us still mistakenly think that liturgy gives truth by way of its art, so we allot our greatest energies to the "truths" that we believe are conveyed—the didactic elements of our worship, like the doctrine preached and the words recited. These are not unimportant matters, to be sure, but to attend to liturgy as if it were still primarily a system of organizing and presenting truths about the world is a sure way to fail—in the same way that Van Gogh would surely have failed if his sole concern had been the recapitulation of each precise angle, color, and ratio that constitutes sunflowers, instead of his own internal artistry that made it possible for us forever after to see sunflowers as he painted them, instead of the other way around. Sunflowers now look different to us because of Van Gogh, just as—thanks to Robert Frost—we are now incapable of passing innocently by "two roads diverging in a wood," or even—courtesy of Andy Warhol—to look naively at a Campbell soup can again.

We should therefore see liturgy as an art form and truth as an artistic construct. What we need now is greater attention to art as a proper, indeed divine, goal of liturgical life. I know that sounds incomplete (at best), and heretical (at worst) at this point, but I shall return to this major theme in the next chapter.

I need first to look briefly at the second alternative suggested above. Alongside art and truth, I mentioned ethics as a specifically human endeavor. Liturgy has functioned in the past not only as a means of truth, but also as a vehicle to inculcate right and wrong.

The concept of ethics is not as old as we might imagine. Though the dichotomy of right vs. wrong must easily stretch back to the beginning of human history, the decision to conceptualize one single specific realm of thought called ethics is not that ancient. Originally the right/wrong axis was assumed to be coterminous with all reality, including areas of human behavior we would never consider ethical. This is best seen in anthropological studies of societies sometimes called "primitive": those which have not gone through the throes of modernity, with its rise of science and splitting of thought into specified realms like medicine, law, art, and physics. These societies still treat knowledge holistically, meaning that they do not parcel it out into categories that only specialists know. Knowledge that we would call ethical (like rules against cheating your neighbor) are not differentiated from knowledge that we consider scientific (like the curing of disease), or ritualistic (like how to offer thanksgiving to the gods), or just plain practical (like how to make bows and arrows for hunting). All of this specialty knowledge is treated as part of one big cauldron of information about the way the world is, and as such, equally governed by what the gods want regarding human meddling with it. People get sick, not because of viral infection, but because they have sinned, or because they have overstepped the bounds in their dealings with others, or for whatever other reason that the society in question provides—all such reasons being utterly irrelevant to moderns who believe in an independent realm of medicine. Similarly, whom you marry, what you do in your leisure time, whether you go to war, how you raise your children, and when you eat your dinner are all constrained not by pure considerations of practicality or of personal predilection, but by what is right and what is wrong.

Not that such societies are purely ethical, not at all. They often do not even know the word ethical. But they are oriented in all their dealing to the same thing that ethics is oriented to, that is, limits. What *truth* is to the kind of system I described above, *limits* are to the social system under discussion now. Every aspect of life is held to be equally divine, and the task of human behavior is to find one's way through the maze of prescriptions and proscriptions that constitute reality. These are not easy to ascertain, since they and their consequences are often invisible. Unlike modern medicine, for example, that proscribes cigarette smoking by pointing to documented evidence that it causes cancer, the link between a divine mandate to light a sacred fire, say, and the presumed punishment for not doing right—a sudden dearth of hunting success or the failure of the crops to come up—is neither documented or documentable. So in these societies revered religious specialists abound to teach these hidden connections. Education there is primarily the means by which ordinary men and women memorize the rules about limits: when, where, and how you go about doing what for whom—and when, where, how, and for whom you do not.

Through the ages Jewish culture has been a limit culture. What truth was to the church, limits were to the synagogue. Whereas Christian learning became doctrinal and its literature theological, Jewish learning was dominated by considerations of what God wanted in terms of right and wrong, and its literature developed into a style that we would call legal. The church knew limit thinking too, naturally, applying it primarily to its chief concern, ideas, and declaring some forms of thought off-limits, or, as the term went, heretical, just as the synagogue knew ideas, but used those ideas in its own case as a buttress for limit mentality that dominated Jewish consciousness. Thus, for example, Judaism did not develop scholastic theologians or doctrinal considerations about ideas the way the church did in its Christologies. But it did have scholastics working in Paris at the same time as the churchmen met in the universities there. Jewish scholastics (called Tosafists) exercised their hermeneutical skill on legal questions, often as hypothetical as the doctrinal points that stretched the minds of their Christian counterparts, but for all that, on a subject matter that was not theological but legal in its essence. Not "How many angels can sit on the head of a pin?" (which is really a question about the nature of mind and spirit as opposed to the nature of materiality), but the following, as an example I will cite in some detail so as to give the reader unfamiliar with rabbinic thought some notion of what I mean.

The festival of Chanukah, kept by Jews around the time of Christmas, derives from a revolt by a group of Jews called Hasmoneans in the second century B.C.E. (Their story is told in the books called Maccabees, carried in the Roman Catholic Bible, but omitted by Jews and Protestants and identified as "apocrypha.") According to a later Jewish tradition, when the Hasmoneans won the war, their first act was to cleanse their sacred sanctuary, which the enemy had polluted with idolatry. One act of that refurbishment was the relighting of a sacred flame that was to be kept burning eternally. Normally oil would have been lit, and then new oil added regularly enough to prevent the flame's going out. However, the Jewish victors discovered only enough oil to last for one day, so they lit it, and dispatched a runner to find more oil. The runner returned after eight days, by which time a miracle had occurred: the oil sufficient for only one day had stayed lit for all eight. Ever since then Jews light candles every night for eight nights, as the rabbis of antiquity explain, "to publicize the miracle."

That was the story and practice of Chanukah that the Middle Ages inherited. The Tosafists, or Jewish scholastics in France, now asked the following question: If the purpose of the Chanukah flames is "to publicize the miracle," why do we light them for eight and not just seven days? After all, there was sufficient oil to last *naturally* for one day, so the miracle was only the last seven days that were tacked on to the one in which the oil would have burned anyway! I won't record here their various answers to the problem they propounded, since the question alone is enough to demonstrate my point, which is simply this: whereas truth was the linchpin of medieval Christian society, right behavior was the focus for Jews at the time. Christians hunted down heretical *believers*, Jews worried about improper *behavers*, that is, people who acted contrary to Jewish law. Christians built theologies; Jews constructed chains of action called *mitzvot*, these being things God wanted Jews to *do*, not necessarily to believe. There were exceptions, of course, especially at times when Judaism came into close enough contact with Christians (or with philosophically oriented Moslems) to be influenced by them. But generally, *what truth was to Christianity, limits were to Judaism*.

Jewish liturgy was thus not primarily a means to arrive at (or even to demonstrate) truth, so much as it was an exercise in limit thinking. Jewish prayer literature rarely discusses the theological meaning implicit in action or word, but it does wax eloquent on how the words are to be said, when they may be recited, who says them, in what bodily posture, and so on—all limit questions regarding right vs. wrong behavior. Jewish art never develops as Christian art does: Jews do know wall paintings from the third century and mosaic floors from late Roman times, as well as illuminated Bibles and prayer books from the Middle Ages; but better known are Jewish artistic ceremonial objects connected practically with doing the *mitzvah* act: swaddling clothes for babies being circumcised, circumcision knives, pointers with which to read the Torah, crowns to adorn the Torah scroll, and so forth. The practically oriented *mitzvah* system was thus elaborated artistically, as art served a practical purpose in Jewish life but remained relatively stunted in terms of its truth-telling function. Here, then, as in medieval Christianity, we have a worship system in which all three human modes of being are represented: limits (= ethics), truth, and art. But art and truth serve *limits* here, whereas in Christianity limits and art serve *truth*.

One word of afterthought is in order regarding the term "ethics," which I have blithely slipped in as the equivalent of limits. What seems to have happened is that, as traditional limit societies learned to differentiate knowledge into various subfields, the area that emerged as the specific subfield to which divine limits still applied was renamed ethics. Food, for example, was now categorized according to scientifically demonstrable practical ends, like whether it was healthy or not. Food taboos with their presupposed intrinsic rights and wrongs were dismissed. But some limit questions about food still existed: whether you should allocate it so as to feed the poor, or whether it is right to harvest grain with advanced technology that strips the land of its nutrients, for example. These are questions that are beyond the ability of botanists and agricultural scientists to answer. So they have been entitled "ethics."

In modern times, then, as the area in which religious competence has narrowed, nonreligious specializations have taken over whole sectors of experience that we once thought religious experts controlled. It is easy to cite examples of this privatization of specialized realms of truth and the anxious reaction to it by religious authorities who, having hitherto controlled all truths, now fought against relinquishing control over them. The Inquisition, for example, tried Galileo for precisely the crime of challenging the church's hold on all knowledge, and to this day creationists and evolutionists argue the respective rights of science and religion to explain the phenomenon of the universe's origins. But the word "truth" has been retained for both scientific and religious explanations of the way things are.

With regard not to the way things in fact *are*, but the way they *ought to be*, however, religion remained in control. Recall the discussion in Chapter Three about moving the chairs. That chairs are movable and how they can be moved are just the way things are, that is, the realm of science. That they ought to be moved *if* we want to achieve some practical end—the example was about helping the maintenance staff clear the room for class the next day—is also science, since the practical relationship between action and its result is also just the way things are. But *whether it is right*, and therefore, desirable, to move chairs ourselves in order to facilitate education the next day and to relieve the maintenance staff of their labor is not a scientific question. In modern times, then, religious thinkers have argued about the extent of that non-utilitarian realm left over from science, the single area about which religion could still rightly talk. Especially was this true of Judaism, where limits had played so commanding a role.

Take food again as an example. In traditional Judaism food was divided (typical limit thinking) into permitted (*kosher*) and forbidden (*t'ref*); but even *kosher* was divided into milk and meat, which could not be mixed, and a third category, *parve*, which was neither, so it could be eaten with either. Throughout the ages volumes have been written on identifying new foods as they come along, trying to determine what category they fall into. Thus chicken, for example, was declared meat, but fish was not. Another example was pork and seafood, which the Hebrew Bible clearly identifies as *t'ref*; but is swordfish a kind of seafood, or just plain fish? And why should seafood or pork products be declared forbidden anyway? As long as we lived in a premodern world, without specialized realms of knowledge, religion could and did justify these prohibitions by practical explanations that could be considered part and parcel of religious knowledge. Thus some authorities said that pork was forbidden because pigs are dirty animals and cause disease. With the rise of science, however, that claim regarding pork was proved wrong. So Jews were left with a dilemma. A new limit system called science had largely displaced the old one called religious law. Some Jews still keep the dietary laws, but no longer because of pseudomedical reasons. The observance of religious limits has become a matter of personal choice.

But religion can hardly justify itself by being a series of optional choices, so an area of religious limits that everyone would accept as mandatory was sought—and found. That area was ethics. Morality, after all, is a system of how things ought to be that is unrelated to mere utilitarian efficiency. Stealing would be wrong even if you could figure out a way to make it pay. And once we decide it is wrong, we don't accept the claim that people can choose to steal or not. The greatest single justification of religion during the heavy onslaught of science thus became the claim that religion alone would decide ethics. In the case of Judaism there was even a time of radical reform in which Judaism's sole function was reduced by some to the inculcation of ethics, with the result that in 1876, one American rabbi, Felix Adler, went so far as to establish the Society for Ethical Culture, a logical "substitute" for what was left of the all-pervasive system of limits that Judaism had once been. To this day American Christians and Jews in great numbers respond to Gallup polls about their religiosity by saying that they are religious just because they are good people.

In sum the grand claims of both Judaism and Christianity were affected adversely by the rise of modernity, with its attack on religion's right to know all truth (on the one hand) and to establish all limits (on the other). The result has been the emphatic rise of yet a third type of religiosity, one founded not primarily on truth or limits, but on art. When I say "art," however, I am thinking of a good deal more than beautiful paintings or sublime music, which, admittedly, have been a part of religious consciousness from the beginning. I have in mind, instead, a basic human propensity that precedes the creation of paintings and music and causes them to come into being. I mean the third area of experience that makes human life distinctively different from that of animals, the way in which we insist on patterning things so that we can even imagine the very categories of beautiful or sublime in the first place. If limit thinking tends to divide the world into good/bad or right/wrong; and truth thinking prefers the dichotomy of true/false; aesthetic thinking differentiates all being into coherent/incoherent, formed/formless, or what I shall call meaningful/empty.

If people come to pray today, it is surely no longer because, in the main, they want as Christians to learn eternal truths; or because as Jews they want to obey yet another set of limits. They may, of course, *have chosen* to want either of these two things, but if so, they are still radically different from their predecessors, for whom the world was presented as one religious whole with no choice whatever implied on it. Our forebears in premodern Europe learned the truths of religion and practiced religious limits because they had to; there were no others. It would never have occurred to them to do otherwise; to ignore the only obvious and taken-for-granted set of truths and laws around was unthinkable. For millions of people today, on the other hand, it is very thinkable. Other truths beckon; other laws summon. We can be secular through and through, satisfying ourselves with religion's minimal claim that at least ethics comes from God. But astoundingly, Americans still come to worship, if not for truths and limits, then for something else. That something else is the satisfaction of the urge for order, form, coherence—what I have called the aesthetic side of life, and what I shall hereafter describe as the will to find meaning in a world that is oversaturated in truths and laws, but still threatens (more than ever) to break down into chaotic emptiness, meaningless entropy.

This chapter of Interlude has come full circle. We began by explaining ritual as part of the universal human will to convert entropy into order. After surveying religious systems in which that will to order was organized as either a system of interlocking eternal truths (Christianity) or a grid of divinely willed legal limits (Judaism), we arrived at our time, when the very pattern of worship is magnified in importance. The starting point for correcting our worship ills is to note what worship's function really is for us. In our age worship serves to demonstrate that, even when chaos seems overwhelming, we can find meaning that sustains us. It is to religion as a system of art, and worship as the demonstration of meaning that we now turn.

7

Worship as Art

THE COLLEGE AT WHICH I WORK is situated precisely on the fringes of
fabled Greenwich Village, one-time den of Bohemians, then, in
turn, the Beat generation of the fifties, and finally, the flower
children of the Age of Aquarius. As early as the Civil War days,
avant-garde artists found their way here. Walt Whitman walked
these streets often on his way home to Brooklyn from the opera,
which was just up on 14th Street. Roughly one hundred years
later, Pete Seeger and the Weavers sang of unions and socialism
down at the Village Gate—which, incidentally, is still around, but
features ordinary theater now, not the rich live human drama that
made Bleeker Street a legend. Washington Square Park, New
York's Hyde Park soapbox equivalent, has heard a lot of poetry in
its time and loaned its name to the Washington Square Players,
arguably the most important semi-amateur theater group in
American stage history. Henry James spent his childhood on the
Village's northern fringes, dreaming presciently about the fancy
people who would inhabit the Park and naming his 1881 novel
after it: *Washington Square*. Throughout the middle and late 1800s,
though, radical Walt Whitman to the contrary, the Park was still
where the beautiful people promenaded. Only later did the "ar-
tistes" find their way there, and by then the Village was becoming
widely reputed as the center of the art crowd, a reputation it has
tried to maintain over the years. As I say, I work there, and I find it
hard, as I walk its streets, to pay attention to the present, so rich is
the Village's artistic legacy from its past.

More than a monument to art, Greenwich Village is a reminder of our ambivalence about art, for western minds have become attuned not only to appreciate art, but to despise it as well. So the Village's cultural allure has gone hand in hand with its seedy reputation, which attracted as it repelled, excited even as it frightened. Get behind the glitter of the sidewalk cafés that cater to the tourist crowd, and you find that the streets are dirty, the tenements infested, the artists poor. Most of the latter, in any event, have left by now, moving south of the Village's downtown boundary (Houston St.), to SoHo (the So[uth] Ho[uston St.] area), where row after row of art galleries offer what everyone hopes will be tomorrow's masterpieces.

It's even poorer in SoHo. That's why the artists moved here. This is what it's really like to be an artist: you're on a perpetual merry-go-round stretching for the golden ring of fame and fortune only to find it elusively slipping just beyond your every reach. Fanatically devoted to your art, you take jobs at night to make ends meet, but save your days for rehearsals, auditions, voice lessons, exercising, or making the rounds to dealers who might give you the big break you need. It almost never comes, and eventually you begin to understand that Americans *say* they value art, even though, in truth, it would be fairer to say they suspect it.

Suspicion of art and artists goes very deep in our western psyche. Precisely because they knew art's power, philosophers of Greek antiquity were wary of it. As Plato conceived of it, poets have insight beyond ordinary men and women. Captured by a type of madness, they are positively possessed, entranced by ecstasy itself, whence flows their artistic inspiration. On the other hand, because they have a hold on our own more mortal imagination, artists must be controlled by the ideal state, their imaging censored lest they pollute young minds. For in the last analysis artists do not apprehend direct truths. The truths for Plato are eternal essences we call Ideas or Forms, which are one step beyond the things and thoughts of day-to-day existence. When I think of a particular triangle, for example, it is only a copy of the Idea called Triangleness. And the problem with art is that what artists render is even one step removed from that, a picture of the particular triangle that the artist just happens to have in mind at the time.

This is hardly a book on Plato, whose philosophy on art I hope I have not unjustly simplified, or, for that matter, on art itself, but if I am going to claim that worship is an art, I have to contend with the reality of art's lowly status in American society. If people object to the idea of treating worship as an art, they have good precedent behind them. Even people who have never heard of Plato want society's lawmakers to watch carefully over our artists, who are somehow suspected of moral sedition. Widely stereotyped as "flakes," temperamental, of dubious character, or just plain odd (at best), artists are relegated to the slums and the margins of our cities, where they can paint, sing, play, and dance without getting in the way of the "serious pursuits of the state." Compare the two columns below: on the left are words that warm the cockles of a parent's heart; on the right are equivalent phrases destined to make the same parent's blood run cold.

"Positive"	"Negative"
Mom, my marketing professor says I have real potential for business.	Mom, my art teacher says that if I work hard enough, I can become famous.
I'm buying one of those new executive condos they're advertising.	I'm moving into a loft in Greenwich Village.
I've decided to pursue graduate work at Harvard.	Is it all right if I pass up college? I have a once-in-a-lifetime opportunity to star in this nightclub in Paris.
Dad, Mom, meet my fiancé; he works for Chase Manhattan Bank.	Dad, Mom, I've met this perfectly divine dancer, and I think we're going to get married.

In our public and private lives, then, we give art and artists a wide berth. They are mad like Van Gogh, poor like Mozart, wild-eyed like the T-shirt caricatures of Beethoven. The important things in life are assumed to have nothing to do with their pursuits, which may be pretty, even sublime, but insubstantial when compared to hardheaded statecraft, business negotiations, contract law, medical diagnoses, and scientific research. Besides, we reason (going back again to Plato, whether we know it or not), true artists are possessed by genius, so how can we possibly expect artistry of ourselves?

But *art is not the same thing as "works of art."* Put aside notions of Beethoven's *Fifth* or the *Mona Lisa,* and let us look more carefully at exactly what art is.

In a way we are all artists: whether we call ourselves scientists, athletes, housewives, or students, we are as surely dependent on artistic know-how as musicians, dancers, and architects. Take scientists, for example. Normal "wisdom" on the subject imagines that the laboratories of the nation are filled with hardheaded realists who labor assiduously over microscopic slides collecting millions of tiny readings, which come together to make a theory of the way things are. Such is the myth of scientific method that they teach about in schools. Scientists know they don't work that way, however. A few years ago a scientist wrote a letter to the editor of the *New York Times,* asking the rhetorical question, "What would happen if someone discovered some evidence that a major theory, say the theory of relativity, were wrong?" The answer, to quote Nobel Prize winner Murray Gell-Mann, is that, "when you have something simple that agrees with all the rest of physics and really seems to explain what's going on, a few experimental data against it are no objection whatsoever." So nothing would happen at all. The theory would still stand, and the disconcerting contrary evidence would be held in abeyance in the hope that somehow it would eventually fit in. New theories come before, not after, the evidence for them. They are artistic constructs created by men and women of vision who see what everyone else has seen, but see it differently. Naturally, the theories must work. Continuous evidence of their failure will most assuredly do them in. But in a curious way theories prepare us to observe facts we would otherwise completely miss; facts do not by themselves make theories.

Imagine the world as a gigantic pile of jigsaw puzzle pieces that somehow fit together to make a whole picture. Scientists charged with understanding reality are in the business of putting together the pieces. But the pieces are endless, so scientists work through the ages trying to build on the picture inherited from past generations. Contrary evidence to a theory is like finding pieces that should fit, but do not. Only when the number of odd pieces increases to unmanageable proportions do people get concerned that there may be something seriously wrong with the picture they are working on. Eventually a scientific genius passes by the table and somehow imagines what a radical reworking of the parts would look like. Only now that the new theory has been conceived is it tried out, and to the extent that more stray parts now fit congenially together, it is said to be more comprehensive, and therefore, better. The old theory isn't all wrong, since some pieces still fit nicely in it, too. But it isn't as far-reaching in scope. Thus Newtonian physics isn't wrong, compared to Einstein's relativity theory; it still explains a good deal—but it is not *as* true as Einstein's reformulation, which explains much more.

At its best everything we do can become an art—even physics, the most hard-nosed science of them all. Einstein had no new data at his disposal when he postulated relativity as the new jigsaw puzzle plan. Everyone else knew what he knew, but he saw it differently. What is true of physics is easily demonstrable in other areas as well. Robert Nisbet, a historian of ideas, calls the notion that scientists get their ideas from painstaking laboratory experiments "the stork story of science!" Charles Darwin already had the idea of evolution before his ship, the *Beagle,* left harbor. Einstein arrived at his general theory of relativity slowly, from 1906 to 1915, but it wasn't until 1919 that experimenters were able to observe an eclipse of the sun and prove him correct. The astronomer who discovered the basic laws of planetary motion, Johannes Kepler, owed his success, it is sometimes thought, to the fact that the scientist for whom he worked, Tycho Brahe, had invented a technologically advanced instrument (called a sextant— the telescope came later) for observing and measuring the heavens. That's not how Kepler recalled things. He had always been a visionary, who wrote an early work (in 1619) envisioning mathematical harmonies that govern the universe. "The roads by which men arrive at their insights into celestial matters," he declared, "seem to me almost as worthy of wonder as those matters themselves." Similarly the mathematician Marston Morse recalled that "discovery in mathematics is not a matter of logic. It is rather the result of mysterious powers which no one understands, and in which the unconscious recognition of *beauty* [note!] must play an important part." Mathematical proofs are called elegant for the same reason Pete Axthelm has his fictitious hero in a book on basketball say of star Connie Hawkins, "That was the Hawk: just beautiful!"—which was exactly what James Watson reports saying the night of his discovery of DNA, "It's so beautiful, you see, so beautiful!" You don't have to create a work of art to be an artist. Whatever you do well, with all your soul, the odds are that when you do it, you already are one.

But if everybody does it, what is it? We would hate to be in the position of Molière's bourgeois pseudo-intellectual who is amazed at the facility with which he has spoken prose all his life, without even knowing it. When I say we are all artists at what we do best, I don't mean to generalize the term to the point where it can mean anything at all. Theater or art critics who use aesthetic words of praise must mean something specific, you would think. And indeed they do. So even though there may be something artistic about everything we do, not everything we do is art. Moreover, *I want to urge people not only to attend to the specific arts that go into their worship, but to transcend that first step by seeing their worship as a more comprehensive art in and of itself.* By demonstrating the fact that we are all artistic, I have at least avoided two misconceptions of which I spoke earlier: first, that artists are special creatures, rightly suspect of being stranger than the rest of us; and second, that only specially gifted people have the capacity for art, so why should we, who pray regularly as part of our human nature, even imagine that we are like that? What we need to do now is look more closely at the role of artistic vision in our lives generally, and then we will be able to see worship as the art form that it is and ourselves as the worshiping artists that we should like to become.

Start with the ordinary American calendar. If you are in business you probably have a small pocketbook or vest-pocket calendar about 3" × 5" in size, for which you buy refills annually. Each year's refill looks pretty much like the one from the year before, or for the year after, for that matter. If you open any of them at random, you will see a set of double pages that appear to be roughly identical to any other double-page spread. What you may not immediately realize, but what is true nonetheless, is that far from being a mere convenience, your business calendar is actually a material extension of the way the business world conceptualizes the abstract notion of time; its first quality is evident just from the interchangeability of one refill for another and the way any two pages look the same. In this very utilitarian American time scheme, time has no inherent logic of its own, but is an empty ledger beckoning the busy executive to fill it according to his or her own schedule.

Other peoples and cultures would be aghast at the colossal nerve with which we shape time to suit ourselves. For traditional Chinese, for example, the year of the dragon is not the same as the year of the rat or the year of the snake. Or to take another example, the Jewish calendar is marked by Hebrew dates in which the Hebrew letters stand for numbers. The first letter of the alphabet is 1, the second is 2, the tenth is 10, the eleventh is 20, and so on. Thus numerical dates can also (at times) just happen to spell out words. In 1984 the Hebrew year of 5744 occurred, and much to their chagrin, Jews discovered that its Hebrew equivalent (T-SH-M-D) spelled out a variant of the Hebrew word for persecution! Hebrew calendars that year were therefore printed with the last two letters reversed, so as to avoid the "superstitious" consequence entailed by the name "The year of persecution." By contrast, the year 5748 (= T-S-M-CH) spells out, literally, "You will rejoice," so as "the year of rejoicing" it was prominently displayed across Hebrew calendars or on beautifully calligraphed front pages of Jewish New Year cards. Is all this rooted in superstition? Certainly. But the point is not whether individual years really are or are not different from each other because of what they are called. The point is that ordinary American Jews who know better than to think that a year holds joy because of the arbitrary spelling of its Hebrew numbers, nevertheless take advantage of that eventuality to imbue a year with uniqueness.

For the executive, by contrast, time has no reality of its own at all. The only appropriate way to deal with it is to convert it into its own manipulable currency equivalent, so that wise managers can "organize their time" to make the most of it. By itself, then, it is empty, meaningless, aptly symbolized by the blank pages staring at us in as-yet-unused appointment books. The idioms about time in our English language emphasize time's malleability in the hands of wise users, in that "time" usually occurs as the object of verbs, as if it were literally the sand in an hour glass, dependent on the way people handle the glass itself. We "spend time" or "save" it, "lose" it and "make it up" again. If we think "time is getting away from us," we can "take time out," to recuperate (ourselves) and to recoup the losses that threaten to overwhelm us. Appropriate therapy under such conditions is a course on time management. At the opposite end of the spectrum are unindustrious people who have nothing to do: that is to say, they have "time on their hands," meaning that they have "all the time in the world" available, but no understanding of how to use it. They do not know what business teaches: mechanisms of converting empty meaningless time into a commodity that matters. If they are smart, they will not "waste their time," but "use" it wisely by "investing" it in a project like going to school or learning a trade. As the saying goes, "Time is money."

No wonder the executive turns calendar pages that are as blank as time itself, inviting human initiative to fill up the hours in a way that counts. The calendar correctly displays the way time is conceptualized: every twenty-four hours gets its own arbitrary block, each day being the same size as the next, each one broken down into hourly segments big enough for appointments that alone will make the time matter. Monday at 3:00 is essentially the same as Wednesday at 11:00, in that we, time's users, make time valuable by scrawling its meaning across our calendrical maps, imbuing this otherwise empty commodity with its potential cash value.

By contrast, religious traditions evaluate time as having its own intrinsic merit. If you are Irish, March 17 is not like March 16 or March 18; St. Patrick's day falls when it does (note the verb "falls," indicative of the way time "happens upon us"); unlike my appointment with a client, religious feasts and fasts are not movable according to convenience. The Hebrew idiom asking "What time is it?" uses the word *sha'ah*, which means time in the sense of a human clock or arbitrary cultural schedule: the conventional way that I measure the hour in which I choose to do something or other is the *sha'ah*, which is measurable on a clock known as a *sha'on*. On the other hand, the sacred times of the year, that is, holy days (like Passover), are called *zemanim* (singular = *zeman*). A *zeman* is conceptualized not as empty time dependent on human initiative for its quality, but as something with inherent value that humans can choose to recognize or not. The prayers for each *zeman* reflect that *zeman's* inherent quality. Thus, Passover, the season of the Exodus from bondage, is introduced by a prayer entitling it *zeman cherutenu*, "the time of our freedom." *Shavuot* (Pentecost), when according to Jewish lore the Torah was revealed on Mt. Sinai, is *zeman matan toratenu*, "the season of revelation." For Jews alive to the religious system of counting time, days do not pass in simple homogeneity. Each passing season presents us with an opportunity to recognize a different aspect of life's bounty, and if we miss "the season of freedom" or the New Year when "repentance, prayer, and charity" are particularly in order, we impoverish ourselves. We have returned full circle to the traditional notion of the individual years having their own inherent value, only here we are speaking of times within each year that recur annually, allowing us to re-experience a different element in our consciousness.

Here, too, the original rationale of some two thousand years ago was what we moderns would call blatant superstition. The year was conceived astrologically, each segment of it assigned its own inherent quality dependent on the concatenation of the stars. Since each astronomical body moves in perfect geometrical patterns, any given stellar configuration was seen as bound to be repeated at the same time (or *zeman*) once and only once every year. Wise human planning depended not on filling arbitrary slots on an appointment pad, but on making one's personal behavior tally with the heavenly configurations. Each configuration itself, incidentally, was called a *mazal*, the Hebrew word roughly equivalent to what we call a constellation. At critical junctures when new organisms came into being—the birth of a baby, the wedding of a newly married couple—one wished the infant or the bride and groom *mazal tov*, literally, the hope that this moment of birth prove a good constellation, not an evil one. (Jews still use the phrase to mean "Congratulations," though they have forgotten how it originated.) But here too, the original astrological basis for the belief in time's inherent quality is less important than the accompanying observation that western cash-flow objectivity need not be the only way to measure time and its meaning in human society. Religious men or women are members of traditions that have treated time in certain ways for centuries, and therefore, even without accepting the superstitious basis for religious calendration, they sense the quality of a *zeman* when it arrives.

In Chapter One I said that time is unmanageable without some system of structuring it. There I emphasized the way our daily schedules are sorted into appropriate times to do things and ritualized ways of doing them. Now we see that what was true of days is equally true of years. Seasons, like days, are assigned inherent meaning beyond the business ethic that establishes time merely as a useful commodity. For sports buffs, Super Sunday functions like a religious event. It is even packed with its own "Holy Week" ritual leading up to it. It comes at the same time every year, and if you do not know when that is, it can only be because you are not a sports fan "by religion." Modern nation states, too, mark their birth and growth by holy times: Bastille Day, Canada Day, or the Fourth of July, depending on whether you are French, Canadian, or American. The French Revolution that inaugurated modern France was instituted in opposition to "l'Ancien Régime," the medieval class structure in which traditional Christianity loomed large, so Bastille Day was a conscious rebellion against Christianity; in fact, in the full heat of revolutionary ardor, even the way of counting the years was temporarily altered, so that instead of counting from *anno domini*, "the year of the Lord," Jacobin France counted years from 22 September 1792, the day France became a republic, the monarchy having been abolished the day before by the first National Convention. So antagonistic to religion were the revolutionaries that they abolished not only the Gregorian calendar and its saints' days, but Sunday as well. The new nation-states of Canada and the United States, on the other hand, were not forged in rebellions against the church, so their new national calendars supplemented rather than replaced traditional seasons and holy days. But even here the potential conflict between two diverse calendrical systems is obvious. In the "civil religion" of America, citizens of the United States can, and often do, keep purely secular holidays like the Fourth of July and Memorial Day, to which they add Thanksgiving, a product of the cross-fertilization of religious and national consciousness. Even Christmas is now observed by many as an American, but not particularly a Christian, event. Thus everybody has a calendar, and modern societies offer several from which to choose.

One index of religious or cultural health is the extent to which the appropriate holy days are presumed to be movable according to convenience. Have you ever discovered that your anniversary or your child's birthday conflicts with a business trip you wanted to plan? Try telling your husband or wife, or your son or daughter, "Thursday night is inconvenient; let's celebrate on Friday." If you do, it won't work. If you miss recalling the day you were married or the day your children were born, you cannot so easily make up the deficit by arbitrarily declaring another day its equivalent. In the realm of human meaning, days vary in their inherent significance, even if it is not the constellations that cause them to do so. Early twentieth-century Jews in the United States tried to move their Sabbath from Saturday to Sunday; they failed. More people could and did come to pray on Sunday, but try as they might to pretend otherwise, they knew they had missed the Jewish *Shabbat*.

On the other hand, they did *try* to move the Sabbath, a clear indication of the strength of American culture's challenge to traditional Judaism. Holy days present temporal occasions to recognize, and thus to celebrate, values; when those values lose their compelling quality, the times that mark them become shiftable. Jews who forgot what the Hebrew word *Shabbat* implied for Jewish consciousness felt free to move the day when *Shabbat* was celebrated, something they would never have presumed to do for the High Holy Day of Yom Kippur. To the best of my knowledge, no one has ever suggested fasting on the day before or after Yom Kippur, just because it's a weekend, say. In American life we once had immovable feasts called Memorial Day and Washington's Birthday. No longer. Executive mentality now slots those events into convenient long weekends, with the predictable result that no one even knows what those days mean any more. When did the relativizing of the American civil religious calendar take place? Was it a consequence of the Vietnam years, when America turned away from proud recollections of national sacred seasons? Whatever the reason, it is a fact that thirty years ago Memorial Day was the occasion for a vast outpouring of nationalistic sympathy, replete with small town parades, pilgrimages to local cemeteries, ritualistic laying of flower offerings on the graves, political speeches resonant with echoes of national purpose, and (in general) a celebration of America. It is no longer that. For better or worse, the relativization of the American "religious" calendar spelled the weakening of Americanism as a religious rival to the traditional religions of its citizens.

I have "spent a long time" in this discussion of time, so as to show, first, how business rationalizes time by conceiving of it as lacking in inherent value, and second, how people rise above that hard-nosed business sense in order to imbue time with its own innate meaning for their lives. Whether they are eighteenth-century French revolutionaries, proud American patriots, or traditional Jews and Christians, they establish a calendar that is presumed to be sacrosanct. This calendar attracts ritualized observances designed to demonstrate the fact that not all of life is a *tabula rasa,* a mere empty slate awaiting only the imprimatur of individual choice to make it into something. If we wish to believe that life has its own transcendent meaning beyond our individual selves, then time cannot be completely open-ended, at the mercy of every single person's whims. Whether we imagine it as having its own God-given structural qualities (like the traditional Jewish *zeman* that is inherently a season of freedom or of revelation), or whether we recognize its essence as lying in the events of our people's history (the birth of the church or nation), we agree that time makes its own demands upon us. It has its own "soldered-in" patterns, its own ebb and flow that we only recognize, at best, and around which we plan religious gatherings, traditional meals, and every manner of ritualized celebration that encapsulates the theme of the calendrical period in question, so that individuals can find some consistent shape in their otherwise shapeless days. In that way time is patterned; and we individuals who shape our lives after the cultural patterning of Christianity or Judaism (or for that matter, Americanism or the sports season) are patterners ourselves, which is to say, artists. That is what I mean when I say that religion is not the search for limits and theological truths alone, but for patterns that provide meaning out of chaos: exactly what dancers do with random movement, composers with arbitrary noise, and painters with pointless shape and color—they show us how the raw elements of experience can be envisioned as cohering in meaningful ways. In its essence religion is thus an art, our life of prayer a celebration of the particular artistic patterns that our religious culture has chosen to encode. Nowhere is this feature of religion more evident than in the calendars that provide us with the times of our lives.

A second example, which I can handle more briefly now, is space. Time and space are a continuum, say the physicists. They are inextricably linked in mutual interdependence in a religious sense as well, since the same search for pattern that gives us predetermined times provides specially valued places, too. Space, like time, is, on the one hand, something really real, something "out there" whose reality we take for granted; yet it is also something completely dependent on our own artistic vision, something whose shape we ourselves decide upon.

A group of geographers in England illustrated what I have in mind when they administered the following test to a group of suburban London families. They asked each family member to draw a map of the immediate vicinity. The fathers, who tended to commute by rail into central London drew their home, the road to the train station, and the station itself—not much more than that. The mothers, who consumed much of the day doing all the family errands, drew far more crowded diagrams, complete with schools, doctors' offices, shops, and the hundred-and-one establishments on which a family's daily life depends. The children, however, noted what even the mothers had omitted. They mapped in their school, their home, and their friends' homes (not necessarily to scale, of course), but in addition, they drew the local candy store! What was the "real" neighborhood? Clearly all of the above and none of the above at the same time. Just as we chart our time by selective perception of the relative value inherent in hours, days, months, and years, so we map our space according to what we choose to notice as important for us.

What is true of neighborhoods and families is true also of cultural, national, and religious traditions. The Soviet Union is officially without religion, but Marxism functions like one when it selects May Day as a holy occasion representative of the universal class struggle (call it their sacred myth) and celebrates each May 1 in the sacred confines of Red Square. Socialist farmers who founded the modern state of Israel kept May Day too, which they celebrated in their own idea of holy space, not the age-old Temple mount, but the fields where crops were ripening. As they rediscovered their Judaism, they readopted the biblical harvest festivals and merged them with the socialist-populist idea of work, still keeping the same sacred spaces, but marking their sacrality according to the biblical calendar rather than the socialist one.

Try this experiment: close your eyes and imagine the world. If you are old enough to have gone to school before the space age, you will never think first of the globe as pictured from a spacecraft. Instead, your picture will be the flat earth pictured in your old school textbooks, with England in the middle and Asia split into two equal parts on the extreme left and right side margins. I was raised with that world map, and to this day I have trouble remembering that you can fly from Hawaii (on the "left") to Japan (on the "right") without going through New York and Europe first; and though I know it intellectually, I find it difficult to assimilate the notion that one flies to Moscow from Toronto by going over the top of the world—as if you could turn the pages in the map from bottom to top, instead of from left to right. Why was that map arranged with Europe in the center but Asia on the periphery? Again we have an instance of the artistic structuring of reality, in this case, the selective perception of geography by nineteenth-century Europeans who saw themselves as the center of the universe. The sun never set on the British Empire, it was said, an indubitable fact to anyone who scanned that mercator projection of the world, with its numerous blotches of red (signalling empire countries) in every sector of the earth's surface. The central line of longitude ran right through England, and the International Date Line, a very inconvenient thing requiring a twenty-four-hour readjustment to one's life, was allocated to the other side of the globe, where most English-speaking citizens wouldn't have to worry about it. Victorian England thus controlled both time and space by laying down the rules by which both would be observed by the world's populations.

Other examples of selective space perception come equally to mind, some just humorous satires, like the *New Yorker* magazine cover showing a New Yorker's view of the world, in which individual Manhattan avenues get specific names, but not much past New Jersey even makes it to the map. ("Can civilized life exist outside the metropolitan area?" was the message.)

A far more serious instance of the human penchant to structure space in a meaningful way is the variety of religious conceptions. As a Jew, for example, I know that my mind's eye sees Jerusalem, not London, in the center of things; all roads lead to Jerusalem, not Rome, on my map. Two thousand years ago my ancestors went farther than that. They drew a map of the world consisting of a series of concentric circles: first, the boundaries of Palestine (now the State of Israel, roughly) which they called "The Holy Land"; inside that, and holier still, was the circle representing the walled city of Jerusalem, "the Holy City" in their vocabulary; even holier was the next circle, the Temple site, within which the holiest spot of all was called the Holy of Holies, to be entered only once annually, on the holiest day of the year, Yom Kippur itself, and by the holiest personality, the high priest. Thus were holy time and holy space superimposed on each other.

With the recollection of the high priest entering the Holy of Holies we come to the role of ritual. Believers do more than just recognize holy space and holy time; they re-experience them. For example, when Jews began to realize they could not hope to visit the Temple any more—the Temple was razed by Roman legions in the war of 70 c.e.—they drew on their innate human artistry to extrapolate the pure geometrical model of a sacred site surrounded by concentric circles of decreasing holiness. With this model as their guide they fixed spaces in their own communities that functioned as the Temple had: their homes and their synagogues (which they even called "little sanctuaries"). In both cases the building precinct was endowed with Temple-like sacrality and ritually marked by a sacred sign on the doors (Jews still put these markers, called *mezuzahs*, on their home and synagogue doorposts). Within the home the table was seen as an altar, around which the family, as the "priests," ate sacred meals, which they circumscribed with appropriately sacred blessings; similarly in the synagogue the central space to which all eyes were directed was the ark, designed eventually as a recessed cavity in the wall in which the Torah scroll was kept. No one sacrificed any more, of course, but prayers were called "the offerings of our lips." In this way sacred values were linked to easily accessible sacred spaces, where (at the right sacred times) worshipers could celebrate their people's ancient artistic structuring of time and space, as if the Temple were still standing.

A parallel example from Christianity is the stations of the cross. Ordinary space was converted into sacred space when Jesus walked it on his way to Calvary. Later generations marked its contours, not by recollecting every step of the route, for that would have been impossible, but by selectively perceiving certain critical junctures of that momentous journey, and taking, as it were, collective cultural photographs of the event that occurred there— here Jesus was condemned to death; here he received the cross; here he fell for the first time; and so on. But the exact stations recalled were a matter of choice, and the choice itself reflected religious values and goals. To begin with, there was the decision to choose this particular scriptural event as opposed to others for microscopic study and detailed recollection—a decision prompted by the centrality of the Passion to Christian consciousness. But the actual celebration of the stations owes its origin to the Franciscans who administered the holy places in the fourteenth century. By that time European piety had identified suffering as a positive religious end; church art had replaced old portraiture of Jesus as high priest and ruler with a new emphasis on Jesus suffering on the cross. Already imbued with this new theology of suffering, the Franciscans were prepared to notice the details of the Passion, and when they returned to Europe, they brought with them their own portable reconstruction of the Palestinian route where Jesus suffered in the form of stations erected in their church precincts. The number and content of the stations varied widely until they were standardized in 1731 as fourteen, but a fifteenth one emphasizing the resurrection later came to represent a more contemporary reemphasis on the paschal mystery that transcends death, the necessary continuity between crucifixion and resurrection.

So just as Jews retained the sacred ground of the Temple by transferring it to the synagogue, Christians kept the sacred route that Jesus traveled by moving it to their churches around the world. And in both instances rituals were established to imprint the memory of far-off geography on people who might never in their lives actually see the places in question, but who would know them as truly as they knew the homes in which they dwelt.

Every people has its own artistic construction of a sacred universe, its shrines that command pilgrimage. For ancients the vision extended beyond the earth to include realm after heavenly realm of concentric circles where angels mediated on our behalf with God, and these regions were amenable to visits by the elect who mastered the requisite mystical means of worship. Modern Jews include such places as Auschwitz, where six million died, and the Herodian fortress of Massada, where the zealots perished under Roman might in the war of 70 C.E. Alternative loci that function religiously today include Woodstock (for the generation of the '60s); the intersection of San Francisco's Haight and Ashbury streets (for the flower children of the time); Elvis Presley's home, Graceland, (which features lines of pilgrims well in excess of that enjoyed by any recognized church in the nation); and campuses like the University of Notre Dame or Michigan (where alumni of all ages congregate for "high holy day" rituals at the "holy of holies," the football field.)

I mean these comparisons not lightly. Though of course I am aware that football is not a eucharist, I am equally convinced that the human need to structure time and space in some artistically satisfying way is evident in football fans who travel to the stadium on Super Sunday no less than in Christians pilgrims who visit a cathedral on Easter Sunday. In each case people ritualize their own respective way of punctuating space and time with meaning.

So religion itself is an art, the art of finding shape in time, plotting points of meaning in bare space, and much much more that I've barely touched on here: selecting heroes in our history, for example (St. George, who slew the dragon, if you are a British Anglican, but St. Patrick if you are Irish Catholic; and in national civil religion, George Washington if you are American, Nikolai Lenin if you are Russian, Chairman Mao if you are Chinese). You can declare yourself a high-culturalist by filling your house with Rembrandt prints and listening to Mozart tapes, or you can listen to the Grateful Dead, with Punk Rock posters on the walls. Rabbis, naturally, would prefer that their congregants make visits to New York's Jewish Museum where they purchase Jewish art for their walls and cantorial music for their stereos. And Christian clergy have their own list of preferred cultural tastes. They know the all-important lesson of religion as art, religion as the conveyer of meaning, religion as the guarantor of structure in a world where chaos threatens always to bring the whole human enterprise toppling down into ultimate entropic decay.

If people adopt the limits or the truths of their religious systems, it is because those limits and those truths look congenial in the context of a world with form and pattern. The minute the coherently structured universe that religions presuppose is thrown into doubt, the values they espouse and the theological truths they voice will seem dubious. Once there were no alternatives from which to choose. In the ghettos where my ancestors lived, no one doubted the sanctity of the Sabbath, the incomparable holiness of the Torah, the unquestioned saintliness of Moses or Rabbi Akiba. Now the Sabbath has been confused with a calendar entry marked "Saturday," and though people generally value the Torah and Moses, too, they may barely have heard of Rabbi Akiba. In the ideal world we sculpt our time and space, our history and our heroes, in consensus with our community, affirming together that these are the people, places, times, and things that matter most. These artistic constructs of community consciousness become our "really real" world in which we live and die, secure in the knowledge that, though others may be lost in the anomie of formless void, we need not doubt that life has meaning beyond the apparent randomness of history and nature.

Worship enters here. It is the means by which we picture the really real, celebrating it as the underlying pattern in creation. Public worship is the public recognition of that form of things that we agree is there. It is the artistry by which we paint the canvas of a world shaped not by happenstance but by the way we believe things ultimately cohere. As art it is no different in its essence than van Gogh painting his bedroom at Arles the way he saw it and convincing us, because he was so good at what he did, that rooms look that way—even though, in fact, he painted it tilted on an angle and out of precise proportion! *Above all, men and women charged with liturgy need to be artists, aware of their responsibility not just to intone certain words and move in certain ways, but to fashion through it all a vision of the universe where order is sufficiently compelling to banish all doubt.*

For in the end our ritualizing *articulates* structure, by which I mean it does more than symbolically portray the shapes and ideas we have already been taught to believe. It demonstrates them in advance of our believing in them, actually bringing them into being anew with each liturgical presentation, until we cannot imagine life without them. Ritual is first, not last, in the chain of belief formation. It is not the case that I believe in God and therefore worship; rather, I find worship so compelling that I cannot doubt God's reality. I may even have trouble conceptualizing what God is, but I do not on that account give up my prayers, any more than I abandon the belief in gravity just because I cannot fathom its physics. Through my own participation in the Jewish communal celebration of a certain order to things, I come to see the world with that order already assumed, to the point (in fact) where I am able to see it in no other way. I cannot imagine a world, for example, where there is no Jerusalem; where the days of the week do not lead up to and away from my *Shabbat*, my Sabbath; where I do not picture myself descended from Sarah and

Abraham, Amos and Hosea, and numerous medieval worthies who are as real to me as my great grandparents, whose pictures (as it happens) I have actually seen. But I need no pictures of these distant ancestors, for they appear regularly in my prayers, in my lectionary, in my songs and hymns, in the communal memory I celebrate weekly. Similarly, though I've not yet visited the concentration camps, they are with me daily, as is Sinai, and the great academies where Judaism thrived in Poland, Baghdad, and Spain. These are part of my neighborhood no less than the actual establishments my family or I visit for our daily needs. Others may make pilgrimages to Mecca (they are Moslems) or to the Louvre (they are Culturalists); I go to Jerusalem. Others await high school homecoming day with the intensity I reserve for Passover. For me even colors look different sometimes: yellow paint is, I suppose, yellow paint, but for some Americans it evokes the yellow rose of Texas, whereas for me, at least on Yom Hashoah, my day of memorial for the Holocaust, it is the color of the yellow badge of Auschwitz.

Without our rituals the world pales into universals whose very bland sameness prohibits their fitting together in any coherent way. Jigsaw puzzles depend on the fact that every single piece differs from the others; when properly assembled they combine to present their own picture that can only be guessed at from the pieces viewed singly. That is the essence of worship—when it works: rituals are played out to their end until, like a jigsaw puzzle in time, a window onto reality opens up before the worshiper, who experiences an alternative world to the one he or she faces every day: a world where time and space, past and present, slowly take on a different shape than one finds in business, on the street, and in the markets of daily life. As fractured as the world may appear beyond the walls of public worship, inside its confines a world of wholeness and integrity, hope and vision gradually finds its way to communal expression, and we leave our church or synagogue able now to see that other world outside with the pattern superimposed on it that we knew as certain in the alternative world of our prayers.

In the most diverse places I find remarkable testimonial to the human need to exercise artistic imagination, to define our life's shape as whole, coherent, and endowed with ultimate meaning.

Perhaps the best examples I can think of come from the study of people who have achieved a certain equanimity about life despite circumstances that ought to be enough to challenge anyone's faith in the meaningfulness of existence: I mean those who sense that they are on the verge of death. In 1969, when Elisabeth Kübler Ross first published her landmark study, *On Death and Dying*, we knew almost nothing about the phenomenon of how we come to terms with death. Kübler Ross taught us that dying people go through stages, from denial of their impending doom to a final stage that she called acceptance. Beyond anger and depression, this is the time when patients lapse into a period of "peace and acceptance." I have talked with people like that, not many, but a few, and marveled at the wisdom they attained at the very end. They have made their peace with life's loose ends and see at last a vision of their life now ending as sealed by the proper closure of their imminent demise.

We need not wait to die to find that wisdom. Erik Erikson charts the stages of human life from infancy to old age, describing each period through which we pass as having its own unique perspective that we are challenged to master. Infants learn to trust; teenagers learn identity; and old age brings what Erikson calls integrity.

Integrity is the opposite of despair. Those who fail to master it end their lives in bitter disdain for what they see around them. But others, the lucky ones, rise to life's final challenge and develop what Erikson calls wisdom. With this wisdom that transcends mere knowledge of "the facts" comes "integrity," which "in its simplest meaning is a sense of *coherence* and *wholeness*." Erikson is not necessarily describing the dying. But when these people do finally die, they will be ready for it. They, too, have no loose ends, no unfinished business standing in their way of seeing their lives as artistic wholes lacking only the final brush strokes of their death.

Must we wait until old age to find the serenity implicit in seeing a pattern to things? I do not know for sure, but I think not. Surely the path to such a blissful state is the road known as religion. For what has religion promised other than that very thing: the consciousness of creation's pattern that religionists identify, each in their own traditional way, as the hand of God? Mystics sought—

and still do seek—the ultimate unity with God that they sense must lie behind the incessant patterns linking all creation in one great Whole. Where the pattern is lacking—where war or cruelty mar creation's tapestry—religions strive to eradicate the blemish. Religion is nothing if not the promise of creation's inherent integrity awaiting those who seek it.

And here, too, we return to ritual. Our prayers posit that world of integrity. Our worship rehearses its reality in confident defiance of the injustice, cruelty, suffering, and pain with which humanity is sated. The dying patient, the elderly man or woman of wisdom—they, too, know that people suffer, and their wisdom certainly does not consist in turning a blind eye to human indignity. But they see the world with the eye of God, affirming the pattern that at least is implicit; and so do we when our worship works.

When worship works we are artists in the finest sense of affirming wholeness through the power of our traditional images of time, space, and history. We rise from prayer, with those others in community round about us, ready to impose religious order on the cacophony of the streets and the jangling inconsistencies of our own lives. Religious ritual thus rehearses what the aged eventually know and what the dying must discover: the promise of integrity in the face of despair.

How, practically speaking, we can go about arranging worship to do all that is a matter to which we shall return. We need first to complete the picture of *what* successful worship is, before we can ask *how* it can become that way. Whatever worship says of pattern and promise, wholeness and integrity, it purports above all to speak to God as well. With few exceptions I have avoided God-talk so far, preferring to show first how ritual authenticates experience in general as meaningful rather than empty. But the issue of invoking God's presence cannot be avoided any longer. We predicated our early analysis on the assumption that worship is real and that the worship system, therefore, is not an institutional delusion. The problem with God-talk is that we run the risk of talking like Lewis Carroll, describing an experience of God that is real enough for insiders who have known it, but unable to communicate that reality to outsiders who have not experienced it, and who therefore need it most. How can we talk sensibly about the presence of God in prayer, so that prayer is legitimately prayer and not something else, without at the same time lapsing into religious language that proves useless to people whose worship system is so pathological and dysfunctional that they have difficulty even comprehending what we are talking about? That is the task we take up next.

8

The Presence of God among Us

ONE WAY OF LOOKING AT THE PROBLEM of prayer is to consider it really a problem of faith. If only we moderns could believe in God with the same fervor of those who came before us, goes the argument, we would have no difficulty with our worship. In favor of this approach is its evident simplicity. The reader of Part One will recognize its folly, however: it amounts to blaming well-meaning worshipers for their own inability to pray. Nothing will frustrate people's hopes for prayer more than being told that their persistent failure to find satisfaction in their liturgies is their own fault. Charging worshipers with "If only you had faith" is like saying to children with failing grades, "If only you had brains." *Our inability to believe is the result, not the cause, of worship failure.* Scapegoating worshipers who come to pray anyway may conveniently salve the conscience of frustrated clergy who have trouble facing up to the fact that they are unable to direct meaningful worship for their people, but its only predictable effect will be the gradual aggravation of an already seriously malfunctioning worship system, and a hastening of the drift away from public worship toward alternative public ritualizing, be it sports, nationalism, or pseudoreligious cults. The proper retort to those who advocate solving worship problems by haranguing worshipers to pull themselves up from the morass of their disbelief by their own spiritual bootstraps is H. L. Mencken's acerbic observation: "For every human problem, there is one solution that is simple, neat, and

153

wrong." Assuming we could pray if only we believed is simple and neat; it is also colossally wrong.

People find faith in many ways, to be sure. The old adage that there are no atheists in foxholes expresses the truism that some people turn to God as a last resort when they realize how close they are to a death they cannot prevent. Other people find their faith in exactly the opposite situation: not in moments of existential panic when they suffer a brief vision of their life coming to a quick, premature, and violent end, but in flashes of eternity when nothing seems as certain as the radiant joy of life, when one can almost believe that this moment of perfection will be arrested in its passing and last forever—a glimpse of the sunset over the Grand Canyon or reveling at the moment of a child's miraculous birth. The foxhole syndrome (if we can call it that) is balanced by the Grand Canyon syndrome: both are cases of extreme experiences calling forth faith from deep within us, faith we did not know we had.

No one can seriously deny the catalytic effect of foxholes and Grand Canyons on our detecting faith buried deep down within us. The problem is that these extreme instances of faith discovery rarely prove lasting. Parishes are filled with people who will testify that they have known the presence of God at one or more peak moments in their lives, but who never come to pray because they know they can never find the Grand Canyon in their liturgies. On the other hand, it is exactly that misplaced expectation that leads liturgical planners to the frantic search for worship programming, of which I spoke in Part One, in which they schedule as many extraliturgical events as possible in the vain hope of producing an extravaganza that will bring the equivalent of the Grand Canyon into the sanctuary once a week. If we depend on foxholes, baby births, and setting suns to fill our churches and synagogues, we are in deep trouble.

A more sophisticated argument on the origins of faith comes from psychologists in the relatively new field of faith development. I've already referred to Erik Erikson's plotting of the human life cycle as a succession of stages through which we pass, each one offering its own opportunity for expanding our human potential. Old age brings integrity and wisdom, says Erikson, but the first step on the long road leading to that final stage is infancy, when we learn the value of trust, and thus faith. Other theorists, basing their work on Piaget's studies in conceptual development, have demonstrated that faith is not a single monolithic thing that we either have or not, but a complex character trait that grows through time. The foxhole syndrome by which faith in a supreme deity is evoked by fear of imminent punishment ranks very low on the scale of faith development, for example.

I do not mean to deny, then, that faith is attainable in many ways, or that healthy human nurturing brings with it a parallel maturation of cognition, moral responsibility, and faith, too. But I do want to emphasize the role of ritual in that very development. Ritual is not the result of faith, but one of its causes. This book as a whole seeks to raise our consciousness of the importance of good ritual; we just saw that ritual's power lies in its artistic capacity to present an alternative world where time and space unfold in structured ways indicative of pattern, plan, and purpose—despite the temptation to view the world as random, chaotic, and accidental. Now we have to expand that insight to include an explanation for the common testimonial by people whose worship proves so satisfying that they attest to encountering God in it. First we need to see how the experience of ritualized order leads to faith in general. Then we have to ask how we come to identify the object of our faith as God.

Finding the Pattern

What is faith, if not belief in an eventual outcome of events despite the absence of empirical demonstration that such an outcome is probable? Suppose I drop a fifty-pound weight from a tenth-story window and insist that I have faith it will hit the ground. That is not faith, you will protest, but a conclusion fairly drawn from a simple knowledge of the facts. On the other hand, if the street below is Times Square at lunch hour, it can only be faith—misguided, to be sure—that leads me to drop the weight in blissful confidence that it will not hurt anyone when it lands. Of course it is at least theoretically possible that what has always happened before will not happen again, or at least not this time anyway, so that the law of gravity may be suspended just this once as the weight leaves my hand. Thus in a way scientific prediction and faith in providence are at least on the same continuum, not two altogether different things; to some extent we all operate with faith in every step we take. But we normally reserve the word "faith" for the confidence we have in that which could not be predicted by the scientific evidence before us. Faith in God implies the belief that God is real, despite the failure of science to demonstrate any cogent empirical grounds for believing it.

But faith is not *altogether* different from scientific "knowledge." I know the weight will hit the ground because of my observation of the patterns implicit in nature. A very unsophisticated way of observing pattern is by trial and error; even our primitive cave-dwelling ancestors would have predicted the fall of the weight, though they had no idea that it was "gravity" or a "law" that the falling object typified. A more sophisticated way of expressing pattern is to work out the mathematics of the law even before observing its operation in the actual world of phenomena. That was the genius of Einstein, whose theoretical predictions were proven right only years after their mathematical demonstration was completed, and who is reported to have reacted without emotion to the final experimental proof that he was right, on the grounds that the mathematical demonstration of the potential replication of patterns in creation is far more convincing than any eyewitness observation can ever hope to be. So scientific knowledge depends on the discovery of order, either firsthand (as we observe the same thing happening over and over again) or mathematically (as we jump immediately to the theory of the necessary relationship between things and know that a pattern is there, whether it is actually observed or not).

Faith works the same way. Regardless of when in our life cycle we reach the stage of discovering it, the discovery of pattern generates faith just as surely as it generates science. Through the experience of pattern we come to believe that things eventually work out, that trust in the beginning is rewarded in the end, that an apparently chaotic first step, like a misplaced note in music or an odd brush stroke in painting, will be perfectly coherent when the composition or the canvas is finally complete. I remember as a child watching my mother stir together the recipe ingredients for my favorite cake and making a wry face at the gooey mess in the mixer bowl; at times like that she would inerrantly reassure me of the outcome by citing an old Yiddish proverb that she had heard from her mother: "A fool shouldn't observe work that is only half done." I doubt that she knew she was teaching me faith at the time, but she was.

In that sense it is less the miracle of the unusual—the foxhole and the sunset—than it is the miracle of the everyday that endows us with lasting faith, just as it is the recognition of nature's regularity that generates scientific principles. But there is an important difference between the patterning of experience that leads to religious faith and the same patterning of experience that promotes science: scientific patterns need not embody value; they simply exist as observable phenomena. Hypothetically, at least, we can imagine a world created by a malicious demon in which the sum total of natural laws are evil in their intent, a cruel hoax for people like us, who hope pathetically to create a better world. Scientific confidence would still be possible in that world; religious faith would not. Faith emerges not out of the patterns alone, but from the trust that those patterns are beneficial in the end. The psychologist Gregory Bateson helps us here by differentiating among different levels of pattern.

Take any simple animal, a crab, for example, and note the similarity between the left side of its body and the right or between its right front side, where a front leg protrudes, and the right back side, where a rear leg is found. In the first case we have a pattern known as *bilateral symmetry:* left and right sides are the same. In the second case we see that the front claw and the back claw are similar. Scientists call that relationship *serial homology*. In either case we have a pattern that holds between two different parts of the same animal. We call this *First Order Patterning*.

Now compare the crab with a lobster. What was true of the crab seems also to be true of the lobster. Lobsters, too, are bilaterally symmetrical, and they, too, exhibit similarities between their front and their rear appendages. So a pattern exists between the lobster and the crab, both being examples of the same sets of relationships between left and right and front and back. When two species demonstrate similar patterns, it is called *phylogenetic homology*. But phylogenetic homology differs from serial homology and from bilateral symmetry in that it is a pattern that holds between two patterns. If serial homology is a comparison of an animal's parts, phylogenetic homology is a comparison of those comparisons. It is thus one step higher in the chain of patterns. Bateson calls it *Second Order Patterning.*

Another example of Second Order Patterning is the similarity between a horse and a human being. Horses and humans, too, are characterized by bilateral symmetry and serial homology. We can therefore compare the fact that horses are like humans to the similar fact that crabs are like lobsters, noting that they are alike even in their likenesses. That is to say, we are now making a comparison (horses:people :: crabs:lobsters) of the comparison (crabs: lobsters) of the comparisons (crabs: left and right sides are similar; front and back appendages are similar). Bateson calls this a *Third Order Pattern.*

The point of it all is that when we talk about patterns we are not always discussing the same thing. Patterns exist in an ascending order of increasing abstraction. Any fool can observe First Order Patterns just by holding a crab and noting its symmetry. The idea that the crab might be like the lobster is more difficult to conceptualize, since each animal is sufficiently unlike the other that it might not occur to us to see how they are the same. By the time we get to Third Order Patterns, it is not even clear that we are in the realm of empirical evidence at all, since here we are comparing not the animals themselves, but *the similarity of relationships between the animals.* I can see a horse and I can see a human being; I might even be said to see the similarity between horses and humans; but I surely do not literally *see* the similarity between that similarity and another one, namely, the similarity between crabs and lobsters. The similarity of similarities is something I understand or deduce from the evidence, not something I actually see in the same way that I see the evidence itself.

Theoretically we can go even farther, into the realm of a Fourth Order Pattern, whereby the patterns of patterns of patterns are held together in one more pattern still. At that point we are so far removed from the evidence that it becomes virtually impossible even to picture what we are talking about. Here we enter the realm of faith. Religious believers hold to the proposition that the cosmos is a masterwork where somehow, despite death and disaster, "it all makes sense." To the inevitability of human mortality, for example, Christianity teaches that Jesus overcame death on our behalf, and Judaism—as early as Jesus' day—preached resurrection of the dead and reward and punishment in a world to come. My favorite image in this regard is the Jewish tradition that imputes to Elijah the Prophet the secrets of what I have called the metapatterns of the universe. Jewish folklore holds that when the medieval rabbinic scholastics found themselves led by equally compelling logic to two mutually incompatible solutions, they suspended their discussion, but retained their respective positions. Holding the ultimate solution in abeyance, they are said to have announced, "Elijah will harmonize conflicting conclusions." The very word "harmonize" is instructive here, in that it is an artistic term expressive of our faith that facts must cohere in the long run, just as musical notes must flow together melodiously, or colors on a palette blend like a rainbow. Things *must* be so, we hold, even in the face of the most boggling evidence to the contrary.

We may not see the metapattern that connects all the lower level patterning round about us, not yet anyway, but Jews and Christians, anyway, have been raised to take it on faith that such a plan exists.

One very common first step toward a lasting faith in God, then, is a far cry from the momentary excitement of peak events like Grand Canyon sunsets. It is the discovery, first, of elementary patterns, and then of second-level patterns, and so on until one has a momentous vision of the top of the ladder, the existence of a metapattern linking all the patterns. The world now makes sense; it coheres, totally and absolutely; it forms a balanced whole with everything in relationship to everything else—like the point at which the composition of a painting is completed, or the final moments when the resolving chords of a symphony are sounded. Not only coherent, it is comprehensive, too, in that it assumes not just an island of order here or there, but everywhere and at all times, completely beyond the possibility of experiential confirmation.

In their very essence rituals mean pattern. To begin with, their *content* amounts largely to an affirmation of resolution, completion, and continuity. Rites of passage, for example, affirm continuity despite the obvious discontinuity of generational turnover and the wrenching metamorphosis of our stage-by-stage development from birth to death. Similarly in political ritual, the Democratic Party's supporters of competing presidential nominees may threaten temporarily to tear apart their party at its pre-election

national convention, but old pols know that in the end everyone will embrace to the singing of "Happy Days Are Here Again";
and no matter how bitterly contested the election turns out to
be, at the ritualistic swearing-in ceremony the president calls
invariably for unity and takes the oath as the president of all
the people. Anthropologists around the world document "rituals
of reversal" that allow the underdog to experience what it is like
to be on top for just a while and "rituals of conflict resolution"
where internal strains in society are played out in a ritual script
that decreases the odds that they will lie dormant, festering beneath the surface of social life, until eventually they dismember
society completely. Even when violent social change does occur, it
does so not at random, but with its own rituals that demonstrate,
better than words, the righting of wrongs for which the revolution
stands.

Even more important than its content, however, is ritual's essential *form:* the ordered, inexorable unfolding of an ancient, time-
less script in words we've heard before and songs we know and
love. If we leave the ritual arena convinced of our faith in God's
plan, it is because the ritual we leave was a successful microcosm
of that order, so much so that, at the time, at least, we could not
doubt its reality in the world about us.

In similar fashion it was from the form as much as the content of
the universe that Einstein drew his faith in the absolute necessity
of an ultimately comprehensive pattern in the universe. Despite
the opposition of many of his colleagues who made up the elite
echelon of the scientific community, he dedicated the efforts of his
later years to arriving at a grand field theory that would have
united all experience in a master synthesis of patterning. He never
accepted the claim of quantum mechanics that the subatomic
world works according to probability rather than by absolute
mechanistic necessity. He is credited with saying that God doesn't
play dice.

But Einstein did not believe in God. I said before that this
chapter would explore the relationship between ritual and
faith. Our first step has been the discovery of how it is that the
experience of ritualized order leads to faith in general. Now we
have to ask how we learn to identify the object of that faith as
God.

From Faith "in General" to Faith in God

According to the foxhole theory of faith, finding God is easy. Revelation comes automatically as your life flashes before your eyes. Similarly with Grand Canyon sunsets: who can doubt God's reality in a blaze of incomparable glory? In truth, however, even there, if you are not ready to recognize God's presence, you'll miss it. A Jewish folktale records the rabbi who is asked where God is found, and replies, "Wherever people let God in." I take that tale not as a moralistic implication that people who don't know God are themselves responsible for deliberately putting up defenses against God's entering their lives, but as an insightful commentary on the fact that even people who want to know God fail in their efforts because they have not been taught to recognize the divine presence even when its comes knocking on their door. In that sense they miss the opportunity to let God in. By analogy imagine a child who is raised never to feel sad. Every time tears well up inside, anxious parents say, "You've eaten forbidden food; what you are feeling is like heartburn, a type of indigestion that will go away." If we later ask the child, now grown to adulthood, "Have you ever known sadness?" we will get a certain answer, "Never." Of course it would be very difficult to put over this ruse on someone, since literature, television, and the movies present the same feelings as "sadness," and eventually the child would realize we were lying.

With religious experience, on the other hand, people are victimized precisely this way all the time. Popular religious literature and media presentation have stereotyped the experience called "knowing God," so that it is assumed that God appears only in sunsets and foxholes, the very, very grand and the very, very frightening. When people have religious experiences that are neither of these, it never occurs to them to think they are experiencing God's presence—any more than our theoretical child-become-adult thinks to identify silent tears with sadness. What we need is a "generic" conceptualization of the ways in which people identify God, one that is free of specific religious images and therefore applicable to all times and places. That will enable us not to confuse God's presence in general with any particular cultural manifestation thereof; then freed from the need to look for God in situations that might have been satisfactory examples in one era but may not be so any longer, we can look afresh at our time and see where God is most likely to be found for us. That insight will have major implications for our worship policy. (To name but two in advance: if God is no longer to be found predominantly in the realm of the magnificent, we need to take a new look at magnificent music's centrality in our services. If God is to be identified in the presence of common human caring, the love that passes silently and humbly between two people who decide to be strangers to each other no more, we may have to rethink seating plans that impose separation and anonymity on people. I return to both of these themes in later chapters.)

The key to finding God in American worship is located in the word "community." The following anecdote illustrates what I mean. Earlier this year I was scheduled to give a speech at the old convention center in downtown Minneapolis. As I entered the building, I marveled at its stately quality. Sitting majestically on a full square block of land just beyond the downtown tourist hub, the center seemed to symbolize the full depth of local tradition that makes the Twin Cities the unique part of America that they are. Appropriately enough, an inscription chiseled into the granite on its upper facade read, " . . . Built for community." On the other hand, people were quick to tell me that the building was slated for imminent destruction, its place to be taken by a bigger and better structure. Would it, too, be dedicated to "community," I wondered, or would the new inscription read just "Bigger and Better"?

The fate of the Minneapolis convention center is a sad but effective symbol for a sort of cultural conflict being played out in synagogue and church worship as the twentieth century draws to a close. There is first of all the view that the most meaningful human experiences are to be found in the warmth of human relationship, so that if God is to be experienced anywhere, it must be in the caring communities where a person's loneliness and need are assuaged by virtue of the remarkable fact that people who might just as easily choose to be virtual strangers elect instead to reach out in love. On that model worship ought to strive to replicate patterns of loving care. It should break down the formal distinctions of social distance that set one person off from another and enforce individualism and anonymity. Spirituality here is something shared with others. Openness and trust in others, as well as human bonding across the arbitrary divisions of class, race, age, and gender, rank high on the list of signs of spiritual being.

In contrast are the traditional European models of religious worship, primarily those associated with cathedral architecture and high culture. That model is a form of individualistic spirituality, in which it is assumed that individuals go to pray—or should, anyway—to escape the fetters of communal life and to commune directly with a God who is beyond human society. God is seen as mighty, transcendent, and far indeed from the madding crowd. Advocates of this approach are quick to point out that the opposite model typified the countercultural reaction to institutional life of all kinds during the '60s and '70s. We all know the extremes—sexually permissive or drug related communes that received so much attention in the Vietnam era, for example. What one group calls community, the other brands as groupieness reminiscent of the hippie generation. Even those who recognize the emotional sterility of religious institutions, and who therefore support our efforts at replacing their depersonalization with caring, loving environments, argue that as lofty a goal as it may be, community building can hardly be associated with the search for God, since God, they say, is present among us only in the grand and the beautiful—that is to say, the bigger and the better. What we need (always) by that philosophy is lofty music, sweeping drama, and high culture of impeccable artistic taste: bigger, better, grander, and larger—as if only in a retreat from current populism will the worshiper find the presence of God.

Is that true? Or can God be present (as Elijah learned) "in the still small voice?" Is God really available only in the stratosphere? Or have we been so conditioned to think in those terms that, even when we know God, we fail to see it, and thus identify genuinely spiritual experiences with less than spiritual names. Is God present beyond us? Or among us? How, that is, do we in our time find God in prayer?

Finding God

Before answering for ourselves, let us examine some personal testimony of others far back in history's memory. That will enable us to unravel a pattern of our own—not just the way this group or that one discovered God, but the common feature to all groups' discovery of the divine in their worship. By applying that pattern to our own case, we will see both how we are the same as those who came before us and how we are different. By adding those insights to the ones we already have, we will be in a position to proceed to the final chapters on our worship, a discussion of what worship must become for us if we are to make it the functional thing it still promises to be.

In the latter part of the last century a German scholar named Bloch discovered an incredible communication indicating that there once were Jews who believed that by fasting for a stipulated number of days, and then by muttering prayers at the ground while bent upside down, their heads between their knees, they would catch a glimpse of God in supreme glory, surrounded by angels, saying the words of praise we know so well from our own liturgies, "Holy, holy, holy, is the Lord of hosts."

The religious community in which Bloch lived, nineteenth-century German Jewish rationalism, was far removed from the sort of mystical contemplation of God suggested by his discovery. Its members had, in fact, already accepted the faulty presumption that classical rabbinic Judaism must have been similarly opposed to mystical "excesses." They therefore faced this newfound discovery with a certain ambivalence. While the find was obviously important and welcome from an objective academic perspective, it constituted simultaneously a severe threat to nineteenth-century religiosity, since it was the very antithesis of the staid rationalistic experience typical of enlightened synagogues then. Reflecting this dilemma, Bloch himself found it difficult to imagine that the worshipers whose practice he had unearthed could be indicative of what he took to be the essential Jewish spirit inherited from the past, and he therefore concluded that the people he was studying, though indeed mystics, had been marginal to mainstream Jewish tradition. For one thing, he dated them late, after the formative influences of rabbinic Judaism had been laid; for another, he situated them in "distant regions of the East," that is to say, outside of Palestine (bad enough), and in Babylonia, which scholars associated then with mystery cults and vague religious tendencies lumped together as "orientalism" (worse still). By implication, therefore, these people constituted a "special case" that one might reasonably assume was irrelevant to modern-day religiosity.

Nevertheless, he painted a fascinating picture of their worship life. Their prayers were marked not by their content, but by their form, which exhibited a certain rhythmic regularity—like a mantra—leading to the conclusion that what mattered most to them was not what the words meant, but how they sounded. Their prayer verbiage was often excessively lengthy, composed chiefly of several chains of synonyms in apposition to each other and selected for their poetic value. The total cognitive message, such as it was, could be captured in one simple sentence: "Praise God." Worshipers seem to have been caught up in the rhythmic flow of the words, which, together with the lightheadedness brought on by fasting and the blood rushing to the head as a consequence of their inverted body posture, invoked a state of trance, whereby they hoped to lose their sense of standing on the earth and, if you like, "to trip" through heaven to see God.

We now know that these worshipers were not marginal to ancient Jewish spirituality, but central to the age that gave us the nascent church and the rabbinic tradition at the very same time. Bloch was wrong on both his proposed date and the place of their activity. We now date these "mystics" as early as the second century, and we place them in the very heart of Palestine itself.

We should look more carefully also at the word "mystic" that has been used to describe them. It sounds at first like an innocent description, but in reality, the word "mystic" is neither innocent nor descriptive. In the nineteenth century, to pin the label "mystic" on someone was, in effect, to stigmatize them. Bloch's selection of the term functioned the same way his faulty date and place for them did: it distanced them from his contemporaries. Even today, when our appreciation of the variety of authentic religious experience has increased dramatically, calling people "mystics" evokes a suspicious sense that they are at the very least, not entirely normal like the rest of us. Find somebody who is really religious, and you say, "Ah, yes . . . well, s/he's a mystic"; as if to say, "Don't hold me responsible for being like that." My unofficial dictionary translation of "mystic" is "off the wall," meaning "all right for them, but not for us." By calling our great spiritual ancestors mystics, we imply that theirs was an interesting sect for its time, but you wouldn't want to join it.

But do you think *they* knew they were mystics? Did they belong to a National Association of Mystical Worshipers, pay dues to a mystics' guild, or go to mystics' conventions? Just to ask these silly questions is to answer them. These so-called "mystics" were just the rabbis, the same ones known to us in imperfect fashion from the New Testament, and the ones who gave us the earliest corpus of rabbinic literature, which is nothing if not rationally conceived and arranged. Like anyone else in any other time, they had families, held jobs, and lived a rational existence; and they gave us, along the way, the very logical system of Jewish law that stands even now at Judaism's very core. Yet when they prayed, they temporarily stepped out of their daily routine, hoping to stand, like the angels, face to face with the Holy One of Blessing, there to lose themselves in uninhibited praise of the God of light, and then to return to their tasks in this, the world below, which God had created and given over to their care.

It is misleading even to believe that there is such a thing as a mystic. In truth there is only a mystical temperament, available to all men and women at all times. Not that the mystical temperament is universally expressed the same way, any more than the universal human potential for music results in just one kind of melody. The forms change, even though the human expression in general does not. So I am not arguing that we should emulate the specific *forms* of worship that I have described thus far. We are challenged to discover *our own* "mystical" forms of prayer that will achieve the same spiritual goal as theirs. Toward that end I must now introduce three technical terms into our discussion.

First, *cultural backdrop,* by which I mean something akin to the backdrop of a play: the balcony for the balcony scene of *Romeo and Juliet,* for example. Backdrop is the context that allows actors to play their roles. As Shakespeare recognized, "All the world's a stage, and all the men and women merely players," so backdrop is necessary for the roles we play in real life no less than for those contrived by playwrights. The whole point of backdrop, however, is that it be so designed as not to draw attention to itself. It must remain unnoticed while the drama is being played out on the stage. If you doubt that, imagine that your best friend is playing Juliet, and she asks how you enjoyed the performance. Can you imagine responding, "I liked it; the balcony was beautiful!" Yet without the balcony as a backdrop, there could be no balcony scene. Our very lives depend on the unconscious setting, or backdrop, offered by our culture. But we generally take it so for granted that we are hardly even aware of what that backdrop is, unless expert observers like social critics draw it to our attention.

In the first two centuries of our era the cultural backdrop of what was then called Palestine was Hellenism. Among other things this philosophy divided the universe into two warring forces, light and darkness. God as light thus became a dominant image in the so-called mystery cults, as well as in Christianity and Judaism, none of which escaped the influence of Hellenism as its common cultural backdrop. (They were all, if you like, actors on the same cultural stage.) Thus, for example, Jesus was regularly portrayed as light, a dominant liturgical metaphor in Christian liturgy even to this very day.

Now we understand why the early synagogue worshipers we have been describing sound so strange to us. They believed in a universe with the earth at the center, but with concentric circles of light around it, the outermost circles being the heavens themselves, which God, the radiant source of light, inhabited. The worshipers' goal, toward which the trancelike state contributed, was temporarily to break loose from the limitations imposed by their earthbound condition—a mixture of light (or soul) and darkness (body)—so as to travel to the regions of pure true light, for which the soul had an affinity anyway. There they would join the angels, who, unlike humans, are composed of nothing but light, in rapturous glorification of the God of light. My point is that as strange as that may sound to us, it was perfectly consistent in a culture where the dichotomy of light vs. darkness was taken for granted.

Consider now just the image of God enthroned in light, surrounded by light-like beings called angels who, dazzled by God's brightness—we call it "glory"—do nothing but utter praise after praise of God. We have no trouble recognizing that image, too, as one that has survived the centuries. Now picture religion as a film that we make of reality; like any other film it is composed of a series of frames that pass rapidly through the camera to give us the illusion of motion. Suppose, now, you could collapse all the frames and assemble a "master frame" expressive of a religion's central image of God. I want to call that hypothetical single frame by the second of my three technical terms, the *master image.*

A master image must be congruent with the cultural backdrop it expresses. The master image we have been describing here—God enthroned in light—is typical of the cultural backdrop of Hellenism. But other cultures at other times have provided their own unique master images. Again the analogy of a play will prove useful. The "master image" of *Romeo and Juliet* (the picture you would expect to see on a *Playbill,* or the one you think of first as typifying the play's content) is the balcony scene; the reason it fits so well, however, is not that there is something innately striking about balconies. Its success as a master image of the play is largely due to the fact that the physical distance between Juliet on the balcony and Romeo in the garden is symbolic of the play as a whole, whose theme, after all, is the unconquerable gulf between the two warring families of which Romeo and Juliet are members. Similarly, though our abundant familiarity with the image of God as light being adored by angels of light might make us think otherwise, there is really nothing inherently necessary about it, either. Its popularity in the critical formative period of Judaism and Christianity was due to its success at evoking a dominant cultural theme of the Hellenistic world in which the two faiths took shape. It was thus permanently encoded in the classical liturgies of the two faiths and persists to this day, even though, much as we may appreciate the image, it can hardly be said to have the same power for us as it did for people in its original Hellenistic context.

Finally I come to my last technical term: *synecdochal vocabulary.* We normally think of vocabulary as words, but it is really a lot more than that. Vocabulary is any means we use to convey a message. Shaking hands, nodding formally, and kissing passionately are all diverse vocabulary items that we use to greet people; they indicate very different messages about relationships that we do well not to confuse! So vocabulary can be soundless movement and gesture. Vocabulary includes objects too: for Christians, a cross; for Jews, a Torah scroll. If you combine movements and gestures with objects, you get actions: raising the chalice, carrying the Torah, and so on. *Through gesture, action, and object, we say as much as we do with words.*

Vocabulary can be further divided into those instances in which the message-bearing item (whether word, gesture, object, or action) wholly contains the message, and cases where it merely points to the message in some agreed-upon fashion. If, for example, I indicate a book, commenting, "This is a good book to read," you may note the advice and read the book, but that is all there is to it. Imagine, however, climbing Mt. Everest to find a guru, whom you ask, "Tell me the secret of life, O Holy One." The Guru produces a worn object from beneath a cloak, and says, "Read this; it is *The Book*." Here we have a common noun "book," used not to identify a simple object but to point beyond that object to something further. Similarly with the word "cross" for Christians; "Torah" for Jews. Words—and gestures, actions, and objects as well—can point beyond themselves to a reality that vocabulary cannot describe, but only suggest. As we saw above, in its extreme instance, when that to which we point is so deeply rooted in our psyche that it is not even amenable to conscious definition, we get vocabulary that we call "symbolic."

There is, however, a medium position, too. Suppose I say, "The pen is mightier than the sword." It is highly unlikely that I have such depth of attachment either to pens or to swords that either word should really "symbolize." On the other hand, by a "pen" I mean not just a pen, but the act of writing, by which, further, I have in mind literature and the human spirit. Similarly the word "sword" here is not just a sword, but an image suggesting violence and war. What I really mean to say is that in the long run spirit is more powerful that brute force. In this medium range usage, a word points beyond its most literal meaning, but not so deeply that it has no specific referent at all. Literary criticism calls such usage "synecdoche," meaning, roughly, the use of a part of a thing to suggest the whole. So I can call my third technical term "synecdochal vocabulary," by which I mean words, gestures, actions and things that point beyond themselves to definable concepts.

We will be looking more deeply at language in a later chapter, but for now we can add to what we noted in Chapter Two (on symbols) by observing three different referring uses of liturgical language.

1) *Signifying function:* a word signifies when it stands for a particular literal concrete referent.

2) *Synecdochal function:* a word "synecdochizes" (to coin a verb)

when it goes beyond the particular literal sign value to suggest that of which the particular sign value referent is only a suggestive part.

3) *Symbolizing function:* a word symbolizes when it goes beyond any particular referent at all, including any conceivable whole of which the sign value referent is a part. It functions primarily to evoke depth of commitment.

Our liturgies rely on all three uses, but the one that particularly interests us here is synecdoche. Synecdochal vocabulary consists of words, objects, actions, and gestures that suggest a whole greater than themselves; so with regard to God we can say that liturgy provides synecdochal vocabulary pointing to the master image. Trained by our cultural context to recognize the reality of God in that image, we invoke God's presence in our worship using synecdochal language.

We can observe the system working in the concrete instance of the worshipers we have been describing thus far. Let us picture a particular community, a group of third-century Jews praying in the ancient synagogue of Beth Alpha which is located on the northern shore of the Sea of Galilee. You can still see the remnants of the place, a brilliant floor mosaic, one section of which displays God as the sun surrounded by the zodiac signs designating the heavens. The *cultural backdrop* of the time is Hellenism, and the *master image* is God arrayed in radiant glory. For *synecdochal vocabulary* worshipers depended on such things as body posture, words as mantras, and the mosaic floor's light imagery. For example, they recited their poems of praise, culminating in the words from Isaiah's vision, "Holy, holy, holy," as, simultaneously, they looked at their synagogue mosaics that displayed God as master of the sun. They would thus have been led to the reality of God's commanding presence in the radiant heavens, which they would have experienced as a mystical journey beyond their earthbound selves.

How are we aware of God in prayer? Through the synecdochal vocabulary of our time that best suggests the reality of a master image that itself best reflects the cultural backdrop in which we stand. It would never occur to us to fast for three days to induce a vision, but that is only because our cultural backdrop is different from that of

Hellenistic Palestine; our master image is no longer a God of light circling the globe in the farthest heaven; and the synecdochal vocabulary that worked so well once will not do so still. *But this model of worship as composed of cultural backdrop, master image, and synecdochal vocabulary holds for Christian as for Jew, and in all ages, even though the particular content of each of these items changes.*

My second example, much closer to home, is nineteenth- and early twentieth-century western Europe, especially Germany. A famous treatise called *The Idea of the Holy* describes worship then. Its author, Rudolph Otto, was a theologian who observed that in his day to pray was, above all, to be radically aware of one's "creatureliness." It was to stand before the ineffable Deity in absolute awe. Otto thus described God as utterly transcendent. I think we can all agree that Otto accurately described the churches and synagogues we know best from our youth, those most influenced by the European spirit. You didn't walk into church and talk, or smile and say, "Hi, there." You entered it aware of your creatureliness, waiting for the God of awe to appear. Why, we should ask, was that kind of worship typical of Germany?

We can begin with Germany's *cultural backdrop,* which was no longer Hellenism with its overriding concern with light versus darkness, but instead, the cultural theme of order: a place for everything and everything in its place; a German penchant for pigeonholing experience; arranging, classifying, and organizing people, places, and things. In such a system what stood out for a European was the importance of putting people in their respective categories, too, that is to say, class consciousness, the social distance, if you like, that separated one class from another and told people their place.

The image of God as an awesome distant Being was therefore not something arrived at out of the theological blue, but an extrapolation from the exaggerated social distance that marked human relationships in German society. Social classes retained their distinctiveness by erecting impenetrable barriers between themselves and others. Formal titles and strict dress codes, for example, militated against easy social mingling across class lines. Paralleling the space separating one social class from another was a veritable social chasm separating the totality of social classes, people in general, from God. Thus was born the *master image* of God as transcendent, God the ultimately distant Being. So successful was this European redefinition of God in terms of European society that many of us still take it for granted, as if the master image of God were not just image but God's very being. In fact a transcendent deity is really just another imperfect way of imaging the divine, favored by one society in one particular time and place. Still our liturgy was reconstructed on that image only a century ago, and then transmitted that way to us, as if it were inevitable that only by celebrating God's regal distance from us would worship successfully invoke God's presence.

We all know very well the *synecdochal vocabulary* that European, and then American, worship developed for the purpose of invoking transcendence: grand churches; the glorification of Baroque architecture; music piped from a hidden choir that sang so well that parishioners didn't dare join in; and enhanced social distance between officiating minister and people. To be sure, this was no invention of the nineteenth century alone; it had been building through the very centuries that made the nineteenth century what it was. But we emerged from that period with architecture that pointed to God in the distance, with masterful choirs singing four-part harmony composed in a key marked "angels only."

It is fascinating to speculate on whether the people who prayed in those lavish structures, sitting formally through endless services without participating, were mystics. Surely Jews and Christians who thought of themselves as the epitome of rationality would have denied such an allegation. But should we believe them? No less than the worshipers in antiquity described above, they emerged with a sense that God was present in their prayers. They differed only in the way God's presence was conceived, and therefore known. If by definition "mystical" means "oddly (and irrationally) religious," then they were not mystics, of course, and that is what they meant when they told us as much. But if "mystical" refers only to the tendency within us all to find God in our own way, our own time, and our own place, then they were as mystical as their predecessors who celebrated God's light-giving capacity by fasting and joining the bands of praising angels in the heavens surrounding the earth.

After this brief stopover in Europe, we arrive back home in America, with the debate over the relative significance of "community." The threefold schematization of worship works here as well. What is the *cultural backdrop* of America, if not just the opposite of Europe? Europeans understood the grand art of Monet's water lilies, while we have Andy Warhol's Campbell's Soup Cans. Music has changed, too. America has given us jazz, the people-music of Black spirituals, and Pete Seeger's folk idiom. We've been raised on the folk guitar, not the organ; on Copland's *Rodeo,* not Handel's *Messiah.* All of this bespeaks a cultural backdrop of an America that was founded on the notion of eradicating the very class distinctiveness on which Europe was based. Here we have worked to obliterate social distance, using first names, addressing envelopes without particular care for titles, building universally accessible public schools, and jettisoning dress codes that mark off one person from another. As we live now in a cultural back-drop of theoretical equality, our *master image* can hardly feature a God of transcendence. For us God will not be imaged as distant, therefore, but as immanently present among us. And our *synec-dochal vocabulary* will be words, gestures, actions, and objects that deny the distance driving God from our midst.

Synecdochal vocabulary for American worship, therefore, must point to intimacy, not distance. That is the point of "community," a term we use to mark any gathering of people where we feel we belong sufficiently to hope for the intimacy of love, of friendship, and of mutual care. Far from destroying community, we need more than anything else to build it up, because that is where God will be present among us.

In the last few decades our greatest threat has been the destruc-tion of community. The century began with natural communities in abundance: native farming communities or enclaves of im-migrants from tiny towns in Europe. In these communities (Gar-rison Keillor's *Lake Wobegon,* for example), people grew up, married and grew old together. By the turn of the century these natural communities were going the way of the dinosaur. Ur-banization brought people to huge metropolises, where they gave up their ethnic enclaves. For a while, at least, we lived in neighborhoods and kept up ties with extended family members, who remembered what it was like to be related to a common set of ancestors and blessed with a common memory stretching back to distant days together. With the '50s, we moved out farther still, to suburbs where we soon lost track even of our neighbors and learned to race in anonymous cars down endless thruways to im-personal destinations. People who once sat on front porches hailing friends and passers-by now build backyard decks to protect their privacy from strangers. Extended families have disappeared, and even the nuclear family is in trouble. Most observers would agree that if there is one crying need in our time, it is for us to know one another again, to rebuild neighborhoods, to know a place where we can greet one another in all the intimacy that America promises—and that is where the church and synagogue come in.

The kind of society we inhabit has been described as one of limited liability. By that I mean we join organizations and hold them responsible, or liable, for a limited list of duties. The "Y" must have a pool, or I might quit. The PTA is responsible for audio-visual equipment in school, and if it doesn't come through, I threaten to withhold my dues. Our lives have become a series of interlocking limited liability associations, which we join with specific ends in mind. But where is the place we do not join, the place where we just belong, like the natural community, the neighborhood, or the family, marked by the potential for total liability, where we simply care for one another? Where indeed, if not our churches and synagogues? People complain that churches are too impersonal. One woman captured the sentiment in a phrase that haunts me still: "The Baptist church on the corner is so big," she said, "we call it 'Fort Baptist'." What she didn't say is that across the road was "Fort Catholic," and on the other side, "Fort Jewish." The staff at work within the fort are so busy that it has taken some time to become aware that people hardly come any more. But those who have assimilated that bitter truth argue now—across the country, in Jewish, Protestant, and Catholic circles, interchangeably—that we must renovate the fort to create community. The question with which we began haunts us still: Is community mere groupieness, or is it theologically resonant with the presence of God? Is community mere sociology, or is it ecclesiology, the "still small voice" of our time?

Clearly my own conclusion is most emphatically the latter: what God enthroned in glorious light was to worshipers of the second century; what God transcendent was to nineteenth- and early twentieth-century Europe; that God we find in intimate community. We have our own newly favored synecdochal vocabulary as well: not necessarily the most technically sophisticated music, but music people can sing; humble everyday language, not elegant linguistic dinosaurs; spatial design to connect, not separate the people in the pews—in general the patterned liturgical celebration of a new social reality, a community that cares for its members as families and neighborhoods once did. For my part I have no trouble at all seeing here our rediscovery of God's presence.

I began this chapter by talking about ritual's role in presenting the reality of cosmic design to worshipers. Out of the discovery of pattern in prayer—what I called the microcosm—worshipers extrapolate the competence to posit pattern in the universe—the macrocosm. From the celebration of ritualized patterns that cohere endlessly and are repeated regularly, we internalize expectations that even the chaos of life is actually but a small part of a larger pattern, if we only look hard enough to find it. Thus we learn to have the faith that prohibits our giving up on life in the middle of its inconsistencies.

Whether our faith stops at faith in general or goes on to become faith in God depends largely on what we mean by God, what evidence of God we expect to find, and whether we would recognize God sufficiently "to let God in." If God is seen by us exactly as we imagined in our childhood, we may not find in our prayers clear and ample demonstration of God's reality. Similarly if we look only for the grand triumphant fingerprints that a mighty transcendent God must surely leave behind, we may be making the error of looking for God in today's world through the lenses of eyeglasses that became blurred with age almost a century ago.

If faith in God's presence arises liturgically from the ritualized presentation of meaningful pattern, we ought to differentiate the kinds of patterns and correlate them with images of God they are capable of suggesting. In Hellenistic times the prime desideratum was a pattern projected externally on the environment of the universe at large. Scientists and philosophers alike asked incessantly about the nature of the macrocosm, finding patterns to explain how the grand and glorious whole we call the universe had come into being. The same is true of the rise of science in the nineteenth century, when in the full flush of faith in the physical sciences, it was confidently predicted that we would know the full truth as well—how the universe had been born, and how it functions now. In both these cases God too was projected beyond the world, the master image in one case being a God of universal light, and in the other, God transcendent. But there was a difference. Hellenistic society was fluid; people moved easily from class to class, and traders brought an international interchange of ideas, so that cosmopolitan religion was the norm as well. Moreover, within Greek thought there was no hard and fast distinction between natural and supernatural, no firm and fixed boundaries separating the gods from their human protégés. Greek gods entered freely into earthly affairs, and why not, given the many layers of semidivine-semihuman beings that were said to populate the cosmic space between the heights of Olympus and the depths of earth's most material substratum, watered (if you can use that term here) by the underworld's tributary, the River Styx? By contrast, German society one hundred years ago was, as we have said, relatively closed to interclass movement and, in fact, quite intolerant of other societies in general, so not particularly interested in furthering intergroup contact of any kind. In Hellenistic Palestine, therefore, the master image of God was an extension of the pattern of cosmopolitanism, on the one hand, and of the permeable cosmology, on the other. God was beyond, therefore, up in the ethereal realm of pure light, but by no means unapproachable. In fact the very goal of worship was the adoration of God not from afar, but from the very heavens themselves that were as open to us as they are to the angels. That is what worshipers meant when they described their prayer as a journey. But nineteenth-century spirituality differed in that God the transcendent was, by definition, so distant as to be unreachable. In each case, however, the master image was a synecdochal confirmation of a certain preferential pattern favored by the society in question.

In our own time we have encountered a new preferred pattern. Old certainties are questionable now, especially the human certainties that we once took for granted. I return to the transience of certainty symptomized by the razing of the Minneapolis Convention Center: it was built to last forever, and they are tearing it down. The God we envision will be consonant with whatever patterns we prefer to display, and since the '60s we have sought to display the pattern of meaningful human relationships that may have fallen apart in the old order, but can nevertheless be reconstituted in the new. Moreover, our time in general has replaced projection with introjection as its dominant mode of picturing the world. By that I mean that our cosmology is relatively impoverished in terms of extrahuman but not-yet-divine beings like angels and demons, whereas we have no trouble at all speaking about internal constructs like an id, ego, and superego. Christians in antiquity required a rite of exorcism to cast out invading devils; we, by contrast, go to therapists who locate emotional aberration within ourselves to start with. No wonder then that God is seen by many today not only to be intimately involved in community, as I have been claiming, but even more—immanent in each human being. That causes theologians many difficulties, I know, but as far as functional worship goes, God-within is not inherently worse than God-without. People can manage to get around the logical inconsistency of praying to a God within themselves very nicely, especially when they recognize that a master image does not purport actually *to be* God, but only to *represent* God by means of an image that is consonant with current cultural expression. Images of God as 1) a Person-like partner in dialogue whom we meet in community and 2) an internal Presence within each person are but two positions on a spectrum paralleling the older conceptions of God as 1) a Person who is distant from us and 2) an utterly transcendent Being beyond our knowledge at all. I do not mean to imply that immanence is the only way possible for us to envision God these days. We are nothing if not pluralistic, and that goes for our image repertoire as well as anything else. Probably the most satisfying master image is somewhere between absolute transcendence and complete immanence in the philosophical sense of the word: not God as an impersonal force far beyond us, nor God as the inner voice of conscience, but God as friend and comforter, who meets us in the human encounters that matter. When our worship develops a ritualized display of those human moments on which we base all hope of meaning, we will have discovered worship that works.

I could end my account here and move on directly to the artistic considerations of space, music, language, and so on that we need to keep in mind if we are to develop real community worship. That is in fact the next step. But perhaps the reader will not mind if I indulge myself by concluding this chapter with a biblical story that well illustrates what I think we need so desperately.

It is easily my favorite tale in all the Bible, and maybe yours too: the story of Jacob who steals his brother's birthright and blessing, fleeing lest Esau kill him. In the dark of night, utterly exhausted from flight, he falls asleep on the desert's barren landscape, where he dreams of a ladder stretching from heaven to earth and angels going up and down it. Awakening in this apparently Godforsaken terrain, he utters what is perhaps the most sublime line in the whole Bible: "Surely God is in this place, and I did not know it."

There lies our challenge. In today's churches and synagogues people see reflected not their dreams, but their nightmares of lonely days and nights that have become the reality of their lives. They wake up, and unlike Jacob, say, "Maybe God is in this place, but you'd never know it."

We need to transform the barren landscape of our communal lives into *real* communities of total liability; there, in the intimacy of mutual care, we will know the reality of God. Let people rise from their worship, then, and looking in each other's eyes say, as Jacob did—or maybe even better—"Surely God is in this place, and we knew it all along."

9

Themes, Conventions, and Frames

IF WORSHIP IS AN ART, then the men and women charged with leading it should be artists. Here we come up against a major stumbling block that stands in the way of successful prayer, namely, the presumption that artists are born, not made, so that either we are innate liturgical geniuses, in which case learning how to facilitate prayer is redundant, or we are by nature so far removed from liturgical artistry that further education in it is useless. Echoes of Plato's theory of artists as divinely inspired geniuses are not hard to find in this skewed portrait of ourselves. What, we wonder, is the point of artistic training if artistry is either graciously and miraculously included or inexplicably and cruelly withheld from our congenital endowment in the first place?

There is some truth here: some people are by nature more suited to liturgical artistry; they have a flair for the right poetry, declamatory language, and sermonic images that move us to tears or laughter. Some people can inerrantly recognize just the right song, convert an empty room into appropriate liturgical space, and translate ancient texts into stirring contemporary poetry. Some people are just automatically more comfortable working with the vast range of considerations that go into the event we call liturgy. Why indeed should we even imagine it to be otherwise? Why should everyone be equally talented in this field, when we are not equally suited for every other one?

But that is only half the truth. To begin with, there is a vast difference between claiming some competence in an art form and

179

being a world-renowned master. To say that liturgical planners must be artists at what they do is not to demand that they all write hymns as if they were Haydn and arrange sanctuary space the way Frank Lloyd Wright would have done it. It is merely to say that you cannot hope to lead people in meaningful ritual if you are ignorant of elementary artistic considerations that go into the selection of music and space; or proclaim its prayers if you know nothing of how the language of worship functions; or direct the whole without a vision of the liturgical event as sacred drama. In *A Little Night Music* Gerald White Johnson says that a person who "has tried to play Mozart and failed, through that vain effort, comes to understand the man who tried to paint the Sistine Madonna, and did." We don't all have to do what great artists appreciate; we do have to appreciate what great artists do.

Moreover, and most important, we should not confuse the arts of worship with worship as an art. The hope that we secretly harbor the potential to be Sistine artists is indeed vain, but it is not the issue. In fact one of the most detrimental forces at work over the last century has been the assumption that since worship involves the arts, it requires art and artists of the highest artistic quality. Insofar as the art under discussion is the actual art of worship, that is the case, in that all liturgical planners ought to strive to become masters of that particular art called prayer. But insofar as people have in mind an allied art like music, it simply is not true that the most sophisticated music is also the music best suited for worship. What we do not need is a team of musicians, painters, poets, architects, dancers, and sculptors—all practicing their own art independently of the worship service in which their several arts are embedded. What we do need is a worship team, people who appreciate the arts that go into successful ritual, but who know how to make them serve the art of which they are masters: worship. When I say, then, that liturgical planners have to master their art, I mean only that they have to comprehend how the various arts come together to constitute worship, and that they must develop a sense of the criteria relevant to the appropriate employment of those arts in the service of communal prayer.

We want to avoid the twin vices that lie at two opposite ends of the spectrum: at one extreme lies the mistaken notion that worship is no art at all, but some purely cognitive enterprise calling on worshipers only to exercise the right theology, say the right words, and go through the prescribed actions called for in the liturgical text; equally dangerous, though, is the other extreme, whereby one assumes that worship is a collection of arts, but not an independent art in its own right, so that liturgists abandon their own obligation to decide anything, giving all decisions over to musicians, poets, and practitioners of the various other arts with whom they work.

Most people are guilty of the former sin; they go through the prescribed ritual with barely any artistic considerations at all, presuming that since they lead the worship every week, they must be good at it—as if playing the piano with the same mistakes daily will in and of itself make one a pianist.

What follows, then, is a short guide to the arts in worship, though not to the individual arts themselves. It is based on the presumption that worship is its own art form, calling on other arts for service. Liturgical planners need not master all those arts, but they have to know how to bring what they have to offer to bear on the liturgy. They should think of themselves as artists in the context of the following analogy.

We can begin by imagining painters working with themes and conventions. Broadly speaking, a *theme* is something the artist tries to portray, and a *convention* is the accepted way it is portrayed. The only problem with this rather open and shut distinction between *theme* as the idea being expressed and *convention* as the favored mode of expression is that it is sometimes hard to distinguish between the idea and its expression. The very notion that our ideas are independent entities burrowing somewhere down deep in our brain cells, awaiting some separate mechanism called expression, is a gross oversimplification—as the following example shows.

When I advise students on how to write sermons, I ask them to divide their outline into two columns, the left column labeled "Ideas," and the right column labeled "Illustrations." In the "idea" column they are to put the syllogisms and simple declarative sentences that constitute the "point" they want to get across. In the "Illustration" column they put the metaphors, quotations, illustrative parables, and biblical proof texts that demonstrate what the left-hand column contains. Thus, for example, a sermon on aging might contain a left-column statement like "Caring for the aged who cannot care for themselves does as much for the people who care as it does for the aged whom they are helping." The right-side illustrations may include a story about a young executive who found meaning in life by visiting an elderly neighbor in a rest home; or an appropriate exegesis of Leviticus 19:32, "You shall rise before the aged and show deference to the old." If the left side of the page is full but the right is not, they probably have something significant they want to say, but only a dull way of saying it, a logically consistent message perhaps, but nothing anyone will listen to, certainly nothing they will become committed to, and (perhaps) nothing they will even understand. On the other hand, if the right column overshadows the left, they may face the problem of having lots of beautiful illustrations illustrative of something, but exactly of what, no one, including the preacher, is able to say. In the first case, people will leave the sermon saying their preacher is a brilliant intellect whom they cannot, however, comprehend, and who, therefore, probably should have become a professor teaching mathematics, not a minister preaching morals. In the second case, they will recognize the preacher as a fascinating raconteur with plenty of entertaining tales, which, unfortunately, don't go anywhere. We can conceive of the left-side preacher as operating solely with the left side of the brain, the hemisphere that is responsible for linear logic, the ideas that I have loosely entitled *themes;* the right-sided preacher uses the right side of the brain, the hemisphere that sees things holistically, and prefers nonlinear presentations of reality, the things we call illustrations, which I have been calling *conventions.*

The ideal sermon preaches the left brain's ideas (or *themes*) using the right brain's illustrations (or *conventions*). Successful communication presupposes that the two sides work together.

Unfortunately this simple breakdown into logically cogent ideas and convincing illustrations is not as simple as it sounds. Eventually the student comes across something that could fit equally well into either column. Suppose the sermon calls for this citation of Shakespeare:

> All the world's a stage
> And all the men and women merely players,
> And one man in his time plays many parts . . .
>   Last scene of all,
> That ends this strange eventful history

Is second childishness and mere oblivion,
Sans teeth, sans eyes, sans taste, sans everything.

Is Shakespeare's description of old-age dependency a mere illustration of an idea that exists outside of the description itself? Or
is dependency as an idea so connected to its image that it would
never have emerged without this or a similar illustration to shape
it? Obviously idea and illustration are not as separate as they appear. The same thing can be both theme and convention, therefore, depending on the context in which it is used. If it illustrates
something else, it is convention. If something else is used to illustrate it, it is theme.

Biblical motifs like "the Exodus" or "Jesus as Christ" are themes
in their own right and conventions of other themes, too. The Gospel of John begins with "In the beginning was the Word, and the
Word was with God, and the Word was God." The reader soon
discovers that the Word is to be identified with the Word made
flesh, the incarnated Jesus Christ, who, moreover, is also described (by Philip, later in the chapter) as "Him of whom Moses in
the Law and the Prophets spoke" and (by Nathanael) as "the King
of Israel" (John 1:45, 49). Both "The Word" and "King of Israel"
were commonly accepted Hellenistic and Jewish themes (respectively) when the gospel was written. The writer of John expresses
them, but uses a new convention in doing so. He draws a verbal
picture of The Word and the King of Israel, but what emerges in
his picture is the new convention of the Word and the King newly
portrayed as Jesus of Nazareth. When he has finished, the image
of "Jesus" functions as novel convention, a new identification of
an old idea.

Eventually, however, the figure of Jesus becomes so well accepted that it emerges separately as a theme in its own right. It
need not be identified as an example of something else. Rather,
artists now learn to portray this or that sort of Jesus; that is, they
develop a series of conventions for portraying Jesus. Thus one
standard, early, conventional portrayal is Christ sitting on a
throne as the Ruler of the universe; another is Christ on the Cross.
But eventually even this latter convention—the crucified Christ—
emerges as an independent theme open to artistic alteration, so
that it, too, attracts first a very stylized human body with arms
outstretched at right angles to the torso, but with no notion of suf-

fering, then later a suffering Christ, the body sagging under its own weight, Christ's head twisting in agony on the cross.

So traditions are made of a continually spiraling chain of theme and convention, with each successive variation on a convention eventually becoming a separate theme itself, attracting its own variations. Change is possible because the act by which tradition is transmitted is not static but dynamic, an ongoing process of portraying accepted themes in different conventions, which then become themes themselves. I have been calling the changed themes or conventions *variations.*

There is still one more measuring rod necessary: *style.* We have so far discussed traditions as a whole, but what about their specific representatives, the individual people who either pioneer new conventions or who remain happy interpreting the old ones, but who, in any case, remain distinguishable as individual artists? We can say that within traditions individuals—and sometimes whole groups—stand out by virtue of the fact that they have their own *style.* Unlike themes and conventions, which are understandings inherited from the past, style emerges out of the influences of the artist's present. Often it derives from some technological breakthrough unique to the time in question. In the sixteenth century, for example, people learned how to master copper plate, not just wood engraving, a technique that permitted finer lines and thus more detailed storytelling on the final engraving. This led to a new style of art, personified best, perhaps, in the work of Albrecht Dürer (d. 1528). But he was not alone in developing copper plate engravings. Style cuts horizontally across space uniting even artists who work in different traditions, but who all inhabit the same time and place and are equally influenced by the same technology.

Eventually we say that a new style is "stylized," or that it becomes a "conventional style," by which we mean it has crystallized into a commonly recognized convention on given themes in specific traditions. We speak of the styles of German Expressionism or of Art Deco, for example, by which we mean that a certain approach to art was common at particular times, even among people of different artistic traditions, people, that is, who used the same style, but depicted different variations of theme and convention. But stylization is a late development. At first we have only style, which is an idiosyncratic artistic foray by a generation of artists, some of whom emerge as particularly representative of the new art form.

Theme, convention, and style are all relevant considerations for worship, which is, after all, an art. As worshipers in the closing years of the twentieth century, we stand within our respective traditions, committed to the ongoing evolution of variations in the themes and conventions that make our traditions uniquely what they are. At the same time we are members of our own age, and thus experimenters in the styles that differentiate our generation from others. Style cuts across tradition lines, and that is why the comments I will make below apply equally to Jews and Christians, Protestants and Catholics. One stylistic device of our age is the conscious application of the principles of art and the social sciences to worship. And that is exactly what follows: some stylistic considerations drawn from theater, spatial design, music, and language theory.

Worship as Sacred Drama

We have seen how the liturgical whole is a single unified statement made by the worshiping community to itself about the world it envisions. The service is similar to a dramatic presentation in which an alternative world is presented by the actors, who are (in this case) the community of worshipers gathered for the occasion. Their liturgy is the script, handed down by tradition for use on this single occasion. Though the same script may be used on other occasions, too, this day's particular performance will never happen again. When a Broadway cast gives a performance, no one in the audience cares much that in general the script is good, or that other audiences liked it very much. Everything depends on how well *this* performance goes.

Imagine yourself attending *Death of a Salesman, J.B.,* or *Julius Caesar*. If today's performance is successful, you will cry at the pretensions of Willy Loman, cry out with rage at *J.B.*'s afflictions, and decry the ambition (or marvel at the nobility) of Shakespeare's Caesar. The world of Willy Loman is pure invention, the work of his creator, Arthur Miller; *J.B.* is the biblical Job revisited in modern guise, but as fictional a person as Willy, fabricated through and through, first by an unknown biblical author, and then again by

Archibald Macleish; of the three protagonists, only Julius Caesar actually lived, but Shakespeare's Caesar didn't. He too is a fictitious character invented by one genius's insight into the human condition. Their stories are therefore not really true. Nonetheless they are replete with meaning for us, and that is why we go to see them. All three characters, though untrue, are real to us; they are windows into our own inner world, and their unfolding stories capture not only our attention, but our shared involvement in lives that for an hour or two approximate our own.

Theater thus presents _alternative worlds of reality:_ fictitious worlds, one might say, but no less real than the workaday worlds in which the audience has its more prosaic identity. We see ourselves in Willy, feel our outrage over _J.B.,_ and mourn the tragedy of Brutus being turned against his old friend, Caesar. And when we leave the theater, we may see the world and ourselves differently.

Worship is not simply theater, of course, but it is very much like a sacred drama. It presents not the imaginative musings of this or that playwright, however, but the constructed world of the accumulated thinking of an entire tradition. _When I say that we are all artists creating a vision of coherence out of chaos, I mean this above all: we use the insights of our religious tradition to force the inchoate flow of personal and world events into recognizable patterns. It is those patterns that the drama of worship presents as the really real, so that worshipers leaving church or synagogue are prepared to observe the world with those patterns in mind._

Traditions, we said, deal in _themes_ and _conventions._ A theme is a pattern imposed on reality and then portrayed in conventional ways. A good example of a theme is "the city." There have been cities for centuries, but only in the nineteenth century did the city emerge as an obvious point on the skyline of the world's imagination. From Moscow to London, Dostoevski and Dickens were recording images of city life, while simultaneously, more or less, the sociologist George Simmel studied German cities for what would be his classic essay, _Metropolis and Mental Life._ Far off at the University of Chicago, meanwhile, Robert Park and his students were surveying life in American cities. Were there cities before there was a cultural theme of "The City"? Yes and no. There were conglomerates of people living in conditions we would recognize as urban, but cities never look the same again for people who have internalized the poverty of *Oliver Twist;* the murder by Raskolnikov; the alienation of Simmel's city "strangers" whose sophistication strangles their emotional relationships; or the contrast between the luxury of Chicago's posh Gold Coast and the underside of Greenwich Village's Bohemia. An objective event in nature and the way we capture that event in our cultural mind's eye are two different things impacting on each other. They both exist in their own right, but there is no way we can disentangle them. We experience the world not as it is, but only insofar as we have framed it as a recognizable theme and then characterized it in some conventional conceptualization that from then on, we take for granted.

As an instance of a religious theme take the concept of time, which we have discussed twice already in this book. Though time probably does exist in some independent form or other, it is not clear exactly what that form is. You can't see time. But you can see its effects: things wear out; they are replaced or renovated; they wear out again. And so on. Observing what time seems to do to us, both Jewish and Christian traditions conceptualize "time" as if it existed externally, in a theme that we can call *renewal*. Renewal is thus a religious *thematization* of time, by which the effects of time (which are visible) are transferred to time itself (which is not). We then portray the *theme* of renewal in our liturgical dramas according to the *conventions* of a calendar. In Jewish tradition the *theme* of renewal is pictured and celebrated at every new month, with the visible regeneration of the moon. Originally the new moon was actually sighted by witnesses and then followed by celebration. New months are still considered holy days in the Jewish calendar and include (especially) festivities for women, who associate the moon's cycle with their own. Thus time is translated into a theme of renewal and characterized by the calendrical convention of new moon days.

The theme of renewal is selected for religious observation primarily because of its relevance to the ebbs and flows and ultimate mortality of human life. Jews celebrate their hope for renewal in the annual new year drama of Rosh Hashanah, which includes conventions of a special musical chant, a lectionary celebrating the miraculous conception of Isaac, the sounding of the *shofar* (the ram's horn) in association with legends of its being blown as God's call to Israel on Mt. Sinai, and prayers reiterating the message that on Rosh Hashanah, the entire universe was conceived: thus humans singly, the Jewish people communally, and the universe as a whole are together reinvigorated at one time. In the same way that we cannot help but see the city differently after we finish reading Dickens, so too, the Jew's image of time is conditioned by Rosh Hashanah. When Jews rise from their High Holy Day services, they should be able to see the world beginning again, their lives remade, their hopes reborn.

Christians, too, have adopted the *theme* of renewal, but they have shifted *conventions*. For Christians renewal is portrayed neither by the new year nor by creation at Genesis, but by the new creation implicit in the incarnation, life, death, and resurrection of Jesus Christ. So the high point of Christian worship is Easter Sunday, as Christians, too, rise from worship with the promise of new life.

The theme of renewal is not limited to specific calendrical occasions that mark actual beginnings, whether annual or monthly. Religious convention extends the theme by generalizing the promise of rebirth through liturgical dramas that are performed with regularity, every Sabbath throughout the year, but without the intensity that the primary celebration on Rosh Hashanah or Easter Sunday provides. Thus Shabbat for Jews is introduced by a prayer heralding the seventh day as a "memory of creation," just as every eucharist echoes Jesus' admonition, "Do this in memory of me." So Christian and Jewish liturgies play out their respective dramas of faith in weekly worship settings that present their respective prisms through which the world exists.

It is important to realize that the only way we have for seeing the world is the conventionalized portraits carried in whatever tradition we adopt as our own. We cannot view experience "raw." A "generic" service that speaks only of promise and wholeness in the abstract will be as unmoving as a critic's synthetic statement of the meaning of a drama. You have to see—or better, live through—a particular drama, as you have to live through the liturgy, which commits you to this or that particular way of seeing reality: the way of St. Francis, Maimonides, Amos, Micah, Isaiah, or the other great visionaries who are the sum and substance of the liturgical "theater" in which we find ourselves. We rise from prayer changed in our essence, committed to a new perspective on an old world.

So above all, liturgical planners must see the liturgy as a drama, and therefore, they must conceptualize it as a whole. It is not just the music, or the space, or the lines we read, or the lesson for the morning, or the sermon of the day, or any other single thing. It is only the *totality* of the liturgical event that will present a coherent image of an alternative world, the world for Christians or the world for Jews: a world that will become so convincing in its presentation, so involving of those in attendance, that they will freely commit themselves to an acknowledgement of its truths and return to lives reshaped by the liturgy's religious-artistic vision.

The very first step for planning a liturgy, then, is to envision its dramatic scope.

Every liturgy begins with a setting of the stage, in which the worshipers as the "audience" come to terms with the kind of play it is. The church interior will be altered for its feasts and fasts, for example, white vestments and Easter lilies for Easter Sunday, but violet for holy week, and red for Good Friday. Similarly synagogues' arks on Rosh Hashanah feature the Torah scrolls in white covers, not the usual ones. Liturgies, like plays, have their props: the candles, altar covers, seasonal prayer books or hymn sheets, seating plans for the cast of characters, and even costumes appropriate to the roles: I don't mean just the clergy and "officials" but the entire assembly of worshipers, who are no passive audience, remember, but active players in the drama that will unfold. They know how to dress—Easter Sunday finery is paralleled by new Rosh Hashanah suits and dresses, all costumes symbolizing refreshment and renewal (the day's theme, remember). People know where to sit, too, in family pews, the "regulars'" section, or wherever church and synagogue tradition or local custom dictates.

Playwrights and directors know the significance of their stage settings, and they use the device of *framing* to let the audience know what to expect: whether they should laugh or cry, expect romance or tragedy. Liturgy uses framing, too, and worship leaders have to take it as seriously as dramatists do.

The first means, historically speaking, of foreshadowing the play's content is *verbal framing*. Greek and Elizabethan dramatists could not count on standardized sets, so they depended on opening choruses or monologues that *told* the audience in words what they were about to see. Euripides, for example, couldn't expect to

189

have real pyramids on stage, so he introduced his *Helen* with a monologue, telling us the site and season of what was to follow.

> These are the shining virgin streams of the river Nile
> Who, with the white snow melting, take the place of rain
> From heaven, and waters all of Egypt's level fields.

Shakespeare's *Tempest* features a single word as an opening line, as the shipmaster calls out, "Boatswain!" and thus informs us that the scene is a ship. The opening scene of *Julius Caesar* is a series of comic puns that set the scene in Rome, putting us on guard that the time is a "holiday to see Caesar and rejoice in his triumph." Shakespeare's *Henry V*, perhaps the best example of a verbal frame, features an opening chorus that puts the matter forthrightly. Recognizing the difficulty of turning a bare stage into the requisite series of sets, the opening monologue proclaims:

> But pardon, gentles all,
> The flat unraised spirits that hath dar'd
> On this unworthy scaffold to bring forth
> So great an object: can this cockpit hold
> The vasty fields of France?
> . . . .
> . . . let us . . . on your imaginary forces work.
> Suppose within the girdle of these walls
> Are now confin'd two mighty monarchies.
> . . . .
> Think when we talk of horses that you see them
> Printing their proud hoofs i' the receiving earth.

Liturgies, too, require verbal frames. They don't always have them, but when they do, they should not be peremptorily thrown away like unimportant one-liners. The current official Passover Haggadah of the Reform Movement thus begins with:

> Now in the presence of loved ones and friends
> before us the emblems of festive rejoicing
> we gather for our sacred celebration . . .

The Palm Sunday liturgy in the English translation of the Roman Sacramentary introduces its theme in the procession and opening antiphon from Matthew 21:9:

Hosanna to the Son of David, the King of Israel. Blessed is He who comes in the name of the Lord. Hosanna in the highest.

Then the priest greets the people with an explicit framing of the occasion that draws them together:

Dear friends in Christ,
for five weeks of Lent we have been preparing,
by works of charity and self-sacrifice,
for the celebration of our Lord's paschal mystery.
Today we come together to begin this solemn celebration . . .

When I say that the speaker of these frames has to act as if they introduced theatrical performances, I mean that the same dramatic considerations that go into an actor's successful creation of the scene must characterize the liturgical speaker as well. I have been present at Passover seders where I wondered if the leader had even read the script in advance or asked the question, "How shall I convey greeting, joy, and the sense of solemn assembly as we all sit down here?" At least the seder leader's place at the table is probably established, whereas the priest at Easter has the additional responsibility of deciding not only *how* but *where* to speak his framing texts. Standing behind the altar or at a significant distance from the assembly, he may *say* words of greeting, but they will be heard as warmly as similar words uttered by a host or hostess who greets us from across the room when we enter their home, instead of stepping forward and greeting us at the door. That may be the effect the priest desires: formality, distance, invitation as regal command. But it is not the only dramatic option available. What would happen if the priest re-evaluated the space in which he "speaks his lines"? Instead of defining just one place from which to speak, he might break down the space into several centers of dramatic action. What would happen if he began the liturgy not from behind an altar or pulpit, but by stepping into the very front rows of the assembled worshipers to voice the invitational frame?

In modern drama a second means of framing began to take priority, based on the fact that playwrights could expect their explicit directions regarding props and scenery to be followed by complex technical crews housed in permanent theaters. With stage sets in place, the whole burden of forewarning the audience does not fall solely on the shoulders of the introductory spoken lines. A mere look around the stage is enough to know whether the scene is a haunted house, a city slum, or an ancient Roman amphitheater. Writers know better than to depend *entirely* on the props, of course. In his introduction to *Saint Joan,* George Bernard Shaw addressed typically acerbic remarks to those who offered "some well-meant proposals for the improvement of the play." He had in mind "the experienced knights of the blue pencil" who want to "disembowel the play" by "building elaborate scenery, having real water in the river Loire, and a real bridge across it . . . " and in return, "blue-pencilling" out an hour-and-a-half of the actual lines. So even the most lavish realism in scenery cannot replace the need for the script; and in fact some modern playwrights prefer doing without any scenery at all, or at least, as in the case of Thornton Wilder, they return to the twin principles of verbal cues and active imagination rather than completely defined settings for the action. But nonetheless, given the props for which the dialogue calls, we would be foolish to disregard their proper use as markers for what is to come in the play that is about to unfold.

That is especially true for props or scenery that have been associated with a play for so long that the play can almost not stand without them. *Macbeth* without a cauldron? *Pygmalion* or *My Fair Lady* without Eliza Doolittle's flowers? *Romeo and Juliet* without a balcony? Almost unimaginable. So, too, in worship. In my Jewish tradition, can I even imagine Rosh Hashanah without a shofar? Passover without a seder tray and matsah? Certainly not, as, I am sure, every Christian worshiper associates church rituals with specific objects, sets, colors, and sounds. But liturgical planners often mistakenly treat these necessary objects as mere accoutrements, leaving them lying here and there at random, or hidden away until they are needed, or otherwise just any old place, instead of seeing them as a necessary means of introducing or framing the themes of the day, visual cues of what to expect next. Sometimes the play as a whole requires framing, and sometimes just one act or scene in it does—only familiarity with the actual religious script itself will tell—but in any case, when necessary props are called for because they signify the nature of the liturgical celebration, we are foolhardy not to think carefully how best to display them in advance of the ritual action they frame and how then to use them to our best advantage.

Above all we should recall the roll of symbol as opposed to sign in creating meaningful worship services. Mere words will probably be perceived as sign. But more often than not, the colors, sounds, and objects that surround the words are what actually symbolize for people; it is things like the shofar, the candles, the white vestments, or some other object specific to the day's liturgy that people remember from their childhood. The children present today will remember these items in the future, far after the specific words of prayer have been uttered, heard, and forgotten.

Before summarizing this chapter, which has taken only one aspect of theater—framing—as its lesson to be learned for worship, we need to return to the analysis of modern theater voiced by Thornton Wilder. In the preface to his *Three Plays* (*Our Town, The Matchmaker,* and *The Skin of our Teeth*) Wilder explained,

> Toward the end of the twenties, I began to lose pleasure in going to the theatre. I ceased to believe in the stories I saw presented there... The tragic had no heat; the comic had no bite; the social criticism failed to indict us with responsibility. I began to search for the point where the theatre had run off the track, where it had chosen—and been permitted—to become a minor diversion.

Where had it gone wrong? The answer, thought Wilder, was framing. As playwrights became dependent on props and scenery, they began to "overframe" their creations, in the sense that they developed the box stage in which all the action occurred. The world on the stage was overdefined, artificially lit, completely separated from the audience that was relegated to the role of passive observer of the story being enacted. How did people manage to "smother the theatre?"

> They... boxed the action; they increasingly shut the play up into a museum showcase... They loaded the stage with specific objects, because every concrete object on the stage fixes and narrows the action to one moment in time and place. (Have you ever noticed that in the plays of Shakespeare no one—except occasionally the ruler—ever sits down? There were not even chairs on the English or Spanish stages in the time of Elizabeth I.) ... When you emphasize *place* in the theatre, you drag down and limit and harness

time to it . . . Under such production methods, the characters are all dead before the action starts.

Wilder's observation is particularly apt for the sacred drama of worship. "The box stage," he concluded, "stifles the life in drama and *militates against belief.*" *Belief,* mind you! By overframing, by depending on the arbitrary frame of a box stage filled with props, the theater became unbelievable to an audience that easily dissociated itself from the action.

The point here is that churches and synagogues have gone the same route, often emulating the very same box sets that had become fashionable in American theater, and that Thornton Wilder decried as "militating against belief." By contrast Wilder draws our attention to the Shakespearean stage that demanded imagination and involved the audience in what transpired on a set thrust out directly into the midst of those beholding the play. People there could not so easily detach themselves from what they saw. They were a part of it, if only by virtue of the fact that the action took place immediately before them and with their necessary acquiescence—they were not eradicated by the darkened house lights that lull actors into thinking people are out there, when in fact they may be sleeping.

So, too, with our worship settings. We would go a long way to restoring worship to a sacred drama of believable consequence if we were only to remove the front few pews of our large worship spaces and, in their place, extend the "stage" forward, until we could rearrange as many people as possible into a "theater in the round" design.

So I draw my first practical lessons for worship that works, lessons drawn from the theater. Worship is like drama. The principles of successful drama are applicable to public prayer as well. Among the many dramatic principles worth mentioning is the need to take framing seriously, either verbal framing or framing by means of props and scenery. On the other hand, to rely on the box stage effect to frame the action is to kill the sense that people off the stage are part of the action being portrayed. They may watch intently, but it will take a herculean effort for them to internalize the message of the drama as their own, rather than as an unengrossing display of what someone else thinks about reality.

How best to utilize liturgical props, where best to speak the framing lines, and how to stage the event we call worship bring us to the second practical lesson: the use of space. Space is obviously of vital concern to directors, who must confine action within a specified area. Proper use of space is also a principle central to other arts—architecture, for example, and dance. It deserves its own discussion as another consideration that most liturgists pay no heed to at all, even though, more than the worship itself, the way people relate to the space in which worship will unfold often determines how satisfactory their experience of prayer will be.

10

Sacred Space: The Message of Design

MOST OF US TAKE FOR GRANTED the spaces that we occupy. With few exceptions, we are content to accept them as they are, labeling one place "the living room" and another "the den," as if the definition of their qualities were derived from a source higher than ourselves. The easy chair, we think, goes only here, for the simple reason that it has always gone here. Every season we change our clothes with casual abandon, spending small fortunes to keep up with new styles; but rearranging the spaces in which we live goes distinctly against the grain. We relate to the spaces we occupy as if they had an objective life of their own, sometimes to the point that we allow ourselves to be overwhelmed by their arbitrary limitations that permit some activities and prohibit others. One of the first requirements of successful worship, then, is the careful shaping of our environment so as to help, rather than hinder, community prayer. Some spaces are fixed, determinative of what you can do in them; but some spaces are not. We have to be able to see the difference.

A useful starting point is a fuller appreciation of the way we allow space to determine our activity rather than the other way around. Everyone has had the experience of visiting someone's home, only to find that the "living" room is furnished in such a way that it is impossible to live in it. Sometimes the furniture is so formal that you feel uncomfortable just being there; or the chairs and sofa are arranged so that only four people can easily converse together, while everyone who arrives after that must be seated on the periphery of the room, where they can talk to each other but not to the people in the middle. Consider further how even the names we give our spaces predetermine what we do in them. Some years ago my own family added an extension to our house, so we had to decide what to call the room we built. Was it a den or a study? If the former, we would install a television set and encourage family gatherings and conversations. If the latter, it would hold bookcases, a computer, and a desk, and feature a working ambience antipathetic to conversation. Clearly what we label our spaces, how we interpret those labels, and how we then arrange the space to accord with those interpretations are critical factors in determining whether the spaces work for us, or whether we remain enslaved to them.

These are rarely just personal decisions. They are sociocultural perceptions, never clearly articulated, but deeply ingrained within us nonetheless. Think of the old-time cowboy singing "Home, Home on the Range," or closer to home for Jewish readers of this book, a Jew listening to *Yerushalayim shel Zahav* ("Jerusalem the Golden"—a song composed to celebrate the unification of Jerusalem and the restoration of Jewish access to the holy places in the Old City after a hiatus of twenty years under Jordanian rule, when Jews were not allowed in). The first example may seem trivial, unless you really are a cowboy raised on the wide open plains and unable to bear the closed-in city feeling that native New Yorkers, say, take for granted. As for Jerusalem, over the centuries Jews had so internalized the very idea of Jerusalem's space—praying at the conclusion of their Passover seder for a return to Jerusalem, for example, and decorating their synagogue sanctuaries to look like models of Jerusalem's sacred sites—that when the 1968 song came out, it immediately captured Jewish imagination, to the point where it was transferred directly from the secular realm in which it was composed to the synagogue, where it quickly became a favored hymn in Sabbath services. In the language developed earlier in this book, we can say that the idea of "a golden city of Jerusalem" *symbolizes* deeply within Jews, who do not see Jerusalem the way the rest of the world does.

We all come from some background or other, so we all have some spaces we love and some we loathe; favored ways of treating backyards, kitchens, offices, and porches; our own "certainties" about who should have access to what parts of our house, how they should dress there, what they may say and do in these "hallowed" precincts, and why. We may not be able to articulate these beliefs about our spaces, but they are very real. Let someone break a spatial taboo, and we have no trouble recognizing it with dispatch, for boundaries symptomize the most strongly held notions of our own worth as well as the worth of everyone and everything we hold dear.

Some cultures, for example, freely encourage their members to entertain guests in their kitchens; they are then surprised to find that friends from other backgrounds or ethnic groups bitterly resent being relegated to what they consider second-rate space. Alternatively, recall the award-winning television program exploring class and culture in Victorian and Edwardian England; it bore the title "Upstairs-Downstairs," a spatial metaphor, and therefore the best metaphor possible for the class structure of the era being portrayed. Another example (closer to home) of communication via an assumed spatial code is pre-civil-rights America, whose two-tiered racial system was never more blatantly displayed than when the Supreme Court ruled that a New Orleans black man named Homer Plessy was not permitted by the fourteenth amendment to sit in a "whites only" section of the East Louisiana Railroad. That was in 1896; and thus was born an official American doctrine of spatial access, "separate but equal." In the 1954 decision of "Brown vs. the Board of Education of Topeka," the Supreme Court ruled, in effect, that separate spaces are by nature *not* equal. They cannot be—such is the very essence of the determinative effect that space has upon us. Of all the symbolic gestures that people remember as marking America's breaking loose from its racial straitjacket—a spatial image itself, by the way—the revolt against arbitrary spatial regulations comes first to mind, namely, a black woman's refusal to give up her seat to a white person and move to the back of the bus.

Look, finally, at our own cultural imagery, which is loaded with expressions in which our situation in space marks off who and what we are:

—Go to the head of the class
—Jockeying for position

—To be off in left field
—Front runners, underdogs, top of the heap
—To be someone's "right hand man/woman"

Roman orgies differed widely from modern state dinners, and both of these have little in common with Sabbath seating arrangements on a synagogue pulpit or a high school graduation ceremony. But all alike are public displays of order in their respective universes, so they all share at least a concern that the symbolic dimension of space be monitored with care. Who gets to sit where tells everyone involved more about the occasion than do all the speeches that officially mark the program. The "Watchers" at worship—of whom we spoke in Chapter Five—know better than to walk freely around the sanctuary during services or even to sit in the front rows where the Regulars meet and greet each other. The language of space may be subtle, but it dominates our message system whenever we get together for group events.

As subcultures in society, religions have their own perceptions of the way their spaces should be treated. Take just the word "sanctuary." In medieval churches, communion was for a long time the prerogative of the clergy, who celebrated the liturgy privately, not so much *on behalf of* the assembled multitude, as *instead of* the assembly, who were often not present in a multitudinous way at all, and whose involvement in the Mass amounted to being present for the consecration of the elements, but not in partaking of them. The result was the gradual splitting off of the clergy from the laity into sharply divided classes, with the clergy occupying a separate room at one end of the church, and the laity inhabiting the main space. Laypeople could see the clergy through a door or over an intervening screen, but could not enter the latter's specially designed space. The word "sanctuary," hitherto used to designate the area around the altar, now was used for the separate room itself. In both instances, however, it was seen as a subsection of the church's "worship space," namely, that section where the sacred elements were housed and where the sacralizing activity itself occurred. By contrast, Calvinist theology denied the sacrificial intent of the Mass and emphasized the essential equality of all believers, so the Reformed Church took steps to reverse the separation implicit in a "sanctuary" reserved for ordained persons only and redesigned churches in which the whole worshiping space—wherever the liturgy of the word could reach—became known as the sanctuary. That same development had already occurred in Judaism. In the ancient Jerusalem temple, the sanctuary was a separate area where only the priests could go. It was, moreover, further subdivided into several discrete zones, each with its own degree of sanctity and accompanying rules of access. For example, the most sacred zone was the "Holy of Holies," which only the high priest was allowed to enter, and only once, on the most holy day of the year. By contrast, the synagogue, where the word superseded sacrifice, designated the entire room where worship occurred as the sanctuary.

How different religious traditions decide to utilize their worship space at any given time is not a matter dependent on personal whim. We said above that, in general, ritual provides a microcosmic reflection of the religious pattern imposed on the universe, in that worship is a sacred drama whose script plays out the way the liturgical participants are trained to see their world. The worship space is thus both the stage for the drama being enacted and a paradigmatic pattern of the world as a whole. Where, for example, a religion preaches huge class, or even racial, divisions, it will enact a liturgy where those divisions are evident in its use of space. If it sees the world as a hierarchy of forces spiraling upward to heaven, it will develop a ritual featuring hierarchies. In these cases it reflects and sustains the social world round about. If, on the other hand, it preaches a gospel of radical equality, it will break down spatial privileges on its liturgical stage, thus signaling that all are equal here before God and so must be granted the same equality outside church or synagogue walls as well.

The liturgical use of space thus articulates religious values and poses a nonverbal argument for the imposition of those values on the society we inhabit. The argument is of necessity silent; but precisely for that reason it is beyond discussion, powerful in its very "givenness," something we just take for granted—in short, more effective than any verbal rhetoric could be.

We should ask ourselves how people know what the spatial message of their worship is. To be sure, sending people with lesser privilege to the back of the room (or a bus) is blatant enough, but sometimes the message implicit in liturgical space has to be decoded by means of a far less obvious key to meaning.

At times the message is so subtle we get it without even knowing how; we pick up cues, that is, which elude consciousness. Again the history of church architecture provides us with excellent examples.

At first, Christianity was an unofficial rebellious faith that met in private households. The church space was therefore the home itself, often just its biggest room, where the worshipers could best be accommodated.

After Constantine's momentous decision to support it, however, Christianity became an official imperial religion. It therefore moved out of the realm of private household observance and took up liturgical residence in spaces called basilicas (see Figure One), which were long halls supported by two weight-bearing rows of columns running from front to back. The basilica was like a throne room, at the front of which those in authority could address the subject people. Originally part of the imperial pomp and ceremony, in that it allowed for regal processions from the entrance in the back to the throne area in the front, the church as basilica now signaled the movement of Christianity into the very upper reaches of the late Roman Empire. Within its imperial spatial con-

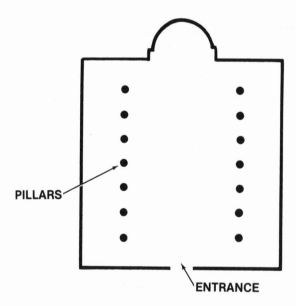

Floor Plan of Basilica

[Figure One]

tours, the liturgy unfolded a new play now, one in which great regal splendor had replaced Christianity's simple home origins.

The Counter Reformation favored a new kind of high-church space, no longer a long basilica, but now more like an enormous theater, in which the liturgy's message was to be delivered to the masses with all the pomp not of a court, but of an operatic performance (see Figure Two). Seated far away, but with an uninterrupted view of the proceedings (as if in a gallery at a great operatic spectacle), people now observed what the liturgical scholar J. G. Davies has called "a sort of heavenly grand opera." In this new Baroque church style, a forerunner of the grand European tradition that we looked at in Chapter Eight, artists like Bernini painted ceilings that emphasized the pre-Copernican cosmology for which the Counter Reformation stood. Just by sitting in their seats, surrounded by the vast artistic panoply of Baroque worship, those who came to pray felt first-hand the spacial impact of knowing that the earth was the center of the universe. Their seats were the earth, around which swirled the painted angels on the ceiling, and even the heavens themselves, with all their hosts. The spacial design thus left the assembled multitude with little

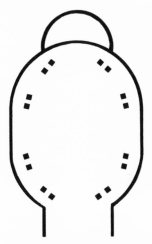

Floor Plan of Baroque Church

[Figure Two]

doubt that despite the claims by some that a new age had dawned, the truth, like God and the universe, was as unchanging as the great cosmic drama being played out before their eyes.

In each of these diverse cases, we find a different church structure, rooted both in church tradition and in a particular historical era. In the fourth century even a fool knew enough to recognize the basilica structure as a sign of imperial splendor; so the movement of the church liturgy from homes to basilicas translated into the message of the church supreme at last. The Baroque grand opera floor plan was similarly conditioned by the larger society in which the church resided; its affirmation of the cosmos depended on the fact that the particular class of men and women who attended worship were trained to appreciate the artistic *conventions* featured by the painted ceilings, and by Baroque music as well, for that matter. All the arts conspired, in this latter case, to give the unified picture of the universe favored by the building design itself.

To revert to the categories we laid down above, we can say that basilican architecture and Baroque art were both *styles* of their time that cut across religious lines, the former being used by pagan ceremonial as well as Christian worship, and the latter common to churches, theaters, and palaces alike. But the church tradition in each case applied the new styles to the *conventionalized* displays of its own old and favored liturgical *themes*, which now came out tinged with new design cues that spoke in fresh accents to the assembled crowds. These assemblies recognized the messages precisely because their experience in society at large had already socialized them to the point that they had internalized the language of space typical of their own culture at their own time and place in history.

Particularly in times of rapid social change—such as the age we inhabit now—worshipers find themselves locked in a conflict between current *style* and inherited *convention*. Like it or not, they are members of the society in which they live; they inhabit traditions, too—Christian tradition, in this example, with its inherited *themes* of sanctuary sanctity, worship as sacrifice, word as prophetic message to humankind, and the favored *conventions* by which those themes have been expressed. Worshipers today must negotiate a complicated interplay between the age in which the religion finds itself and the religion as it has been handed down through time. In the drama of worship, space itself is a channel of communication in which the favored traditional *themes* can be expressed in the context of recognizable *conventions*, but according to the newly dominant *style*.

To be a member of any society, and of any subgroup within that society, means learning to recognize spatial cues, even though we cannot consciously describe what they are. We associate room size, seating arrangements, color schemes, lighting intensity—and all the many subtle things that go into our perception of space— with certain culturally conditioned meaning systems. The people trained as professional liturgical planners are necessarily steeped in the liturgical traditions that provide the traditional spatial code. They learn the rules of sanctuaries, pews, choir lofts, and pulpits, until they are able to arrange the space in accordance with all the canons of their glorious past. What they may not recognize, however, is that the rules in question were part of a code whose message, however valuable once upon a time, may now be lost on worshipers, or even be detrimental to worship in a new age. Seeing only the "traditional," historically oriented axis of interpretation—the standard spatial *conventions* already ingrained through time—and failing to recognize that even those taken-for-granted conventions were once just hotly debated new *styles*, they may fail to appreciate the contemporary axis of their own age, the spatial language typical of the *style* which *today's* worshipers "speak."

To put the matter bluntly: five hundred years of basilican architecture generated a religious tradition rooted in basilican space. But eventually people charged with sacred space had to decide whether basilicas were *inherently* necessary for proper Christian prayer, or whether they were just historical accidents evolved to provide a spatial message consistent with Christian ascendance in late antiquity, but whose continual use would have proved dysfunctional to the Christian worship of a later period. More immediate to our own time is the parallel question about the awe-inspiring transcendent spaces we have inherited from the nineteenth century and before. In the last chapter we saw that transcendent structures promote a message of a transcendent God. Should we retain them without alteration? Or should we pass the same negative judgment on them that an earlier age once passed on basilicas? Can we afford to emphasize the nineteenth-century *convention* of viewing God as transcendent, when the twentieth-century *style* argues that God is best known in our very midst? I have listened intently as rabbis of grand synagogue sanctuaries speak glowingly of the beauty of their worship environment without considering the possibility that, as much as *they* may be accustomed to "read" the message of their space as grandly transcendent and therefore spiritually uplifting, *their congregants* decode the message of space in contemporary American terms that deny the very spirituality that the rabbis affirm. When all is said and done, those same rabbis may decide on theological grounds to retain their grand designs—and the nineteenth-century liturgical style that went with it—but they should at least know in advance of making that decision that American style reads space differently. At stake is our own conflict between *convention* and *style;* vertical axis and horizontal axis; two different language systems, each of which renders the meaning of space differently.

All of which brings us to our own time and place in history. We too have internalized a language of space, which we can call American space. It is a spatial code that differs from imperial Rome as it does from European Baroque, and nineteenth-century transcendence. The question is not so much what a given church or synagogue structure says in the abstract, as what it says to *us, the people who frequent its confines now.* What is the American code that *we* use to translate the meaning of the design cues in our worship spaces?

By now we know quite a bit about the American code by which we translate space into messages about ourselves. To be sure, it is not the same for all Americans. Any language is both a function of the rules in effect in a given time—the particular language *style* in vogue, if you like—and the *conventions* inherited from the past, which differ from community to community. Thus, to take but one obvious example, Catholics and Jews will see different messages inherent in the same spatial structures; what is positive for one may be negative for the other, simply by virtue of the fact they use different historically developed conventions to express their spirituality; on the other hand, the longer they both root their own respective religious experience in America, the closer they both will come to applying American style to those inherited differences, and the more they will each tend to see the different spatial designs of synagogue and church according to a common interpretative code that governs what space means to Americans at large.

Whether in the long run Catholics or Jews want to retain old conventions of spatial representation without change, or whether they want to alter them, will depend on the kind of universe they want to display in the drama of their worship. I repeat what I said above: the appropriate criteria are theological. But whatever they decide, they cannot avoid facing the fact that Americans will have increasingly less choice about interpreting spatial messages according to the American code. To direct worship without taking into consideration the way worshipers will perceive what you direct would be like sending messages in Morse code, even though you know the receivers at the other end no longer organize the dots and dashes the way you do. We have to ask how space is perceived in the "dots and dashes" of American perception, or we will always be in the position of holding worship in spaces that provide messages which other people decipher differently than we do.

The first step to an appreciation of space is the ability to see it, not just to accept it. A fresh look at any given worship space will reveal certain categories of appreciation.

Fixed, Semifixed, and Personally Negotiable Space Patterns

Space is fixed, semifixed, or personally negotiable. *Fixed* space includes things like the total area, the shape of the perimeter, the built-in fixtures like the ark and the lighting—things, in short, that cannot be altered without structurally revising the entire nature of the area in question. Fixity comes about through design or accident; the design may be theologically sound—most synagogues face east, for example—or just structurally required—the doorway opens onto the street, say (see Figure Three).

Semifixed space includes movable furniture, things that can more easily be altered by worshipers who want to change their space but who, for financial or other reasons, cannot consider renovating the whole place. Many new churches and synagogues have semifixed movable chairs, for example, instead of fixed pews bolted into the floors. Some have large stagelike altar (or pulpit) areas that are fixed, but increasingly, they have begun adding semifixed additions that extend those fixed areas into the

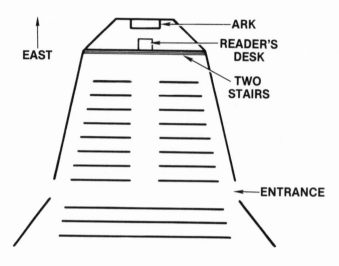

Floor Plan of Hebrew Union College Sanctuary in New York

(The necessity to face east results in fixed space with a dysfunctional narrowing of space around the pulpit. It lacks "thrust stage" effect that would allow the liturgy to be acted out in the midst of the congregation.)

[Figure Three]

congregation, thus serving as an additional focus (see Figure Four).

Finally, *personally negotiable* space is space that individuals establish as their own boundaries for individual transactions. When fixed space limits us, we may try to modify the situation by semifixed alterations: chairs instead of pews, a readers' desk in the middle of the congregation, and the like (see Figure Five). Innovative worship often requires overcoming fixity by individual action alone: a preacher who leaves the lectern to draw closer to the congregation; a cantor who walks out into the assembly to invite group singing; or framing words of invitation by standing on the stairs leading to the congregation rather than from behind the pulpit or altar.

The first step to appreciating our worship spaces is to learn to see them differently. What parts are fixed, and what does the fixing pattern lock in (or out)? What semifixed areas exist, and

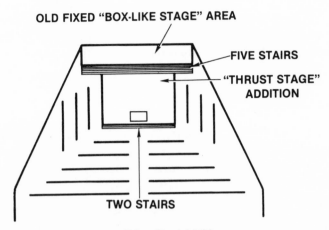

OLD FIXED "BOX-LIKE STAGE" AREA

FIVE STAIRS

"THRUST STAGE" ADDITION

TWO STAIRS

**"Thrust-stage" Semifixed Addition
to Fixed Pulpit Space**

(The space folds back under the raised pulpit where it can be stored if all the liturgical action is to take place from the high pulpit. On average days it can be used as a second "community" focus in addition to the primary formal focus of the original fixed structure.)

[Figure Four]

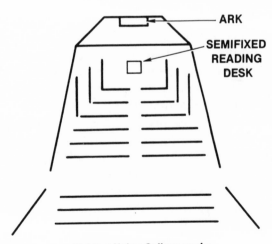

ARK

SEMIFIXED READING DESK

**Hebrew Union College again,
showing Semifixed Reading Desk**

(Recognizing the impossibility of adding a thrust stage in the narrow east end of the sanctuary, students customarily ignore the formal focus entirely and conduct worship from this movable pulpit, which can be repositioned on the fixed raised area for formal occasions.)

[Figure Five]

what alternatives can we take advantage of? How can we use our own freedom of movement to negotiate space personally, thus adding a dimension that transcends the spatial limitations of structure?

Distance: Intimate, Personal, Social, and Public

The anthropologist Edward Hall has applied to humans insights into the way animals perceive space. Left to their own devices, all animals exhibit patterns of territoriality, after all, and human beings are no different in that regard. Compare a crowded elevator with a backyard barbecue. In the former, people have no choice but to squeeze closely together. In less crowded circumstances, they would naturally choose to inhabit the four different corners of the elevator—that is the usual pattern of occupation when the first few people get in; in that way, they retain an "appropriate" distance between themselves and "strangers." The crowded elevator, however, exemplifies *intimate space,* in this case, intimate space that is enforced on people who manage it only by staring straight ahead, engaging in no conversation with the person next to them, and in general pretending that even the people whose very body heat they can feel do not really exist. By contrast, an aerial photograph of the barbecue crowd would demonstrate that they congregate in little clumps of conversationalists, with the members of the conversations being a little farther apart than in the crowded elevator, yet not so far apart as the extreme corner distancing that elevator occupants favor when they get in. The barbecue conversationalists automatically deploy themselves with *personal space* separating them. The initial elevator distance, a little greater still, is like the distance we use when engaging in initial business meetings with strangers—not yet personal, but close enough to be *social space.* If the hostess at the barbecue is our boss, she might come out to welcome us: we would hardly expect her to appear on the balcony and give us a speech! But she might stand at *social [space]* distance from us, with ourselves gathered all around her, and from there tell us how good it is to have the whole corporate team assembled. The balcony talk—more likely from a balconylike podium assembled on a stage for the occasion—would characterize a political speaker who comes to address the crowd; in which case, we would have an example of *public space*.

According to Hall, each of these spatial designs has its lower and higher end, and each of those characterizes certain human transactions.

Space Type		Distance	Typical Activity
Intimate	Low End	Touching	lovemaking, wrestling
Intimate	High End	6"–18"	intimate conversation
Personal	Low End	18"–2½'	spouses or family members standing together
Personal	High End	2½'–4'	normal friendly conversation, the way people who are never intimate stand together
Social	Low End	4'–7'	impersonal business, counseling or therapy session
Social	High End	7'–12'	formal business with the boss, who sits behind a desk farther away

Space Type		Distance	Typical Activity
Public	Low End	12'–25'	
			different degrees of formal addresses
Public	High End	25' and up	

If we consider the space separating the people reading and directing worship—the ones we called Professionals—from the nearest pew—where the Regulars usually sit—we can see that most worship operates at high social to public distance, usually the latter. Certainly it is perceived as public by the majority of the worshipers, who sit far away from the front row. That perception, however, is only partly explainable by the real distance involved. It is also due to the way in which the professionals use their voice and other verbal cues. Attuned to a distant orientation, they speak in what has been called "formal style," characterized by a somewhat stilted manner and stylized speech patterns. Martin Joos, who coined the phrase, points out that as public distance increases, "formal style" becomes "frozen style," which, he says, is perceived as the appropriate way to relate to strangers. Thus clergy may prefer transcendent architecture because they associate it with church or synagogue tradition; the laity in the pews, however, are more likely to identify it with frozen style and a feeling of not being "at home." Add the fact that the "public address" mode of prayer under discussion normally occurs in fixed-feature space where the average worshiper—who may only be a Watcher, remember—is not permitted the luxury of personally negotiating some spatial relationship with the others in the room; and you have an environment that alienates people from each other.

Contrast an infant's baptism or a wedding liturgy. The first is a small gathering of people who of necessity must hold another person—the baby—at low-end intimate distance. The priest or minister probably knows better than to address the assembly from a distance. And the feeling tone is normally and naturally warmer. The wedding group, by contrast, may be very large indeed. But the ministering official may be moved by his or her familiarity with the couple and by the intimate nature of the occasion to speak directly to the bride and groom who stand only at high-end personal distance away. Thus the wedding address, too, will be warmer, devoid of the formal (let alone, the frozen!) style that would normally typify an event of such size. In other words, even in a formal setting, it is possible to break down a sense of alienation. Much depends on whom the speaker selects as the focus for his or her remarks. When Romeo sees Juliet through her balcony window, he says,

> But soft! what light through yonder window breaks?
> It is the east, and Juliet is the sun!
> . . . .
> See! how she leans her cheek upon her hand:
> O! that I were a glove upon that hand,
> That I might touch that cheek.

If those lines are recited well, even members of the audience sitting in the very last row do not feel distant from the stage, because Romeo addresses his remarks softly to himself; his mental focus is Juliet, to whom he wishes he were speaking in the most intimate way possible. Similarly when the liturgical speaker focuses his or her remarks on the wedding couple, or on the baby about to be baptized, or even on some imaginary parishioner sitting in the front row, rather than on the masses assembled anonymously "out there," a different feeling tone results. That warmer tone is not always desirable, of course: the liturgy features grand announcements as well as intimate invitations. My purpose here is not to argue for any single way of saying everything, but simply to introduce the elusive influence of space as a contributing factor to the way the liturgical lines are heard. Not only what we say, but how we say it, matters; and part of "how we say things" is the way we focus remarks on particular others rather than on everyone all at once.

Focus

The concept of focus is as simply grasped as it is normally overlooked. Performing artists practice it: so do athletes, courtroom lawyers, expert speakers, and notable debaters; architects and interior decorators use focus too, not for themselves, but for the people who will occupy the spaces they organize.

For performers, focus is the practice of mental concentration. Some performances—a pianist's recital, for example—require focus on the particular piece being played. In like fashion a batter focuses complete attention on the ball being pitched, and a tennis pro waits in absolute awareness of the opponent who is about to serve. In these instances focus is directed at a particular blueprint of anticipated action, so to speak, the musical score about to be interpreted or the aerial course of a ball about to be returned with bat or racquet. Focus is the ability to filter out all extraneous thoughts and perceptions, and instead, to sharpen the center of one's focal awareness at the expense of the periphery.

Some performances, however, require focus not on the blueprint of action alone, but on the people for whom the action is about to be performed. At issue are two forms of communication. Communication involves a) a sender, b) a receiver, and c) a message sent. Morse code expertise requires no concern whatever for the receiver on the other end, but may necessitate focus on the message being transcribed into code—like the pianist concentrating on the exact reverse process, decoding the musical score into music. That is the first kind of communication, action by a sender, but no immediate feedback reaction from the receiver. On the other hand, consider two lovers in intimate conversation about their future. Their focus is on each other, not on their words alone, and though they obviously have to worry about saying the right thing, the more important consideration is the knowledge that they are speaking directly and personally to each other, not daydreaming off in space even as they profess their love. That kind of necessary focusing on the receiver as well as the message is what characterizes courtroom argumentation, parliamentary debate, or a stand-up comedian—who may even interrupt the evening's standard repertoire to inquire of a nonresponding audience, "Are you sure you are out there?" In this second kind of communication pattern, the speaker (or sender) learns to focus on a person or persons representative of the whole audience, talking directly to them and looking, at the very least, for some eye contact or other sign that they have received the message. In the baptism and wedding examples, the child and the couple constitute the obvious focal receivers—though it is surprising how many clergy fail to talk to the child being held, preferring instead to address impersonal theological remarks to the roomful of people in general. In a large assembly of people, a Sabbath liturgy, for example, the sermon has to be delivered, not to everyone indiscriminately all at once, but to each one of the people specifically—that is to say, a practiced speaker focuses on first one and then another specific listener, looking them each in the eyes long enough to establish contact. Unpracticed speakers make the mistake of thinking they are talking to everybody all at once: they either look into the impersonal distance, or they let their eyes wander around the room, darting from one person to the next, but never focusing on anyone. Regardless of the content of their message, their speech fails.

So focus in these latter examples is the practice of concentration through space by a message sender to a message receiver. The message's receipt is acknowledged directly by the receiver, who nods, looks the receiver in the eye, tightens the embrace, or performs some similar response in body language that is unmistakable to the sender. Or sometimes, when the receiver is only imagined to have understood the message—the baby at the baptism who is probably either sleeping or crying at the time, for example—the response is merely imagined, as if the baby would be responding if he or she were old enough. The very fact that the baby is a point of focus for the speaker is sufficient to establish it as a point of focus for everyone else at the same time, and even though the baby cannot acknowledge the message's receipt, the assembly's common attention—what I shall call, in a moment, the fusion of everyone's focus on a common focal point of action—is enough to establish positive feedback to the speaker that the message is getting through.

But worship differs in one important respect from examples like the law court or a comedian on stage, in that we said worship is a sacred drama in which everyone is an actor. It follows that to "play their parts" well, even parishioners in the last row have to develop focused attention. Moreover, worship is a group event, not merely a series of individuals going through their motions in serial fashion until the script is done. When it succeeds, the attention of all the participants is riveted together, in what I shall call *fused focus*. The best parallel here is the actors on a stage, who together provide the illusion called for by the script. In a monologue, only one person speaks, but a cardinal rule for the others is not to upstage the speaker, by which is meant that they are required to hold their pose, whether sitting or standing, and to remain absolutely stock-still, their attention riveted on the speaker. In that way, all the characters on stage fuse their focus on one central point of action. The actors are not independent but interdependent, requiring the focus of each other if they are to succeed in drawing the audience's attention to what they say. They, too, are a system, no less than worship is, the only difference being that in worship everyone present is an actor, called to focus attention on the speaker of the moment. Ross Speck and Carolyn Attneave, two psychotherapists describing a systems approach to therapy, include the following report of a jazz session that indicates what I mean when I say that religious ritual, too, requires fusion of focus.

> In Preservation Hall in New Orleans, old black men from the early Dixieland era improvise and invent jazz nightly. The audience of habitués and tourists begins the evening relatively unrelated to one another, at separate tables and in couples or small groups. Under the mystical, religious, tribal, hypnotic, musical spell they become closely knitted together. They sit tightly pressed. The small group boundaries dissolve. They clap, sway, beat out rhythms, and move their bodies in a united complex response. The group mood is a euphoric "high," and the conventional bonds dissolve. New relationships melt away the conventional barriers of status, generation, territory and sex. Young middle-class white women, black street people, elderly spinsters, and hippy youths recognize a mutuality and express it in gesture, contact and words. This lasts until the musicians give out and the people depart. Many leave in groups they might never have contemplated before they came. *For those brief hours they have become involved with one another and with humanity in general in new ways, with new feelings, new relationships, and new bonds.* However briefly, they have been a part of a social network. They have experienced the network effect.

To be sure, not every characteristic of the jazz session is applicable to worship. We saw above that some rituals do produce a "euphoric high,"—the presidential nomination with its "Happy days are here again ... " refrain; others produce a cathartic "low"—the funeral; and there are others that produce no intensive emotional involvement at all—seeing friends for the daily lunch. It all depends on the nature of the Ritual Moment, which is defined by the script of the particular ritual. But every one of these group rituals, regardless of the emotional intensity of their desired Moments, must at least unify the participants around some commonly conceived scripted requirement, and the jazz session demonstrates one such example beautifully. The people entered the room as lone individuals or (at best) small groups of two or three. But as the music put them "in sync" with one another, they found their individual focus fusing—like several flashlight beams splaying at random around a ceiling, until they eventually land together superimposed in one brilliant burst of light. Their experience became one of being "involved with one another and with humanity in general."

Good liturgical leaders learn to sense the rhythm of their worship, to discover whether everyone is progressing together through the liturgy. There is nothing mystical about it. Lawyers sway a jury by getting their combined rapt attention fused on that all-important final argument. Teachers know when their class is working together. Football teams, if they want to win, depend on fusing their members' individual focus. And worshipers require it, too.

Of the many things that go into fusing congregational focus, space ranks among the highest. If you doubt it, take a look at the knickknacks you have collected on your mantel or window sill. Every decorator knows that if you group the various objects together here and there, rather than space them out one by one at regular intervals, the room will look balanced and orderly, inviting attention rather than defusing it. Similarly every teacher knows that some classrooms support classroom attention, and some do not. The same is true of worship spaces. They either draw our attention together or they diffuse it.

Recall the examples above of baptism, marriage ceremony, and funeral. In each case the ritual was arranged around a perceptual center, or focus: the baby, the wedding couple, or the casket being placed in the earth. We can say that in rituals, *the fusion of the worshiping group's focus is enhanced to the extent that its members can concentrate on a central visible object of attention.* Sometimes the person addressed fulfills that role; sometimes it is an object, like the skull Hamlet lifts up before he says, "Alas! poor Yorick. I knew him, Horatio." Most religions use their own set of significant objects—the C-system—to accomplish this end: the raising of the cup; the procession with a Bible, cross, or candle; the Torah scroll carried around the room and then proclaimed from a central reading desk. All of these are to their own sacred scripts what the skull is to Hamlet's graveyard: visible points of focus for the group.

We saw before that people often fail to appreciate how the appropriate use of liturgical props can frame an action. Now we see that it is equally easy to forget their role in facilitating the fused focus of the congregation. Jews, for example, have a beautiful ceremony for ending the Sabbath, called *Havdalah*. It features a spicebox, a cup of wine, and a tall braided candle. No one could ask for a more attractive possibility for a ritual, and though many Jews ignored it for years, it has lately made a comeback. Some rabbis understand the almost magical quality inherent in the *Havdalah* symbolism: it is twilight Saturday evening; the sun is setting, and the room is getting dark. The candle, wine, and spicebox sit on an unobtrusive central table, around which people stand shoulder to shoulder, in almost intimate distance from one another. Together they recite the appropriate blessings and sing the traditional songs for the occasion. They pass the sweet-smelling spices from hand to hand, and watch the bright flame of the candle dance in the darkening room. Staring intently at a common focal point, they are fusing their focus into a common spiritual goal. As the ritual moves toward its high point, the Ritual Moment, they are usually moved to hold hands around the circle, and at the end, with the last song sung, the candle's flames doused in what remains of the wine, the Ritual Moment behind them, they turn warmly to their neighbors in the circle, people who just a few moments before were strangers, and embrace them with the traditional greeting, "A good week!" They, too, have experienced the "network effect."

Too many rabbis do everything wrong, starting with their failure to use the ritual props as a common focusing point. Instead, they put the objects on a table near the front of the room, where they can hardly be seen. Then, standing at public distance away from the worshipers, they adopt a frozen style of speech and explain the cognitive meaning of the symbols, which (at that point) cease being symbols at all and become mere signs, about

218

which no one in the room cares one whit. People leave the room with a brilliant opportunity for worship wasted.

Spatial Analogues and Cultural Ecosystems

Specialized spaces provide the opportunity for specialized activities, or so they should. If we are not careful, they may equally well militate against them. Robert Sommer, a psychologist specializing in the influences of spatial design on behavior, studied schools, bars, hospitals, and airports, to see how each one constituted what he called a cultural ecosystem, that is, an arrangement of a population in a certain unique way designed to accomplish certain ends consistent with the ecology. Nature's own ecosystems are determined by a give-and-take between the evolutionary requirements of a species and the environment's ability to support those requirements. In human society our needs are not just physical, but cultural. We design environments supportive of some activities and destructive of others.

A women's ward of a long-term state hospital, for example, featured halls with long rows of chairs side by side, in which more than fifty residents could sit at one time. But even with all the chairs filled, Sommer rarely noted more than two conversations in progress. The paucity of dialogue was due to the fact that people do not converse when they have to sit shoulder to shoulder. Such a row design of furniture is called *sociofugal* (like the word "centrifugal"), meaning that it orients people away from each other. Chairs in the airport function similarly to discourage waiting passengers from talking to each other. The same is true of lunch counters and bars; the media display bars as happy places where people wander in off the street to meet strangers over drinks, but the reality is otherwise. Bars where people engage in animated conversation depend on the fact that the clientele resides in the neighborhood, already has much in common, often knows each other, and has become accustomed to meeting in this particular central watering hole. The real bars, the average ones where strangers go to drink, are described by Sommer as "featuring lonely men sitting speechless on a row of bar stools, with their arms triangled on the bar before a bottle of beer ... If anyone speaks to his neighbor under these circumstances, he is likely to receive a suspicious stare." If people want to talk together in the

219

bar, they go to the booths, where they can sit across from each other at narrow tables that do not separate them too much, or at larger tables they can sit diagonally and at right angles to one another—these being the very opposite of sociofugal arrangements, that is, *sociopetal* designs intended to focus people's attention toward the center and to encourage their social interaction around a common *fused focus*. When Sommer rearranged the hospital so that the residents had small attractive square tables at which to meet, conversations doubled.

Straight lines of chairs, especially hard unmovable ones bolted to the floor—which Sommer calls "hard architecture"—epitomize the very opposite of what we called "community." Airports, he says, feature sociofugal seating because they want to drive people out of the free waiting areas into the shops and restaurants; the hospital preferred the row by row design because it was easier for the maintenance staff to clean the floors that way; bars find it profitable because their goal is not to encourage long conversations by people nursing a single drink, but to get them to order round after round unencumbered by interruptive socializing. In other words, hospitals, airports, and bars may *seem* inefficient in their discouragement of personal interaction and the comforting of one human being by another, but in each case the "Law of Systems" is operative here no less than it was in the dysfunctional worship systems at which we looked some chapters back: namely, "These systems are mostly efficient most of the time; if they appear to be inefficient, we are probably not looking at what they do efficiently."

People respond to similar furniture arrangements in similar ways partially because of that furniture's common physiological fallout. Chairs arranged side by side anywhere necessitate that the inhabitants twist their heads on a ninety-degree angle if they want to converse with the people beside them. But there is a great deal more to the phenomenon than physiology. People learn to associate spatial arrangements with particular emotions and activities. They use successful instances of negotiating behavior in old familiar environments as cues to what may be expected of them in new and unfamiliar ones. Straight rows once encountered serve, by analogy, to tell us what to do when we find straight rows a second time. When one environment with which we are familiar serves as a model for what to do in an environment new to us, the model environment is called a *cultural analogue.*

The greatest single impediment to fulfilling worship in our churches and synagogues is the insidious effect of the cultural analogues by which people are conditioned to act in certain prescribed ways during worship. Our structures were designed with Rudolf Otto's model of transcendence in mind. Worshipers were to be overwhelmed by their lonely, finite creatureliness and absolute dependence on a God before whom they could only stand in awe. With the Baroque theater model as a basis, the worship space was made over into the most sociofugal environment imaginable.

We have therefore inherited a model in which the sacred action frequently occurs in a "picture box" stage design. Our cultural analogues include the theater, a movie, or (if singing is featured) an opera. People are thus encouraged to sit quietly and passively in rows designed for watching but not for interacting either with each other or with the drama being staged before their eyes. They know better than to participate! The metacommunication of the stage design tells them to take our urging to the contrary as just part of the dramatic script, not a genuine request for involvement.

To begin with, normally there are pews, long wooden benches permanently installed in the floor—"hard architecture" if there is any! To make matters worse, there are no designated individual seats on pews, so that in crowded conditions, people will be jammed together in a way that magnifies the difficulty of turning to look at the person beside them. When Sommer assigned students to straight-line crowded arrangements, he observed them engaging in "escape behavior," asking their teacher to move the class outdoors, for example. When people cannot physically escape, they develop internal escape mechanisms—not unlike the crowded elevator phenomenon described above. That is, they ignore each other, pretending that no one is around. At the same time, they count the panels in the ceiling, make up mental shopping lists, review the birth dates of their great uncles in Europe, or turn their attention to any other task that will effectively remove them from the proceedings "on stage." They will not make the same mistake of sitting here next time. Instead, they will prefer Watcher spots on the aisles at the back, where, even though they cannot see or hear the preacher, they can at least tune out with ease and move out if necessary. They develop what Sommer calls "passivity in the face of an environment" that makes undue demands on them, but which is not their own to change: "prison-itis, hospitalism, and institutional neurosis," he calls it. If he had studied churches and synagogues, would he have recognized "sanctuary neurosis" as well?

The problem is that people relate to institutions in general as if they were renters of the space there, but not its owners. "They accept the idea," says Sommer, "that the existing arrangement is justified according to some mysterious principle known only to the space owners." In our case we can call it "the mysterious principle of theology," which relegates the worshipers to the status of temporary nonowners of worship space. It is only a short distance from that assumption to the idea that they are nonowners of the liturgy as well.

To be sure, this sociofugal message of pews may once have been functional. Certainly Reform Jews worked very hard in the nineteenth century to do away with the medieval lay involvement in the liturgy. The masses were noisy, individualistic, and unappreciative of the higher artistry that characterized western aesthetics. But we have come a long way from that position. If worship today requires community; if God is known as present among us; then the metacommunication implicit in synagogue and church architecture may be the first thing we should question. The people charged with worship need to remain ever watchful for the cues people offer regarding their comfort or discomfort about the spaces in which they pray. We should not assume that the nonprofessionals who cannot walk around and who have not internalized theological reasons for their spaces share our own positive attitudes toward even the most beautiful sanctuary; or even if they say they do, that they mean it; or even if they mean it, that we know what they mean *by* it. They think the sets for productions of the Metropolitan Opera are gorgeous also. And never having experienced really compelling worship that works, they may unwittingly be telling us that they are willing to settle for poor opera in church or synagogue as the best of a series of bad options.

The theologians themselves would be appalled to think worship was confused with opera, of course. But spatial concerns are only partially responsible for that misunderstanding. Sacred text is the subject of the next chapter. We have seen how significant the metamessage of space can be. We now can turn to the sacred script enacted within it.

11

The Script of Prayer:
Words Spoken

The Prayers We Say

DESPITE THE IMPORTANCE OF SPACE to meaningful worship, most people remain blissfully unaware of the spaces in which they pray. There are seminaries, for example, where students study liturgy without once discussing the role of sacred architecture in conveying the message of their texts; and traditionally the study of liturgy has been so text-centered that people still act as if knowing the history of the texts we pray is equivalent to knowing what prayer is. For most of us, then, it is the *words* of prayer that come to mind first as best exemplifying worship. The regulars will have memorized favorite prayers and learned to expect standard liturgical one-liners to punctuate the time they spend in worship. Watchers may be unable to follow the progress of what they are watching, but they can, and usually do, read through the liturgical text in their hands to get some quick idea of what the service is all about. Slowly but inevitably people confuse praying with reading, as if the liturgy were a theological treatise, in which case the only thing that matters is the content of the text. They go home either admiring or dismissing what the text that morning said, in the same way that they leave a class in philosophy or psychology as a disciple or a critic of Plato's *Republic* or Freud's trifold division of the psyche.

In part they are right. Most prayer does use a text, after all, and prayer books come packaged like philosophy and psychology books. You can indeed spend your time reading them, and they do in fact say something that we are expected to take seriously. But all literary texts are more than inert words on paper. They were written by someone, once, and were intended to be read, in some way, by someone else at some other time. Texts are messages, then: they may be telegrams, diaries, newspaper editorials, or even prayers, but whatever particular textual form they take, they are part of a complex whole beyond just their literal content. Prayers are a specific genre—or actually, as we shall see, several genres—of communication, part of the communications network that fuels the worship system. They invite us to ask the same questions of them that we might of any conversation.

First—What does the text say?
Second—How does it say it?
Third—What does it mean?
Fourth—How does it get said?

These by no means exhaust the criteria for analyzing texts, but they will serve as our guide in thinking about questions that require consideration if we are to appreciate worship. To exemplify what I mean, let us return to a consideration of the Greeting Ritual we discussed in Chapter Five: you meet someone on the street and recite the prescribed ritual text, "Good morning. How are you?"

What does the text say? This is equivalent to what people normally consider the text's *content*, which at first glance seems self-evident, merely a matter of quoting the words verbatim, "Good morning. How are you?" It would be unlikely that anyone would pay much attention to it beyond that.

There was a time in the study of linguistics, however, when what the text says was thought to depend on the history of the words used to make it up. So early linguists would try to discover how the words were used in the past and then list all their meanings from the beginning of the time people started saying them until now. In studying how long people have been using the phrase, "Good morning," for example, they would have turned up the fact that the English word "morning" goes back at least to the thirteenth century, when it was used only for the period of time before daybreak, however, and was spelled in a variety of ways, including "morwnynge" and "morwene." Around 1400, the King Arthur legends give us the example of "Gode morwene." By Shakespeare's time it had become "Good morning," but the word "good" had not yet become firmly attached only to the specific names assigned to the day's arbitrary divisions; so along with "Good morning," "Good evening," and "Good afternoon" Shakespeare has his characters say (in general) "Good time of day to you." Even the most simple taken-for-granted text has a history, and for a period of time, at least, there were linguists who thought that only its history could reveal what the text really said.

How does a text say what it says? Closely tied to the *what* of a text's content is the *how* of its means of presentation. If the first question was part of classical linguistics, the second was studied by classical philosophy and then literature, usually in the form of logic or rhetoric. You may remember studying Aristotelian syllogisms, for example, or even the rhetorical devices of, say, Lincoln's *Gettysburg Address*, as exemplary ways in which texts argue their case. The key word here is "argue." Here, too, an older, limited understanding of language once governed the way texts were studied. In the case of *how* texts work, philosophers thought that all texts with any sense at all worked by means of argumentation, the "necessarily true" forms of argument being "logical" and the fallacious but nonetheless convincing brands of reason being "clever rhetoric." The issue boiled down to the idea that texts must somehow purport to reflect a state of being that is either true or false. Thus the *how* of a text's saying something was equivalent to its ability to reproduce a true state of affairs. In the case before us, if the time of day was evening instead of morning, or if it was raining, so that the day was hardly "good," the greeting would be judged untrue. Words were believed to be like pictures. They reflect reality and are true or false.

For a long time this single-minded view of language was taken for granted. It was widely recognized that language sometimes functions in other ways, of course. If I say "Good morning," on a rainy afternoon, I might correct myself quickly by adding, "Oh, it's afternoon already; sorry; I meant 'Good afternoon'; and come to think of it, it's not really very good, is it?" But if I get upset with you and cry out, "Good grief! What are you doing?" it's not clear if there are any circumstances that will prompt me to think about whether grief can ever be "good" and thus to emend my remarks appropriately. Obviously "Good grief" says what it says in a way that is different from the way "Good morning" gets its point across. But philosophers warned us not to confuse examples like "Good grief" with language's primary role of providing pictures of truth.

Since the early part of this century we have seen two breakthroughs in the study of language, one in linguistics and the other in philosophy, with the twin results that both the first and the second question about texts can be answered more broadly now. The first breakthrough was a series of lectures given by Ferdinand de Saussure at the University of Geneva between the years 1906 and 1911, pointing out how language is a living, dynamic system very much alive in every speaker's present, quite unrelated to the history of the way the same or similar words were used in the past. You were perfectly able to say "Good morning" adequately, for instance, even before you read the paragraph on the history of "Gode morwene"; and knowing how it was used once upon a time has no necessary impact on your ability to use it in the future. So Saussure argued that linguistics should study the *way* words (he called them verbal signs) are strung together by competent speakers of language systems. *What* a text says is irrelevant to the history of the text's usage; and since the *what* of the text's message is inherently connected to the *way* the words are combined in meaningful sentences—that is, the *how* of a text's being said—we can see further that the two questions of *what* and of *how* are so closely tied together that they may even be one question.

At about the same time that Saussure was lecturing in Geneva, another continental European, Ludwig Wittgenstein, was preparing to take over his father's steel business in Vienna. In order to learn the business thoroughly, he was sent to England to visit the steel factories of Birmingham. While there, however, he gravitated to the study of philosophy and went to visit Bertrand Russell at Cambridge. When World War I broke out, he returned home to fight for the Austrian army, and while holed up in the trenches he wrote the first draft of a philosophical system that would summarize better than any other work the view of language as "pictures of reality." But Wittgenstein was a genius beyond the range of most geniuses. Even as most of Europe's great thinkers were adopting his book as the final word on how language works, he was preparing to leave philosophy altogether, and only after several years during which he taught mathematics, worked as a gardener, and became an accomplished self-taught architect, did he return to the study of language—but this time with a correction of the shortsightedness which assumes that the only sensible way to use language is to develop word-pictures that reflect reality. By the 1930s he, too, was developing a new philosophy of language in his university lectures, the end result of which was a revolution in philosophy equal to Saussure's revolution in linguistics.

Wittgenstein recognized language is only sometimes used to reflect the state of affairs. He compared the use of language to playing a game. Just as many different games are possible with the same pieces, so many different functions are possible with the same words. And just as it would be foolish to judge a chess move by the rules of checkers, so it would be invalid to judge the phrase "good grief" by the rules applicable to saying "good morning," or for that matter, to other word combinations in which the adjective "good" is used (like "My sister is a good sport," or "A good movie is hard to find these days"). We use language in different language games, so before we can pass judgment on whether a given sentence is appropriate, we have to know what the particular game and its rules are.

The end result of the "new Wittgenstein," as his second philosophy of language became known, is that philosophers no longer expect that the texts we use will always give us pictures about reality. They may do that, of course, but word-pictures are only one of the many games we need language for, and not the most important game at that. And again, as with Saussure, we see that the content of a text is not separable from its form. The *what* of the text's message is part and parcel of the rules of the game in which it is being said, the *how*, that is, that constitutes not just text, but *con*text.

In sum, the way people look at the texts we use has changed drastically over the last century. The question of *what* a text says must be asked along with the question of *how* it says it. The history of what a text meant once upon a time can no longer be imagined to have any necessary relationship to what it means now. And the text's content depends on the rules of the language game in which the text passes from message sender (speaker or writer, usually) to message receiver (hearer or reader).

Oddly enough, these lessons about language are alive and well in almost every field of study except liturgy. When people ask what a *prayer* text says, they still expect to receive a lecture on its history; and to the detriment of their worship, they still insist on treating all the sentences in their prayer books as if they were part of one single game called "theological truth," in which (they assume) the sole function of liturgical language is to offer portraits of reality with which they, as readers, are expected to agree. As long as people persist in thinking that liturgy is just theology, a liturgical language game consisting of saying out loud various sentences, the content of which they should be willing to affirm as true, they will be bitterly disappointed by their prayers. They will find many sentences meaningless; and others, boring; and they will feel guilty about the fact that they do not believe in everything they say. If they are really "guilty" of anything, it will be that they have been applying the wrong criteria to prayer— like treating "good grief" as if it were just a variation of "good morning"—and their "punishment" will consist of the consequence, namely, their prayer will always be found wanting.

A new approach to the language of prayer begins with abandoning the simplistic twofold questioning that characterized earlier attitudes. Prayer cannot be studied in terms of its objective content (on the one hand) and the way that content is argued (on the other). So we turn to the latter two questions on our list, subtle but important variations on the first two questions we looked at— not "What does a text say?" but "What does it mean?"; not "How does it say it?" but "How does it get said?" The all-important difference here is the accent on the interaction between the text and those who use it, the readers who come to it with different predetermined designs on what they should be doing with it: study it, proclaim it, read it (like a novel), argue about it, or pray it. Texts do not have purely objective status; they don't say anything on their own. Rather they are read by readers who understand them in certain ways. So instead of asking what the text says in and of itself, we have to ask what the text means to the reader who reads it. Similarly, instead of asking how the text itself says something, we have to ask how the "something" that it says gets said in the first place, that is, what are the rules of the language game that result in "good grief" rather than "good morning"?

These latter questions, too, go together. The question of our prayers is not how the texts that make them up somehow conspire independently to give us a theologically accurate picture of reality, but how worship can be considered a unique human activity in which words are used in special ways to do special things. What are those ways, and what are those things? That is what we have to look at now.

If the truth be told, at our current state of knowledge so little thinking about the problem has taken place that only partial answers can be offered. Still, if only we can avoid the self-defeating notion that the sentences of our prayers are all pictures of reality that demand intellectual assent, we will have gone a long way toward making it possible to say them. If our words of prayer are not photographic representations of "truth," what then are they?

Constituting a Present: Words as Performatives

Perhaps the most popular treatment of liturgical language has uncovered what philosophers have been calling performatives. The term goes back officially to 1955, when a philosopher named Austin gave a series of lectures at Harvard University, but Austin is reported to have said that he had the idea as early as 1939. Whatever the case, few ideas have been so warmly accepted through the years.

The essence of Austin's groundbreaking idea is to be found in the title of the book into which his lectures were transcribed. He called it *How to Do Things with Words,* by which he meant that words do not just report things that exist independently of the reports (that was the old way of thinking, as if words described an independent thing called reality). Instead words actually bring reality into being; they accomplish something; they are powerful tools that establish a state of being, rather than just report on it. Once we get the idea of what he is talking about, we can all think of many instances when liturgical or ritual language especially doesn't just *describe,* but *perform.* Here are the examples Austin offers.

"I do [take this woman/man to be my lawfully wedded wife/ husband]" (as uttered in the course of a marriage ceremony).

"I name this ship 'The Queen Elizabeth'" (as uttered in the course of smashing a bottle against a ship).

"I give and bequeath my watch to my brother" (as occurring in a will).

"I bet you ten dollars it will rain tomorrow."

"Can saying it make it so?" asks Austin of his own examples. It certainly can, he answers, as long as certain conditions are fulfilled. Successful use of these explicit performatives to accomplish some end requires that the rules of the "Performative Game" be followed, namely (among other things): the people involved have to recognize a conventional procedure that includes conventional language said by conventional people; the people saying the performatives must be appropriate and must follow the rules of the convention; they have to mean what they say; and so on. If, for example, the owner of the town liquor store suddenly takes a bottle of wine off the shelf and smashes it over the hull of my boat, declaring, "I name you 'The New Yorker'," his performative fails, even though there is nothing really wrong with the actual words he said. In fact the real naming might just have occurred, and the ship may really have been called "The New Yorker"; but still his statement doesn't count; it isn't so much "wrong" as it is "no good." Similarly, even if I myself were to name my ship The New Yorker, but if I did it with a sly smile on my face and was heard to say afterward that I didn't really mean it, you might be in doubt about what the boat was called, and you might ask, "Is it really called that?" Here, too, the performative doesn't work, even though the right person said it under the right set of circumstances. The question again is not so much whether what I said was true, as whether what I said really counted.

If a five-year-old child says, "I bet you a year's allowance," or if I "give and bequeath to my brother" a watch I do not own, these performatives do not count, that is, they don't perform what they were supposed to perform. In the first case, we don't hold children accountable for foolish vows; in the second, the institution of the law doesn't recognize bequests of nonexistent property. Austin calls such unsuccessful attempts at using language not *untruths* but *infelicities*. John Searle, another philosopher who has studied the matter, calls them just *defective*. He differentiates between "brute facts" that we suppose are out there in nature somewhere (whether they are or not) and "institutional facts," which come about because we have all agreed to recognize them under certain conventional circumstances. Marriage, bets, bequests, and namings are institutional facts, then, that either work out or not, depending on what we can call not just texts but texts in action, the process of saying certain things in certain contexts, or "speech-acts" as they are technically known.

Our initial insight must be a recognition of the large number of cases in which our worship is composed of performative language. Nearly every rite of passage brings an institutional fact into existence, and nearly every worship service features some statement or other in which people say things to establish a fact about themselves—a fact, moreover, that did not exist before they said it. Let me cite some instances of what I mean, this time from the 1978 *Lutheran Book of Worship:*

—I baptize you in the name of the Father and of the Son and of the Holy Spirit.
—(bride and groom to each other) I give you this ring as a sign of my love and faithfulness.
—We commend to almighty God our brother/sister and we commit his/her body to the ground: earth to earth, ashes to ashes, dust to dust.

Moreover it is not just these particular single lines that perform rather than report. By extension, much of the ritual that leads up to and away from these explicit performatives can be considered performative as well. If we look carefully, we see that the explicit performative lines, such as the ones I cited above, are used at precisely that part of the ritual script that corresponds to the Ritual Moment. They often accompany the critical actions that mark the rite's taking place, and they serve to instruct us on how we are supposed to understand the physical actions being undertaken at the time. In baptism the rite calls for water to be poured on the candidate's head, at which time the performative explains how we are to understand the water being poured. In a wedding the bride and groom (who marry each other, technically, according to Lutheran theology) exchange rings and tell us that this is no simple barter of goods, but something that "I give . . . as a sign of my love and faithfulness." At that moment the marriage happens, just as at the parallel moment the baptism occurs. Similarly there is a moment when the body is buried, a physical act we cannot miss, but to tell us how to "read" the physical act, how to understand the *institutional* fact being accomplished, we get an explicit performative that informs us what the funeral actually is, above and beyond the simple action of throwing dirt on a coffin.

In each case an entire ritual has been designed to lead up to and to lead away from a performatively indicated Ritual Moment. If the script is followed with care, we leave with the sense that this liturgy, at least, was felicitous; it worked out. Do people ask whether the state of affairs portrayed in the liturgy is true? Certainly not. That question is irrelevant. The state of affairs becomes true by virtue of the artistic *conventions* that everyone at the ritual agreed on before they came. I can't say to you, "I bet you fifty dollars," if you do not agree in advance on the institution we call "betting," and if you don't accept the commonly held convention that by shaking hands on the deal, you are obligated to follow through on the commitment to which we agreed in advance. It's against the rules to object afterward that bets don't count, or that you don't believe in betting. At the moment of the bet, you and I enter into the universe of betting, in which shaking hands signifies a mutually agreed-upon meaning system. Similarly worship depends on the common acceptance of the conventions under which certain institutional facts are presumed to exist. It is against the rules to object in retrospect that you don't accept marriage covenants or won't go along with Christian burial. Worship, like a play, depends on the willingness of all concerned to suspend their disbelief in the alternative world about to unfold before their eyes, and to give themselves over as willing partners in the words and actions that will bring it about. They commit themselves to be part of a universe in which water is not just sprinkled on people's heads, people are baptized; people don't just live together, they get married; bodies aren't just covered with earth, they are committed to their everlasting rest. A church with baptized members, the state of holy matrimony, and Christian burial are institutional states of being, artistic constructions of physical states that we decide in advance to honor with our recognition. The acted-out words of worship serve to confirm that recognition. Institutional states are born as liturgical words are said. Performatives thus establish an alternative world.

Fleshing out the Past: Words as Stories

The alternative world presented in worship exists beyond the present. By analogy, consider what happens when we read a novel. As we get farther and farther into the story, the characters become real for us; we can practically see them, flesh and blood standing before us. We interpret their behavior as described on any given page in the light of previous events from earlier chapters, until, no less than actual living friends and neighbors, the fictitious men and women in the book develop evolving biographical plot lines that virtually guarantee their success or failure by the book's end. Like actual people, then, they owe their depth of character, if they have any, to their development over time, the way their present arises out of their past and builds a foundation for a future.

In the *Tale of Two Cities*, for example, Charles Dickens portrays the horrors of the reign of terror that gripped the French Revolution. His unlikely hero is Sydney Carton, who lays down his life to save another man from the guillotine. The book begins, as it concludes, with lines that are memorable in the history of the English language. As to the beginning, there is the sweeping judgment that "it was the best of times, it was the worst of times..." Through the rest of the novel we get the kind of painstaking analysis of the worst of times in which Dickens, the social critic, excelled. But at the end we see the "best of times," too, Carton's self-sacrifice memorialized forever in his final words, "It is a far far better thing that I do than I have ever done; it is a far far better rest that I go to than I have ever known." The reason we appreciate his final testimony is that through some four hundred pages we learned to know Sydney Carton; we have entered his universe, along with Madame Defarge and her knitting, the upperclass English gentry, the miseries of French prisons, and all the rest of one particular world that once was—recreated as existing once again, for us, the readers. So we remember that Carton was introduced to us at an earlier time as "the idlest and most unpromising of men"—in a time, moreover, when:

> Those were drinking days, and most men drank hard ... The learned profession of the law was certainly not behind any other learned profession in its Bacchanalian propensities; neither was Mr. Stryver ... , [and] Sydney Carton, idlest and most unpromising of men, was Mr. Stryver's great ally. What the two drank together ... might have floated a king's ship.

Can Sydney Carton who chooses the guillotine be the same Sydney Carton who knew nothing more noble than a life of dissolute luxury? That is the great irony behind Carton's final lines, without which those lines would lose their appeal; and at the same time it is only the genius behind Dickens's art as a storyteller that permits us to see Carton's inner nobility finally shine through, as we realize that he is the symbol of "the best of times" to which the very first line in the book alerted us.

So too with the lines of every liturgy, which we recite not as solitary individuals but as the latest chain in a faith community. They are actually the community's lines, not just our own. The character of the story is the church entire, or the Jewish People forever. Fully to pray the lines of the moment presupposes consciousness of the lines once spoken by those who preceded us in the ongoing story of our faith. To their role as performatives (establishing a present), then, we add now a second function of liturgical language: the establishment also of a past. The words of worship are artistic constructs filling in the background of the community through which we claim descent; the heroes or martyrs whose memory we hold dear—our extended family members, really—and the events of our corporate life as a people or church that we presuppose because without them we would not be here praying as we do. Thus the *Lutheran Book of Worship* says:

> In many and various ways, God spoke to his people of old by the prophets.

> But now, in these last days, he has spoken to us by his son.

And Reform Jews daily read how God

did wonders for us in the Land of Egypt, miracles and marvels in the land of Pharaoh.

Whether God "spoke to his people of old by the prophets" or "did wonders for us in Egypt" is no more demonstrable as a fact "out there in historical reality" than is the "fact" that a child is baptized, a ring is given as "a sign of love and faithfulness," or an aged grandparent "commended to almighty God." We see only water cascading onto a child's head; we cannot see the baptism itself. Baptism occurs only if we care to assent to the convention by which it is said to happen. Similarly we see the ring change hands and the body enter the earth, but not the "love and faithfulness" or the "commendation," which exist only in our unspoken pact to see them there.

Each worship service is a rereading of a sacred script and the establishment of a new sacred reality, a world that did not exist until we willed it to, one that we establish anew with every sacred performance. So part of the script rehearses history as we choose to see it, the people of the past as we care to recollect them, and a selective perception of the events of our people that made us what we are.

Looking to the Future: Words as Hoping, Committing, Inspiring

Worship looks to the future, not just the past. The story we establish as our own has consequences for what we will become, not just for what we were. For analogies, look again at literature. Even in fiction, characters once established are not free to do whatever they wish. Their characters and accumulated experience are, to some extent, determinative of what they will henceforth do. Madame Defarge is described by Dickens as a woman absolutely consumed with the will for revenge:

> There were many women at that time, upon whom the time laid a dreadfully disfiguring hand; but there was not one among them more to be dreaded than this ruthless woman ... Of a strong and fearless character, of shrewd sense and readiness, of great determination, of that kind of beauty which not only seems to impart to its possessor firmness and animosity, but to strike into others an in-

stinctive recognition of those qualities; the troubled time would have heaved her up under any circumstances. But imbued from her childhood with a brooding sense of wrong, and an inveterate hatred of a class, opportunity had developed her into a tigress. She was absolutely without pity. If she had ever had the virtue in her, it had quite gone out of her.

Now at the end of the tale, Madame Defarge has the power to save the innocent prisoner awaiting the guillotine. But she cannot, for the simple reason that even her creator, Dickens, is not free any more to do with her as he wishes. She is the opposite of Carton, a woman unable to use her "strong and fearless character," her "shrewd sense and readiness," or her "great determination," for anything but revenge; she cannot change her nature any more than history's real avengers can. Her character is cast; she cannot be capriciously remade to demonstrate "the best of times"; she epitomizes "the worst," for even at the end:

> It was nothing to her that an innocent man was to die for the sins of his forefathers. She saw, not him, but them. It was nothing to her that his wife was to be made a widow, and his daughter an orphan.

So, true to character, her last orders of the day preceding the guillotining are, "Take you my knitting, and have it ready for me in my usual seat." Fictitious character that she is, she must nonetheless act in character, molding each future action as a natural outgrowth of her past.

In the world we weave through our prayers, we, too, formulate a character that is our own. We become Christians or Jews of such and such a stamp by virtue of the story that we say is ours. To invoke prophetic vision is at the same time to implicate ourselves as believers in all that flows from that vision. To begin the story and then to take it all the way up to the present is also to expect it to end, and not just in any old fashion, but according to the cues for ending that were established along the way. I spoke before of a work of art being both coherent and comprehensive. Our constructed world of reality must be both. The story told in worship, then, must be comprehensive in that we anticipate it will not end abruptly in the middle, now, without the realization of the dramatic foreshadowing given us earlier in the text; and it must be coherent, in that up to and including the final ending the tale must be consistent, as consistent as Defarge who knits by the guillotine until the end.

So worship is filled with anticipations of the future: hope, promise, commitment, inspiration, and the like. Sometimes these are evident:

"God bless you and keep you."
"God have mercy on you."
"Lord, may this eucharist take away our sins."
"Peace be with you." "And also with you."

The wishing form of prayer is explicit in the way we respond. Normally we answer prayers with *Amen* = "May it be so." Jewish prayer sometimes ends also with *Ken yehi ratson* = "May this be God's will." So, too, we pray: "Thy kingdom come, thy will be done," "Hear us, good Lord" (from the Lutheran intercessions), or "God our creator, hear our prayer and bless us" from the equivalent rubric in the Reform Jewish Sabbath service. Sometimes, then, the anticipations are clear: wishing that God fulfill our requests, or explicit statements that "We hope and pray . . . "

But sometimes the hoping aspect of our prayers is only implicit in a statement that we make on faith. Knowing that our story commits us so intensely to a single conceivable outcome at the end of time, we state as a given what has yet to be the case, convinced that it will indeed be the case, just as Madame Defarge had no choice, given her character, but to show up at the scaffold knitting to the rhythm of the guillotine. "On that day," goes the conclusion to the *Alenu*, one of Judaism's closing prayers, "our God shall be one and God's name shall be one." It is not so much a question of "Do we really believe it?" as "How can we really be so bold as to say it?" We dare say it because we have internalized our story of the world in such a way that no other ending could possibly follow. So we say it as hope and as anticipation, as commitment to the story's integrity as well, and as exhortation to ourselves to take the story seriously in our perception of our lives. Similarly we recite creeds that inspire us and commands that exhort us, until in the end, the fullness of the liturgical vision has become so plain that it cannot be denied. We are committed to this sacred way of perceiving reality. We leave our worship with a sense that the world is shaped differently than it was when we entered. Saying has indeed made it so.

I have by no means exhausted the many uses of language in prayer. But I have tried to show that the ways we use language during worship are many, and that they should not be judged by the rules governing the game of scientific description. All along I have reiterated my theme of worship as an art form, and art as the means by which we create alternative realities, transforming emptiness and entropy into meaning and pattern. As soon as this simple lesson is grasped, many other word-oriented worship exercises fit into place, too: the sermon (or homily), for example, which does not really teach us a set of objective facts that we did not know before, so much as it lets us see things we have always known—but in a new light, with new artistic models, stories, and hopes for improvement. By way of example, on New York's upper east side a Lutheran church has been housed in a modern highrise office and shopping mall. The pastor there some years ago used to direct the visitors' attention to the scene across the street, visible directly from within the sanctuary via a window that could have been colored in with a stained-glass biblical scene, but was left transparent instead. The scene through that window is shocking: right across the street sits a pornographic book store advertising xxx reading and videos. The point of it all, the pastor would say, is to see the outside with the vision of the inside, to grasp the message of Christian worship and then to apply it, like a grid, on the hitherto unexamined life we lead on the streets of New York. Before coming to pray, we might have seen the store as just a store offering us merchandise that we might ignore, prefer, purchase, or despise; but after prayer, the world is seen in a new light: and so is the store, which signifies for us now our calling to work prophetically in the world until such evils as pornography shall be ended.

All good art works just that way to establish alternative realities. When I was younger, I used to go to the Museum of Modern Art, where I would sit in front of Picasso's monumental *Guernica*, its visual message of the terrors of war displayed like a wraparound screen in the room that it dominated by its sheer size and conception. When the museum returned the work to Spain, its rightful owner, I understood what they were doing even as I cried at their having to do it. I cannot take my children to sit before *Guernica* as I used to. By comparison, my children learned to watch *MASH* reruns, not just from time to time, but nightly, to the point where they knew in advance how each episode would end. ("Don't miss this one, Dad," they would say, "This is the one where . . . ") The fact that I had memorized the visual script of *Guernica,* so to speak, did not dissuade me from coming to see it again and again; just as they, knowing the dramatic script of *MASH,* nonetheless sat through its reruns without missing a night. When *MASH* finally went off the air, they cried also. Both *Guernica* and *MASH* are works of art establishing their own alternative worlds in which war is unthinkable.

The difference between *Guernica* and *MASH,* on the one hand, and worship, on the other, is this: however compelling the alternative worlds of Picasso and Hawkeye may be, they exist outside of ourselves, created by someone else. They invite us as welcome—or even as involved—observers to share their insights, but we remain observers in their worlds. I am not a "Guernican" or a "Mashie" in the same way that I am a Jew. Religious worship, by contrast, is never fully worship until we who pray go through the script of prayer making it our own. I do not just play-act at being a Jew; or just observe—even in an involved way— the Jewish stories, recollections, and promise of my prayers; or merely *pretend* that my performative life-cycle ceremonies transform people's lives into the categories of marriage or covenanthood. I really am what I pray; that vision of the world is my own; the history I rehearse is not somebody else's, but mine, calling me to a future that is mine as well. We are blessed with freedom of choice, so there is no inherent necessity that we should act according to an ironbound plot devised on the day of our birth; but if, some day, we are able to look back with the wisdom of old age, we should see our lives not as an accumulation of disjointed experiences strung loosely together through time, but as a coherent whole, with the seeds of the future planted at every successive moment of the present. The words of prayer locate us in a continuum between a sacred past that we identify as our own and a vision of a future that we

241

hope to realize as the logical outcome of the story of our lives.

Thus does worship, reiterated according to a sacred script, week in and week out, commit us to a world that we ourselves bring into being: a world of transformed identity, stories and history, promise and hope: none of which is an objective "thing" that liturgy reflects, all of which are institutional facts that worship establishes.

12

The Script of Prayer: Words Sung

The Prayers We Sing

THERE ARE WORSHIP TRADITIONS without any music at all, but they are few. Religions that feature textual recitation usually have at least a favored way of chanting the text. As far as Jews and Christians are concerned, music of one sort or another has been part of our respective traditions since our worship began. Music has thus been central to synagogue and church throughout the centuries.

The word "music" covers a broad spectrum of phenomena, however, even within the Judeo-Christian worship tradition. Just consider the variety of music we have called sacred!

- The ancient Jerusalem Temple in the time of Jesus featured levitical choirs and accompanying instrumentation that included woodwinds, percussion, brass, and strings—a complete orchestra of sorts. The Temple was not unusual in that regard, since the pagan sacrificial systems of the time were similarly outfitted with musical splendor.

- Probably in reaction to that very pagan musical style, the nascent church and synagogue looked less favorably on instrumentation, even though singing certainly continued, and eventually Judaism and Christianity developed their own respective chanting traditions. In Christian worship, that predilection to sing the liturgy was gradually transferred entirely to the monastic orders so that medieval churches were built with large choir sections where monks performed their liturgical hours through song.

• In the European Reformation, however, Christian worship changed in content, form, and the understanding of who was to do it. In keeping with its central focus on the Bible, as on the direct access of individual worshipers to the word of God, Lutheran worship expressed a distinct preference for hymns, which the assembled people as a whole sang, and Calvin wanted to limit the music to biblical texts.

• In the sixteenth century Jewish worship had yet to go through its "reformation period," but that transformation did come some three centuries later, in the wake of Napoleon's sweep across Europe, an event that facilitated the Jewish exit from the ghettos and entry into cultured European society. Jewish music now moved in one of two directions.

• To begin with, there were the "traditionalistic" congregations in which worship proceeded with the inherited premodern Hebrew text in a style unconcerned with "modern" western aesthetics. Particularly in eastern Europe, where the cultural byproducts of Napoleonic conquest never reached, Jews elaborated an already-present cantorial solo mode. The cantor, or *chazzan* in Hebrew, specialized in a finely-crafted and intricately executed recitative filled with melismatic passages. When people speak of Jewish liturgical music they usually mean this specialized cantorial style that was evident even before the Napoleonic revolution, but reached new heights in artistic sophistication thereafter.

Theologically speaking, this cantorial style was rooted in a rabbinic conception of a prayer leader who is the congregation's spiritual representative to God (in Hebrew, literally, "the agent of the congregation"), and as such is charged with singing the liturgy on the people's behalf. The people pray, too: the synagogue never abandoned liturgical celebration to the prerogative of a special class of clerics, as had been the case with Christian monasticism. But on the other hand, it also never developed the monastic tradition of unison singing by those charged with liturgical recitation.

- That brings us to the second direction that music took after the Napoleonic period, the reform of the worship service that constitutes the Jewish "Reformation," so to speak, a reform that differed from the Christian parallel in that Jews did not have a strong unison singing tradition among their clerics, so they never developed the parallel phenomenon, congregational hymns, among their laity. Instead, Judaism created a mutation in the art form that it did have, namely, the cantorial solo role.

  The post-Napoleonic period in western, as opposed to eastern, Europe brought with it lasting cultural reverberations. Jews were released from their ghettos and promised civil rights, with the implicit proviso that they acted "civilly." So they restructured the choreography of their worship according to the canons of western conceptions of spirituality, taking as their model the very forms that had already infiltrated contemporary churches. But Christians and Jews applied modern standards of music differently. We saw that the Protestant Reformation had featured unison singing, which was really just an extension of the chants by the monks transformed, however, into hymns sung by all the people. The Jewish equivalent tended toward an elaboration of the solo mode—generally, the old synagogue favorites that had been based on ancient chant styles, but which were now recast to fit the aesthetic demands of modern western art standards.

- The music of what I have called the nineteenth-century "Jewish Reformation" was typical only of western Europe, beginning perhaps in Vienna, but then moving westward toward the urban capitals of enlightenment culture like Berlin and Hamburg. In Poland, meanwhile, Hasidic Judaism had developed yet a further musical mutation: a tradition of wordless melodies called *niggunim*, rooted in native—and not necessarily Jewish— folk tunes, which were sung slowly at first, and then faster and faster so as to produce a group ecstatic state.

- I haven't even mentioned the Mantuan court musical tradition of Salamone Rossi, whose seventeenth-century Jewish music sounds distinctly "unsynagogual" to the modern ear; or the phenomenon of Jews rising together to conclude a service with *Hatikvah*, the national anthem of the State of Israel, clearly borrowed in terms of melody from *The Moldau*, but expressing in its lyrics "the hope of two thousand years, to be a free people in our land, the land of Zion and Jerusalem"; or, on the Christian side of things, folk-rock services, perhaps the strains of Bob Dylan, heard ubiquitously in coffee-house masses in the '60s.

In sum, Jewish and Christian music has been diverse indeed: we have known chants and modern art songs; solos and hymns; biblical lyrics as well as melodies sung without any words at all; instrumentation and relative bans on instruments. It is difficult to find a single common denominator to unite all instances of church and synagogue music into a single set of music that we call sacred.

What is it that makes music "sacred"? People generally just imagine it must be something in the music itself, by which they mean the particular sound they have in mind when they think about music that "naturally" belongs in church, as opposed to the sound of bars, dance halls, discos, and the stage, which they imagine, just as "naturally" does not. A little thought will demonstrate how subjective that criterion is. It seems hard to imagine that sacrality inheres in certain musical styles, but not in others, since, for example, Black Spirituals sound nothing like Bach chorales; the traditional chanting of Moroccan Jewry is a far cry from measured Gregorian chant, and both of those have little in common with Verdi, Brahms and Mozart, who have, in turn, not much in common with each other.

If we think of *Hatikvah* once again, it might fairly be argued that, no matter what Jews think, the melody is just a poor variation of a theme from *The Moldau*, so the song is not sacred. But try telling that to Jews for whom *Hatikvah* bespeaks their fondest religious aspirations! At a recent service celebrating rabbinic ordination and cantorial investiture, the student-composed service called for *Hatikvah* as the final hymn; before it was sung, one of the officiants rose to say, "In honor of Jerusalem Day [a new Jewish sacred day marking the reunification of the holy city of Jerusalem, and by chance, the day that year on which the service fell], the *choir(!)*

will sing *Hatikvah*." The message was clear: for him, *Hatikvah* was no sacred song, but a national anthem; the liturgical script mandated it, but at least it could be relegated to the choir, which was rehearsed to sing it in a reasonably "spiritual" arrangement, slowly and artistically to an organ accompaniment. The three thousand people present, however, with the front rows of students and faculty leading the way, saw *Hatikvah* as distinctly sacred and refused to stand silently waiting for the organ to catch up to the tune as it ran full speed through their minds. As the anticipation of yet another generation's rabbis and cantors being consecrated to their life work merged with the Jewish people's hope of centuries, they happily broke out in song, several bars ahead of the choir in the loft, naturally. The moment was not one to be recalled for its liturgical synchrony. But it did demonstrate that songs do not come prepackaged as sacred or profane; their sacrality depends largely on something other than purely musical considerations.

If we look at the other extreme, songs that have always been considered sacred, we arrive at the same conclusion. No one would deny that Ernest Bloch's *Sacred Service* and Verdi's *Four Sacred Pieces* are sacred. Their composers proclaimed that fact in the titles themselves, and before Bloch dared to compose his service, he even secluded himself in extended study of the sacred material he was to integrate into his masterwork! But it seems hard to imagine that what prompted their titles is the sacrality of the musical compositions themselves. Palestrina could compose a madrigal today but a motet tomorrow, the former for use in a profane setting and the latter in a sacred one. Are the two *sounds* so different that one is obviously sacred and the other not?

A ready alternative possibility is that the Bloch and Verdi music can be called sacred because of the lyrics, which are obviously sacred texts. That seems true enough, but it can hardly serve as a defining quality of sacred music, since, in that case, any music at all would be sacred as long as the words were sacred, and the whole problem with which we began was the sense that sometimes the same sacred lyrics are put to music that we consider profane—I once heard the Friday night sanctification prayer (the *Kiddush*) sung to the tune of *La Marseillaise,* for example. Would we, by analogy, find it acceptable to have the *Sanctus* or the Jewish *Kedushah* sung to the nationalist strains of *My Country 'tis of Thee,* or, worse, the Soviet Union's *Internationale;* or even *Deutschland, Deutschland, über Alles?* I mention national anthems particularly because they were usually composed as sacred hymns themselves! *Deutschland, Deutschland, über Alles,* for example, which is still sung as a hymn in many churches, dates back to a 1797 melody by none other than Haydn (!), and was used first as the Austrian empire's anthem, entitled *Gott erhalte, Gott beschütze, unsern Kaiser, unser Land* ("God keep and protect our Kaiser and our Land"); and *My Country 'tis of Thee* is just America's version of the more religiously sounding *God save our Gracious King/Queen.* These were sacred songs once, certainly, but are they sacred still? Their melodies haven't changed. Or if you think the problem with a *Sanctus* sung to *Deutschland, Deutschland, über Alles* is precisely the fact that we would be mixing two religious motifs, a sort of modern day syncretism, what about substituting the latest nonreligious hit by the Beatles, Billy Joel, or whoever tomorrow's rock stars will be? Would a *Sanctus* sung to *She Loves You, Yeah Yeah Yeah* be any better? Obviously not; there must be some independent standards to judge the music itself. That puts us back where we started, demanding some musical criterion for "sacred," but unable to locate one that is true for all accepted pieces of sacred music.

At least, people say, we have a right to demand *good* music; that is, we may not know what makes music sacred, but we do know what makes it good. The argument here seems to be that, as the loftiest of human activities, worship demands music of impeccable taste; otherwise, we would not be taking seriously its claims to speak to God. Let us agree, for the sake of argument, on the presumption that we would be able to reach consensus on what is good music—a doubtful hypothesis, I think, but worth granting for a moment anyway. We still have the problem that many religious traditions—Orthodox Judaism and most ethnic churches, to name but two—do not use "good" music. Then, too, not all good music is sacred, obviously. And though it is taken for granted here, it is by no means self-evident that God has the same taste in music that Philharmonic subscription holders do.

Suppose, however, at the very least we adopt the principle that we ought to offer to God only our finest creative accomplishments, so that even though not every good piece of music is sacred, all sacred music must be good; and suppose further that we define "good" according to whatever definition of "good music" we find in the culture we are considering. That would save genuinely ethnic musical preferences as well as ancient or medieval chanting modes, while at the same time providing us with a mandate to do for our time and place whatever others have done for theirs: that is, create new music according to the highest aesthetic criteria available to us. Unfortunately, that won't do either. To begin with, it saves ethnic, ancient, and medieval music all right, but only for ethnics, ancients, and medievals, who, one might imagine, ought certainly by now to acculturate or grow up; and besides, our own recovery of old traditional favorites begins sounding like the musical equivalent of slumming through the neighborhoods of our youth—hardly what we think we are doing when we go back to our musical roots in hymns, chants, or folk melodies. Then, too, even music that all agree is both good and sacred turns out often enough not to facilitate worship. What shall we do with Aaron Copland's *In the Beginning,* Leonard Bernstein's *Kaddish,* or even Bach's *B Minor Mass?* All three are certainly sacred, and the last may even have been used for worship, but I can't imagine using any of them for that purpose now. Bernstein's *Chichester Psalms* contains a gorgeous rendition of Psalm 23 that might be plundered for use as a solo in modern worship, but the rest of the work—much as I may (and in fact do) love it—is probably not likely to receive wide recognition as a liturgical favorite. And by contrast, the great liturgical favorites of all time do not always pass musical muster with connoisseurs of musical taste— which is, of course, the problem we began with in the first place!

In sum, we seem to have gotten nowhere. Not only can we not agree on what makes music sacred, but even if we could, it would not follow that all sacred music is good music, and even if that were true, not all sacred (and therefore good) music is applicable to worship, which seems, in this as in other respects, to be stubbornly intent on advancing its own criteria for what is desirable in synagogue and church.

Yet oddly enough, in the face of all this uncertainty, when people debate the musical merit of their worship, both sides harden into the kind of unbending absolutism that we rarely encounter elsewhere. Keeping in mind what we said in Chapter Two on symbols, we understand the reason for some of the forensic heat:

music reaches deeply inside our psyche; the old standbys of our youth echo in the chambers of our soul long after the sound waves themselves are dead. In a word, music *symbolizes*. And that is why so much of successful worship depends on it and has depended on it for so many centuries. We are in the dilemma of dealing with a channel of communication far more important than the words of prayer we discussed above. There are certain exceptions, to be sure—like sexist language issues, which symbolize as much as music does—but still, it can be said that even though people may object to the *texts* we use, they usually relate to spoken words alone as *signs*, not as *symbols*; and are prepared, therefore, to establish an uneasy truce with their opponents in the realm of what is merely said. With music, on the other hand, they hold definite opinions which they support with great force, using the arguments we have looked at here, even though their strong feelings may be relatively independent of the reasons they advance for them. They may say that we should use the music they like because that music is a) sacred or b) good, whereas in fact, it is rarely possible for them to prove either point, much less to demonstrate why, even if they are right, that has anything to do with the case. In fact, they like the music they do because it *symbolizes* positively.

In the face of such a raging issue it is no surprise to find pastors and laity alike abdicating musical responsibility and delegating it instead to musical specialists who have no understanding of worship, but who presumably know good music, in the same way that theologians know a good doctrine when they see one. This does not always solve the problem. Musicians, after all, have their own musical tastes: musical sounds that symbolize to them no less than music of a different sort may symbolize to others. The truth is, according to the canons of western composition, there is such a thing as good music. Musicians have learned to recognize it, appreciate it, play it, love it, and, often, live it! Sociologists of music demonstrate the extent to which music is its own subculture in America. Music is a demanding taskmaster, and members of musical elites would often rather starve than give up their musical ambition to sing at the Met or play in the Philharmonic. Asking musicians to select music for worship *solely* on the basis of its musical quality is tantamount to asking philosophers to write prayers on the basis of the logical strength of a chain of reasoning.

But in some worship settings that is exactly what happens, with disastrous consequences. I am most emphatically *not* saying that musical expertise should be bypassed when it comes to selecting the music for prayer, but I am saying that musical quality as defined by musical elites is not the sole, nor even the most important, factor to be considered.

As long as we persist in imagining that sacred music means "music that is sacred" in the same way that soft ice cream is "ice cream that is soft," we will get nowhere. "Soft" is the name we give to the consistency of an ice cream compound that corresponds to a certain molecular or chemical makeup of the ice cream itself, whereas "sacred" bears no relationship to any particular quality inherent in the arrangement of sharps, rests, and eighth-notes. If we want to know what criteria to apply to the music of our worship, we have to start the discussion all over again.

Music as Performative

The idea of performatives is a useful new beginning. We saw before that the study of language, too, is befuddled by the simplistic notion that words must inevitably point to an objective thing called "truth" and that this "truth" exists as some metaphysical state of affairs awaiting our linguistic ability to recognize it. But prayer, we decided, is not just a specialized kind of text reflective of theological truths; it is a textual act in which the words we recite accomplish something. The spoken word of prayer does more than mirror an independent reality existing outside itself; it performs.

We can apply that same insight to music. The music of prayer also does more than convey independent truths or ideas; it, too, performs. If we want to know what "sacred" music is, we have to ask first what sacred acts are, since sacred music is not music that is sacred, but music that performs sacred acts.

Going over the diverse list of sacred music that we just looked at will demonstrate that, in every case, *music is considered sacred not on account of what it is, but on account of what it does*. Sometimes it expresses texts that are considered sacred in such a way that the meaning of those texts is enhanced: that is the case with Bloch's *Sacred Service* and Verdi's *Four Sacred Pieces*. The Hasidic song without melody, however, has no text at all, but is sacred still

251

because it is used to attain a sacred state of bliss in the context of Hasidic worship practice. Similarly, Haydn's *Gott erhalte . . . unsern Kaiser*, like the anonymously composed *God Save the King/Queen*, were once sacred songs dedicated to empires seen as divinely willed and rulers blessed with divine rights; they were sung by subject peoples acknowledging their religious support of what God had willed. *Hatikvah* may or may not be a sacred song, depending on whether it is sung by secular Israelis before a soccer match or by Jews affirming an age-old religious vision of a holy land and people reunited after two thousand years of waiting. Copland's *In the Beginning* is sacred because it expresses the sacred text of Genesis, and Bernstein's *Kaddish* is sacred because it expresses a Jewish prayer; yet neither piece is liturgical—even though the latter's text is a prayer—because though these two musical compositions do something religious, what they do religiously is something other than make prayer happen.

In sum, music, too, is performative in its own way. From their religious tradition composers learn the goals of religious life— expressing a sacred text (e.g., the revelation on Mt. Sinai), giving thanks, inducing awe, attaining a trance, or anything else. They create music that accomplishes those goals and then, through a curious feedback loop, the music utilizes its capacity to express the otherwise inexpressible so as to refine further what the goals are. Worship is just one of the goals that Judaism and Christianity define among their favored religious activities. To the extent that music performs "felicitously" in a sacred cause, it is sacred music; to the extent that the cause is worship, it is liturgical sacred music. And the type of worship act that the music is intended to facilitate depends entirely on the theological presumptions of the tradition in question.

We are almost at the end of our analysis of the role of music in worship. But first, one more matter needs clearing up. Must the music of worship be "good" music by specifically musical standards? For centuries now the upper classes of Europe and North America have argued that it must. The assumption seems to have been that artistically excellent music moves us to a higher form of religious consciousness than lower forms of music do. That was the motivating theory behind the conversion of medieval Jewish chants into artistically acceptable western art songs. And the same process can be seen as recently as our own day. Some years ago I was present at the ordination of a rabbi who had composed some simple but effective songs when he was a teenager. At his ordination they played one of his songs—but only after it had been rearranged with sophisticated harmonic structure and set for the organ, at a tempo, incidentally, only about half the speed of the original, which was judged by the experts to be too upbeat, even raucous, for real worship. When the final piece was played, even though it was unquestionably better music, it failed miserably as worship. The musicians present commented on the superior musicianship evident in the new setting: in their view, a miracle had transformed a simple childish melody into a sophisticated musical event. The composer and his friends, however, were disappointed. They had prayed often with the old setting, but found that the new one barely moved them. They would get used to it, they were told; as it now stood, refurbished and recast, the melody would prove lasting; it would be worthy of prayer; it would raise the assembled congregation to levels unattainable by the composition in its original state. The composer remained unconvinced.

Who was right, the critics or the composer?

At issue is whether the composer should take function into consideration when writing a piece of music. By comparison, it is worth recalling the famous debate that occurred in the world of architecture in the early part of this century. In 1895 the Viennese architect Otto Wagner published a book called *Modern Architecture,* in which he argued that buildings should be designed as just the opposite of the neo-Gothic, neo-Baroque, and neo-everything-else that dominated the main boulevard circling the inner city of Vienna. In opposition to the official architectural establishment, he and his colleagues formed a Secessionist school of thought, which championed function over arbitrary form. Before long, others developed their notion in more extreme ways, the best known, perhaps, being the Bauhaus school, often recalled crisply in the curt motto attributed to one of its ideologues, Mies van der Rohe, "Less is more." Much later, the American architect Robert Venturi is recalled as having expressed the artistic conflict beautifully, when he parodied Mies van der Rohe. In response to "Less is more," he retorted, "Less is a bore."

Neither Mies nor Venturi were talking about liturgical music, but they might as well have been recording the headings for the music debate of churches and synagogues in our time. It seems fairly obvious that, from a purely musical perspective, the music that people prefer for their worship is often not the highest possible artistic composition. Worshipers who nonetheless are moved to pray by it would probably judge that, for them, anyway, "less is more"; musicians with trained ears and heightened sophistication to what music can be would hold only that "less is a bore."

They are both right. Musical purists undoubtedly find much of what passes for liturgical music boring, and for them it fails in its function. But musically exciting compositions, though "more" in terms of music, are not necessarily "more" in terms of worship. Texts we sing should be judged along with texts we say simply and solely on the degree to which they facilitate worship, for sacred music is music that performs in a sacred way, and worship is one such performance.

Words and Music: Syntax and Semantics

We saw above a variety of ways in which spoken texts perform: they create a present, establish a shared past, and commit us to an anticipated future. It is not quite so clear that music performs in the same ways.

On the one hand, music is like literature in that they consist of basic elements, called notes or letters, separated by punctuating elements like rests or periods. Neither letters nor notes mean anything in themselves, but they can be combined into patterns that communicate. Thus not only authors, but musicians, too, speak of ideas, musical ideas being a certain pattern of notes; sensitive listeners can follow the "plot line" of a piece by hearing the ideas come together at different times and in different ways. A melody line can be inverted, stretched out, set to different tempi, highlighted by the counterpoint of a second melody heard in the background, scored for different instruments along the way, and so forth. People who know music would therefore testify to music's ability to perform in ways that are at least similar to words.

On the other hand, music differs from literary texts. We can arrive at an appreciation of music's uniqueness as a communicating medium if we differentiate between *syntax* and *semantics* and between *open* and *closed* systems. An ordinary sentence is a series of words that follow each other according to rules of combination.

Take the sentence "The child baked a cake," which has five words divided into three grammatical units: the subject ("the child"), the verb ("baked"), and the object ("a cake"). Theoretically at each step along the way, the speaker assembling the sentence has to stop and decide which word or words will fill the spaces called "subject," "verb," and "object." Is the subject going to be "the child," or "the adult?" If the baker is a ten-year-old boy named George, it must be "the child," but still it could have been "George," or "a child," or maybe (if George is the speaker's son) "my son," or (if the context is a court case, in which the cake turned out to have poisoned the guests, so that George's lawyer wishes to exonerate the defendant), "the minor." The point is that spoken languages provide words with agreed-upon referents in the real world, which we have in mind as the subject of our utterances, and when we make up a sentence about that world, we choose the words that best express what we have in mind. The step by which we choose one word from a theoretical pool of possible words at each stage in the sentence's formation is called *semantics*. *Semantics* is thus the meaning that words have because they already contain a referring value that speaker and hearer share. I can call George "the child," because we both know that "child" *semantically* means a ten-year-old.

The other necessary step in constructing a sentence is to combine all the right words in the right order. Some languages allow speakers great latitude in ordering their words by providing case endings that define the role of the word in question. In English, by contrast, I cannot invert the sentence to say, "A cake baked the child." In both instances, therefore, we see that the meaning of "the child" in our sentence depends on more than its semantic sense; it depends on where it comes in the sentence, or failing that (in languages like German or Latin, which have case endings), on how it is declined as nominative or accusative case. It is either the baker or the thing baked, and the only way I can tell which is by the case ending or in languages without cases by the position it has relative to the other parts of the sentence. Since the rules of word placement in sentences are collectively called *syntax*, we call the meaning each word derives from its position relative to the other elements in the sentence its *syntactical* meaning.

Using what is now a familiar systems approach to study phenomena, we can consider a sentence a system. Insofar as its

255

words (that is, the elements of the system) depend on something outside of themselves to give them the meaning they convey in the system, we have an *open system*; insofar as their meaning depends on the other elements in the system alone, they constitute a *closed system*. Thus, spoken messages perform their function by virtue of the way they combine *semantic* and *syntactic* meaning; semantic meaning depends on word-values that we get from the use of the same words in other contexts, whereas syntactics is the way the word interacts with other words in the sentence in question. So the language of words is to some extent open and to some extent closed. In most cases the semantic value is so strong that even if I were to invert the order incorrectly (as in "the cake made the child") you would probably understand what I meant and presume that I was a new English speaker making a mistake with the word order. So *words perform their function primarily as a semantically dependent, open system.*

By contrast, music is a syntactically dependent, closed system. At the end of a composition, for example, we hear a particular chord resolve the piece because we already have the piece in our ears. It is not the case that the chord in and of itself necessarily means "resolution," since the same chord may have an entirely different message if it is placed somewhere else in the composition. If we were to compare the notes in a symphony to the words in an essay, we could say that a given chord takes its meaning from its position in the score, the way a particular word in a sentence takes its meaning from being the subject or the object of what is being said. Music thus has what we call *syntactic* meaning.

But music does not have *semantic* meaning, and that is where it differs from words. We saw that, when I use a word, I depend on the *semantic* meaning that it already has from other sentences. The single note A, like the single letter A, has, remember, no inherent meaning; the question is how a string of notes, like a string of words, becomes meaningful enough for us to communicate by it. Music is its own unique art form in that it is self-referential; it refers back to itself for its meaning. At first, it may appear otherwise, as, for example, when composers borrow a particular set of notes from one composition and embed it in another, so that, when people hear the new work, they appreciate its relationship to the place where it first occurred. In that sense, the borrowed musical phrase does *seem* to have semantic meaning; I hear your work and I recognize the opening sounds from Beethoven's Fifth Symphony, for example, and I think, "Ah, Beethoven." But the musical meaning is still not semantic; what looks like semantic value is really just my recollection that the notes in question appeared once before somewhere. The musical citation from Beethoven does not point to some entity outside of itself, the way the word "child" does. When I try to figure out where I heard it, I recall, "Oh yes, it was in Beethoven's Fifth." That is a different thing from hearing that "the child baked a cake" and recalling both where I heard the word "child" before and the fact that "child" means something special, namely a young person, but not an adult, or a horse, or whatever else I may want to use it for. The semantic content that I thought existed in the notes is really just syntactic meaning referred to a larger sample of music.

The note A is just the note A, the way the letter A in a word is just the letter A. The meaning in both cases comes from letter or note strings. In music a string of notes, like G G G E-flat, F F F D—the opening bars of Beethoven's Fifth—may be used syntactically to recollect its usage once before, but unlike the letter string C H I L D, the music string remains arbitrary, with the possibility of becoming anything at all that the composer wants it to be in the new composition. G G G E-flat is not limited semantically the way C H I L D is by its usage elsewhere.

I don't want to go so far as to argue that music strings can always be anything we want them to be. They, too, are limited by past usage. Composers may well avoid G G G E-flat precisely because that string will remind people of Beethoven; and musically knowledgeable people who have internalized thousands of musical themes will have a working vocabulary of many more similar combinations that have their own meaning by now. But that meaning is syntactic, not semantic. The notes in question refer back to the place in musical history where we heard them first and remind us of the context of that earlier successful usage. They do not remind us of some outside state of affairs to which the earlier usage pointed. My use of G G G E-flat recalls Beethoven's use, but if I don't mind being accused of plagiarism, I can use it again and make it mean something else by the way I place it in my own work. In fact some composers write "variations" on the work of a prior composer, in which they deliberately borrow someone else's theme and make it over into a newly meaningful composition precisely because there is no fixed semantic content to notes, the way there is with words. In Jewish music, the beginning of a popular melody for a concluding prayer (*Bayom hahu*) is exactly the same as the opening bars of *The Farmer in the Dell*! Thoughtful cantors often try to avoid it because its syntactical meaning reminds us of nurseryrhyme trivia. But people usually don't mind singing it anyhow, because the rest of the piece verges away enough from the conclusion of the nursery rhyme that they can forget its original usage, and because when they sing it, they are not afflicted by any necessary semantic meaning attached to the notes in question. Similarly Jews have often borrowed hymn settings from Christians, but not lyrics; and, the other way around. When the Wesleyan pastor Thomas Oliver heard the Jewish hymn *Yigdal* in an eighteenth-century English synagogue, he was able to borrow the music (which is semantically neutral), but he had to change the words (which are semantically fixed), "giving them as far as I could," he says, "a Christian character." Out came the familiar Christian hymn, *The God of Abraham Praise*!

So if music is a language, it is a different sort of language than words. It is *syntactic*, whereas words are mostly *semantic*. And whereas sentences are *open* systems, musical phrases are *closed* systems. A *verbal* idea is a *semantic* unit of thought embedded in an *open* system. A *musical* idea is a *syntactic* unit of thought embedded in a *closed* system. Music and words are not the same thing at all. Sometimes musicians who hear me describe music as "only" syntactic and closed (but not open) make the mistake of thinking that I must be putting music on a lower level than words; I hasten therefore, to correct any such misunderstanding. Neither "open" nor "closed" is an evaluative term, and semantic meaning can be seen, if anything, as a *defect* in verbal language just as much as it can be viewed as an enrichment. The fact that C H I L D has specific semantic content renders it easily accessible for almost anyone to manipulate in a sentence, whereas musical meaning, which is syntactic only, places music on a much higher level, far beyond the capacity of just anyone to compose with it. Semantics tends to restrict, not enhance, creative potential. Witness poetry, which is widely regarded as the pinnacle of verbal accomplishment precisely because poetry is as close as literary composition ever comes to music! In poetry words begin losing their locked-in semantic meaning, while at the same time they depend increasingly on syntactic recollection. So music is not a lesser form of communication just because it functions differently. But it does function differently, and since we are dealing with the performative nature of communication channels, we have to take music's way of functioning into account when we ask, "How does music perform differently than words?"

How Music Performs in Prayer

1. Music as a Support System for Words

The first thing that comes to mind when we are asked about the role of sacred music is its ability to serve as a support system for the lyrics of prayers. The assumption seems to be that the prayer being expressed musically is saying something in its verbiage, so that the music selected should somehow enhance the verbal message of the text. Thus the usual procedure is for liturgical composers to depend on a prior text, which they are commissioned to set to music, meaning that they are to attempt to outfit the text in question with appropriately expressive sound. I have no quarrel with this familiar rationale for sacred music, but I think people use it in a very limited way. They make the mistake of thinking that the text, which the music illustrates, must be descriptive of some state of affairs that the text describes.

There are two problems with this approach. First, if music has no semantic content, it is hard to see how it can describe any state of affairs at all. That is precisely the problem with advanced program music that purports to describe something outside itself, but does so not just by imitating the bleating of a lamb or the chirping of a bird. I have in mind the great program pieces of the eighteenth century onward, like Berlioz's *Symphonie Fantastique*, Beethoven's *Pastoral Symphony*, or Tchaikovsky's *Romeo and Juliet*. These composers do sometimes merely imitate: think of the cannon fire in Tchaikovsky's *1812 Overture*. But in general these complex program compositions are far more subtle than that. As Aaron Copland, a modern master in the art of program composition, explains:

> There are two kinds of descriptive music. The first comes under the heading of literal description. A composer wishes to recreate the

259

sound of bells in the night. He therefore writes certain chords . . . which actually sound like bells in the night. Something real is being imitated realistically . . . The work has no other *raison d'etre* than mere imitation at that point.

The other type of descriptive music is less literal and more poetic. *No attempt is made to describe a particular scene or event; nevertheless, some outward circumstance arouses certain emotions in the composer which he wishes to communicate to the listener.* It may be clouds or the sea or an airplane. But the point is that instead of literal imitation, one gets a musicopoetic transcription of a phenomenon as reflected in the composer's mind. That constitutes a higher form of program music. The bleating of sheep will always be the bleating of sheep [we would say, the notes that imitate the bleating of sheep have *semantic* content, given by the sound's inseparable association with sheep], but a cloud portrayed in music allows the imagination more freedom.

Composers of advanced music often have to indicate in words what their composition "is about." Tchaikovsky wrote *Romeo and Juliet,* for example, which we can enjoy merely as music. We have to know the story first, however, if we are also to recognize that, more than just an exciting musical notation, the first theme is symbolic of the fight between the Capulets and the Montagues. So, to say that sacred music is primarily intended to express the text of a given prayer presupposes that everyone knows the prayer and that its musical expression works in a subtle way beyond direct description, like the clouds in Copland's example, not the sheep. As I say, I have no quarrel with that, but imagining that the function of sacred music is *only* to express sacred text is as limiting as imagining that symphonic music must always, or even primarily, be programmatic. Surely music goes beyond this narrow definition of function.

There is also a second objection to the usual justification of sacred music as primarily expressive of a prayer's text. This objection is not musical, but textual, for if this simplistic definition of music underestimates the power of music, it also underestimates the scope of words. As we saw above, liturgical sentences are rarely just descriptions of things. They perform in the sense that they bring into being certain states of affairs, or they recollect, or they express hope, or they commit us to a vision, and so on. It is not wrong to think of music as a support for the text, therefore, but insofar as music does so, what it supports is the text's function, not its literal meaning. Take the Song of the Sea, a liturgical staple in Jewish worship wherein God's saving grace in parting the sea before the escaping Israelites is remembered (*mi Khamokha*). The music should not be imagined as actually picturing each and every word of the text that celebrates the crossing. The real question to be asked is what the text *does*, not what it *pictures*. If its performative task is recalling the crossing, for example, the music might be soft and melodic, evocative of fond recollection, rather than a stirring rendition of an actual sea parting its waves; if the text functions as a promise of God's salvation yet to come, the music might express hope or confidence in the future, perhaps making use of a traditional motif expressive of the Jewish historical past or borrowed directly from the cantillation traditionally associated with the Song of the Sea in the Bible. Whatever choice decided on by the composer, the music should *do* what the text does, but not necessarily mean every word that the text literally says.

But the main performative function of music is not dependent on the words of the text at all. Only a word-centered culture like our own would make the mistake of reducing all the arts to alternative expressions of verbal messages! Music has its own way of speaking to us. What appears first to be a weakness—it is a closed system dependent on syntactics, not semantics—is actually no weakness at all, but a strength. We have to move, therefore, to the ways in which music operates purely as music in our worship.

2. Music as the Structuring of Time

Music speaks to us, we said, because of its syntactic connections. We recognize melody lines we have heard before. We hear a sound, think back, and remember that this same set of tones comes to us every year at this time. On New Year's Eve, for example, we hear *Auld Lang Syne* by a different band in a different key to a somewhat altered tempo, but we know what it is, and we think "A new year!" Christmas carols tell Christians it is Christmas again. Shabbat hymns tell Jews the Sabbath is at hand, just as the *Adir Hu* melody tells them it is Passover time and the familiar strains of *Kol Nidre*—whose Aramaic text they do not even understand!—announces Yom Kippur.

How different this is from words! A word that is invested with semantic meaning becomes an independent building block for use in an infinite number of sentences, but loses thereby the intrinsic ability to connect one point in time with another. Music, however, never abandons its syntactic connections with its past. Music thus functions on its own to structure time. Musical tradition is the record of musical syntax, the association of certain sounds with certain events and seasons in the sacred calendar.

3. Music as Communal Bonding

If music binds us to our common past by virtue of its syntactic evocation of temporal associations that we share, it bonds us to other hearers in our present as well. This bonding function is not unlike what we called a *fused focus*. The example was a visual focus by which isolated individuals are led to fuse their individual attention on a common spot or event: Romeo looking at Juliet (in a drama); the priest holding aloft the cup (in the mass). But there is an aural fusion of focus, too. We listen to the same symphony and experience its tensions and resolutions together, so that, even though the concert hall is so dark we cannot even see each other, we emerge as a group—recall last chapter's example of the "network effect," prompted by the Dixieland jazz session, that got everyone moving "in sync." For some music and in some contexts—some of them religious, the tradition in many Black churches, for example—we actually move together, beating time, swaying, clapping, or singing. Sometimes the effect is to fasten everyone's attention on a particular *event* being celebrated in the liturgy; alternatively, it may establish a shared *emotion* or even just a sense of sharing the *experience* of a common melody with common associations for everyone present. Whatever the reason, the music works, as mere words do not, to develop a fused group focus. Music thus acts to convert individuals into a group where they can experience together the message of the alternative world being established in their prayers.

4. Music as Emotion

Without doubt, people get emotional about music in ways that they do not when they hear mere words. Philosophers from the beginning of time have recognized this unique ability of music to move us, sometimes to tears (of sorrow or of joy), sometimes to revolutionary zeal (there is a reason armies march to battle to the strains of drums and bugle), and sometimes to more complex emotional states we never even knew we could realize.

Why music should possess this unique capacity to stir our emotions is not at all clear. Is it something inherent in musical structures? Is such musical power universal, or is it dependent on cultural training? These are examples of questions prompted by the recognition of music's power to soothe or to anger, to satisfy or to antagonize. In part, certainly, music's emotional strength seems related to what it is, music, and therefore to whatever elements constitute music as its own art form. In part, too, it derives from the fact that music is a syntactic code, which recalls the past to memory and serves, therefore, as an ideal medium of recollection. We saw that symbolizing depends on just that uniquely human propensity to remember, and that symbols, by definition, are those items about which we feel most strongly even without rational reasons to justify those feelings. So in addition to whatever inherent technical quality of music stirs us to great feeling, we should not pass lightly over the fact that the sounds we hear today attain meaning because we once heard them somewhere else: in our youth perhaps, as a lullaby sung while we rested in a parent's lap; or on Christmas Eve or *Kol Nidre* night; or in peer groups where, as teenagers, we discovered our first glimpse of independent adulthood.

So the emotions music prompts are really two kinds. First there are compositions that stir our feelings for technical reasons that composers may understand or not, but which they surely set into motion by the insight that constitutes their claim to musical genius. I don't suppose every human being on the face of the earth is automatically moved in the same way by, say, Beethoven's *Violin Concerto,* but in the western world, at least, where ears are trained to hear the same potential sets of sounds the same way, very many people are. And parallels must surely exist in other cultures. Thus, when people trained to appreciate the art of music for its own sake say they want only the finest music in their sacred repertoire of sound, it is because they know the incomparably sublime sense that grips them when they hear good compositions. On the other hand, emotions well up, too, when we recall the very structured sense of time to which I keep returning in chapter after chapter. We human beings cannot bear the thought of senseless anarchy; we need to pattern our lives in terms of recurrent events, from the memory of things that happened long before we were born (religious fasts and feasts) to the recollection of episodes drawn from our biographies (birthday parties, fiftieth wedding anniversaries). True, great music has its own inherent musical structures that somehow speak to us; but ordinary music, too, sometimes *symbolizes*, in that it draws on its syntactic power to bring to mind our past, to remind us of the cyclical passing of the years, and thus of the moments that mattered once and (through musical recapitulation) matter still. This is the second kind of emotionality stirred by music, all music, but sacred music, too, so that sometimes it is not great music we are after in our sacred services, but just music that symbolizes for us: the Christmas carol of our youth or the strains of *Kol Nidre*, without which it would seem that Christmas or Yom Kippur does not even arrive.

* * *

In the last chapter, while dealing with the texts we say, I introduced the name of Ludwig Wittgenstein, an extraordinary genius of our century. Now in concluding the chapter on the texts we sing, I want to invoke the insight of a second creative intellect, the French anthropologist Claude Lévi-Strauss. Lévi-Strauss's interests ranged far and wide, but he retained a lifelong fascination with ritual and saw clearly the necessary complementarity between speech and song in the life of the spirit. His magnum opus is a four-volume *Science of Mythology*, the chapters of which he labeled as if they were sequential parts of a musical score. The introduction was thus called "Overture", and the conclusion (some 1,600 pages later!) he named "Finale."

In the "Finale" Lévi-Strauss turned to a consideration of myth and music, which he conceived as similar to mathematics in that all three are part and parcel of the same human need to structure the universe in meaningful ways. Mathematics is pure structure, just an assemblage of random X's and Y's joined by arbitrary signs signaling functions like addition or subtraction, multiplication or division. The brain must work mathematically as it forces the data of consciousness into logical categories without which we would be overwhelmed by pure chaos, the anomie and entropy of which I have been speaking all along. But human society functions by many channels of communication, not just purely cognitive structures that one brain shares directly with another. So the structures we impose on reality must be communicable from person to person, generation to generation. Lévi-Strauss saw two such communication channels, if you will: pure sound heard without any cognitive content, and pure cognitive content heard without any differentiation in sound. The former ("pure sound") is music; the latter ("pure sense," as he called it) is myth. By myth he meant more than some vague recollection of Greek or Norse stories of heroes. He had in mind the universal practice of telling tales about the world: as diverse as the myth of the chickadee's origin, which he found among the American Indians, and the myth of Oedipus that we inherit from the Greeks. Myths are like our spoken texts in prayer: they are "pure sense" in that they provide cognitive content and depend on the meaning of their words to get their point across. At the other extreme is our repertoire of music in its absolute form, "pure sound," dependent on the mathematical arrangement of notes to communicate its message.

Human beings, however, require both "sound" and "sense" to complete their understanding of reality. We are neither pure mathematical intellects nor pure "sense" or "sound" users; having transformed the brain's pure mathematical logic into scripts that "say" and scores that "sound," we then seek to unite the two into fully satisfying rituals celebrative of the whole human experience. That seems to me to be the essence of how ritual works: the combination of "sense" and "sound," our two primary human channels for communicating to one another the patterned structuring of experience.

Thus it is rare for religious ritual to feature texts that are rendered as if they were pure readings: instead, we develop chants, traditional singsong ways of declaiming them, ways in which the "pure sense" of the text moves toward the satisfying middle ground where sense and sound come together. When I read prayers that worshipers expect to be sung, they are invariably dis-illusioned, as if the prayer wasn't really "said." Of course it was "said," but the whole point of prayer is that "saying texts" is not like "saying the alphabet" or "saying out loud the content of a story." "Saying" a prayer is unlike any other "saying." It cannot be judged the way we judge other reading events in our repertoire of what to do with words. It must be judged for what it is, worship, the ritual recitation of a text, where "sense" must eventually be joined with "sound" in an exercise of imposing structure on chaos.

Similarly it is rare to find pure music in ritual. We have pure in-strumental music here and there, but it does not predominate. As we saw in the first function of sacred music discussed above, most church or synagogue composers attest that their art lies in inter-preting the sense behind a sacred text or teaching, not arranging pure musical notation in such a way that music as "pure sound" occurs. They write musical interpretations "of something": of *Ave Maria*, for example, Psalm 150, or the *Kedushah*. Here, too, then, the "pure" form of the communication is sacrificed as the "pure sound" is outfitted with words. *In ritual, just as the "pure sense" of the spoken text attracts the "sound" of chanting, so the "pure sound" of musi-cal notation is given lyrics that "make sense."*

At its best, ritual is the experience of pattern. In content and form it imposes order, creating what we called an alternative world. That world is expressed through a text that is both spoken and sung. Together sense and sound create a universe that did not exist beforehand.

Huffman,
The Art of Public
Prayer

13

System Intervention

Summary

IT IS TIME TO RETURN to where we began: the twin axes of worship that we laid down in the introductory chapters as the dual focus of worship systems. We said then that group prayer has a *horizontal* axis and a *vertical* one.

The *horizontal* axis is the way in which, as individual worshipers, we feel ourselves drawn together into a single unified group. The group galvanizes our commitment around the vision of its own particular alternative world, in opposition to the many competing loyalties that claim our attention. Establishing the sense of our own worshiping group's ultimate claim on our allegiance depends on the ability of our rituals to articulate the *favorite themes and conventions* of our religious tradition in a convincing way. When we go through the script of our own group's worship, we make it our own, acknowledging that the way it has always seen the world is still our way, albeit with some alterations derived from the contemporary *styles* that govern the way all groups in our culture—not just our own—perceive their past.

In addition we said that worship requires a *vertical* axis, which we defined as the worshipers' recognition of God's presence. It must be clear, in other words, that we really are praying, not just meeting for some alternative end, like marking the close of the bowling season or sitting around a campfire. God's presence today, I indicated, is more likely to be evident in the intimacy of community than it is in the awesome grandeur that marked the ambience of European-based worship styles. That says less about God, mind you, than it does about ourselves. I do not mean to make any philosophical assumptions about God when I pass judgment on styles of prayer; God is, after all, beyond being captured in any particular sensory guise. What is at issue is ourselves, or more particularly the dominant mode of viewing our world in any given time and place. It is almost as if each culture develops its own set of lenses through which to see reality. Earlier ages saw things through glasses that projected everything outward, emphasizing grandeur and might, magnifying distance between people, classes, nations, and even supernatural beings called angelic bands—and beyond even them they saw the reality of God.

We, on the other hand, seem to have exchanged those projecting lenses for a set of eyeglasses that makes everything seem nearer than it was before—like the effect of using an old telescope, but discovering that we have been looking through the wrong end: we turn it around and discover that the distant horizon is not really as far away as we imagined. Indeed the story of the twentieth century is just that: the process of bringing distant horizons closer and shrinking the expanse of space between ourselves and others. We land men and women on the moon and send spacecraft to Jupiter to radio back pictures of what seem like the ends of a galaxy. Television brings us instantaneous images of distant wars and faraway cultures. The world becomes what Marshall McLuhan called a global village, and we begin to think we are more apt to run into God, not in the endless reaches of space and time, but in a global town meeting, along with the other villagers who inhabit the immediate place we call home. Thus is born a new *master image*, as I called it, a vision of God in keeping with the *cultural backdrop* of our age and dependent on the *vocabulary* of communication with which we have easy familiarity.

This expanded conception of *vocabulary* to include more than lists of words in grade-school textbooks evokes our discussion of the many modes of cataloguing reality and relaying to each other the *meaning* we think reality holds. We thus discussed space, text, and song; all of which come together in the unique dramatic art form we call worship. They function somewhat differently from each other, to be sure, since they are rooted in different media. I have mentioned some aspects of each, and surely thoughtful readers can add to my list. But beyond the specific tasks we allot to each one, there is a common criterion for them all, namely, their ability to support a worship system that works. Worshipers must be led to recognize themselves as proud continuers of their religious tradition, bonded together in common pursuit in a way that makes God's presence manifest.

Critiquing Change

So far, we have spoken of worship as if it were simply a matter of appropriate artistic skill: the competent dramatic management of space, words, and music, particularly, but blended together to constitute the composite art we call worship. To a great extent that is exactly the case. Very frequently worship fails because those charged with its presentation lack the requisite skills, usually because they have never even considered what those skills are. On the other hand, it should be quite clear that authentic worship in any of the great religious traditions goes well beyond mere artistic entertainment. *Elmer Gantry* was a great American novel exploring the possibility of what can happen when the artistic potential of worship is misused by someone who manipulates its artistry for the emotional effect it can have on worshipers. Every once in a while, our newspapers or television screens bring us images of modern-day Elmer Gantrys, cult leaders who regularly discover what artistic competence divorced from integrity can do. Religions thus provide their own built-in safeguards against the possibility that their liturgies or sacred assemblies will be misused. These are their *liturgical traditions*.

I want to spend just a moment on the issue of becoming judgmental when it comes to our community's prayer forms. From what I've said so far, it should be clear that the most common error today is our failure to change old and practically comatose habits; but it would be a grave error if we were to solve that problem by a pendulum swing to the opposite but equally undesirable extreme of promoting wholesale change for the sake of instant emotional gratification, without due regard to the safeguards and values that our traditions themselves have established.

We can begin by noting how liturgy is both like and unlike theater. To be sure, like any great play, the liturgical dramas are compelling in their own right, simply by virtue of the insights they contain. Prayer books can, after all, be read and studied for their messages of the human condition, no less than the scripts of great plays can. If we are moved to read or to sing our religious dramas with conviction, it is partly for the same reason that brilliant scripts invite great acting.

The analogy of the world of great theater is not entirely adequate, however. Think of how a play comes into being. A playwright expresses his or her own vision of a human situation, hoping that it will prove convincing enough to attract the attention it deserves. The burden of proof is entirely on the playwright. Of a thousand new plays every year, only a handful are produced successfully, and of those, only one or two, perhaps, prove powerful enough to warrant being called great drama. The liturgical script, on the other hand, is largely unchanging through the ages. Not that new prayers aren't added with some regularity; they are. But the editors of new prayers and prayer books know that the burden of proof is on them to prove not only the literary adequacy of what they have written, but the fact that their creativity is directly linked to their traditions. A poet who writes a eucharistic prayer must demonstrate not only that it is good poetry; it must also be good theology; it must fit the liturgical prescription, so to speak, for the service. Thus, in the long run, prayers are entrusted to committees, while plays never are. The former are seen to be the concern of the community whereas the latter are judged to fall within the domain of the individually creative artist.

Both plays and liturgies stand in lines of traditions, but their traditions have different degrees of moral power associated with them. Take theater first. In earlier chapters we saw how individual pieces of art are linked to one another in an artistic tradition. In music, for example, one composer can write a variation on a theme used by another composer. In films, once a great director (like Alfred Hitchcock) experiments with a novel means of presentation—the shower scene in *Psycho*, for example—any number of later directors will try variations on that cinematographic model. Archibald MacLeish could not have composed *J.B.* had he not read Job first—not as a book of the Bible, mind you, but as a human theme in world literature, since *J.B.* makes no pretense at being sacred writ, but does constitute an artistic variation on an earlier piece of artistry. Like any other art form, then, some dramatic productions stand out from others as constituting their own set of *themes* and *conventions*; that is to say, they represent one theatrical *tradition* rather than another, like theater of the absurd or existential drama. Likewise there are schools of music and fine art, baroque as opposed to romanticism, say, or cubism as opposed to impressionism.

Still, purely theatrical or artistic *traditions* differ from religious traditions in this all-important respect: they do not come packaged with a very strong moral demand upon us to adopt them as our own. Culturally sophisticated parents may instruct their children to develop a taste for Beckett, Brecht, and Bach; but if they opt instead for the "Mad Dog Raving Rock Band and Its Celebrated Light Show," the most they are guilty of is bad taste—a sin only somewhat higher than preferring fast food to French cuisine and considerably lower than exercising moral indiscretions like marital infidelity and stock manipulation.

In sum: religious traditions are different from artistic ones not because they are not also artistic, but because they are not purely so; they share the moral imperative associated not with the arts but with ethics. So the drama of liturgy establishes an alternative world in which we find more than the personal insight of a particular artist, who presents that insight according to his or her own artistic tradition's preferred conventions. It is possible, and even (perhaps) probable, that we will be more likely to avoid alcohol after the conclusion of a performance of *Cat on a Hot Tin Roof*. Tennessee Williams was himself an alcoholic who knew something about the illness that eventually killed him, and he poured all the pathos of his own tormented existence into the character of Brick, who says of life, "I want to dodge away from it." But even though Williams portrayed the pathos of alcoholic addiction while at the same time suffering from it, no one accuses him of hypocrisy. With religious dramas, on the other hand, prophets who steal, commit adultery, or defraud their publics are unmasked, declared false, and disowned by their constituents. Even if they are pardoned for the inherent human frailty to which we all are heir, there is the sense that they should have striven to rise above their failures, for *religious visions make demands on us that purely artistic visions do not*. Liturgies do not present their alternative worlds on a "take it or leave it" basis alone. Even religions that hold alcoholism to be an illness, not a sin, expect parishioners who hear a sermon on the subject to work wholeheartedly to limit drunk driving or to support truth in advertising for glitzy liquor ads that

271

identify adult or even teenage drinking with the broad path to popularity.

Liturgies therefore purport to make moral demands on us that transcend the similar claim of dramas in general. It will be helpful to imagine the choices we make arrayed on a scale ranging from pure taste at the bottom to absolute morality at the top. Food tastes are low down in the scale; you either like artichokes or you don't, and if you want to spend a lot of time growing them, studying them, and cooking with them, even going to the point of joining the local branch of the National Artichoke League, the only quarrel I can have with you is that I fail to see how you can spend all your leisure time that way instead of in the Society of Tomato Growers, which attracts my allegiance.

Higher up on the ladder is artistic taste, where different taste cultures tend actually to hold each other guilty for their bad judgment. The history of rock music, for example, demonstrates how musical taste can even go so far as to signify social conflict, as generation after generation of young people adopted new musical styles. Early British rock drew on Reggae music that had grown out of the black emigration from the West Indies; by the 1970s lower class white "Teddy Boys" erupted in waves of violence against blacks and against the sound of early rock music. The rest of the decade was to see a bewildering assortment of successive styles: Mods; Skinheads; the Glam-rock, Teeny-bob, and Punk-rock of David Bowie or the Sex Pistols: these were movements, not just sounds, that symptomized the way in which tastes in art carry baggage that goes well beyond that of tastes in food.

At the highest rung, however, is religion, which does more than symptomize or even display different judgments on how the world should be arranged. It formulates morals, advocates action, and demands we take stands to make the world over in our own religious image. We saw early on in this book that, generically speaking, everything from "the one true church" to "godless communism" can be a religion in this sense, as each tries to implement its own vision on a world in process.

Religious drama, the ritual we call prayer, stands at the upper end of art and the lower side of religion, combining both in an artistic appeal to religious values. And here is where I think our right to be judgmental in religious drama's behalf enters in. The drama of worship that arises out of *religious*, not artistic, traditions

272

makes its own inherent call on us. It goes beyond the claim of artistic excellence. It demands our allegiance on the grounds that the themes it presents and the conventions in which they are presented are right, just, and necessary for us. In so doing, our worship links us on the vertical axis to God, whence we claim the right to make moral judgments in the first place.

First, tradition presents its own *theological* critique of change that threatens to go too far. Worship always has within it a dialectic between continuity with the past and solidarity with the present. On the one hand, tradition bequeaths to us certain *favored themes, portrayed according to prescribed conventions.* We need its time-honored chants, age-old prayers, standard deployment of space, and familiar sacred objects—all of which establish our worship as rooted in the past and appropriate for the present.

But we cannot avoid filtering these age-old verities of vocabulary through the sieve of *contemporary style.* In complex societies like our own there is, of course, more than one single style appropriate to prayer. Musically, for example, sophisticated worshipers will expect artistically competent compositions, since for them, "less [really is] a bore." But others will clamor for a less sophisticated music: in the idiom (or style) borrowed from folk rock, say, or even youth camps. The style we prefer determines our location on a series of spectrums that graph our place in society: we are highly traditional or relatively open to the winds of change; highly ethnic in our identity or suspicious of old ethnic ties; elitists, culturally speaking, or populists.

In utilitarian terms alone, no position on the spectrum is necessarily dysfunctional to worship, as long as the members of the worshiping community in question agree on the decisions that are made and see themselves correctly represented by them. But at some point the change threatens to be so abrupt or extreme that the worshiping group will no longer be seen or see itself as maintaining any continuity with its roots. If it were only a matter of taste, that would hardly matter at all. But since religious identity carries echoes of obligation, we ought to pause before allowing our contemporary style completely to sever the connections we have with our past. If our worshiping group develops in ways completely different from others, we will soon have little relationship to them; if we stake out brave new directions relative to our ancestors, we may equally well soon share little of the ancestral faith itself. So the artistic considerations laid down throughout this book must always be seen against the appropriate judgmental perspective of the traditions to which they are applied. Granted the scientific fact that artistically competent worship will develop group identity, liturgical planners need always keep in mind the nature of the successful identity that will result, and use the art of worship in the service of religious responsibility.

The same critique can be seen from the perspective of the vertical axis, which I called *locating God among us*. Theology can challenge the experience that worshipers say they have of God, proclaiming that it is really not God whom they experience, but what has traditionally been called "idolatry" or "heresy." Tradition thus tells us at some point that we are going too far, abandoning time-honored practices, or introducing such enormous novelty that the connection between our worship and that worship's roots is being severed. The god we worship is not the God of our ancestral faith, goes the claim.

Secondly, there is a *pragmatic* critique that must be borne in mind, particularly regarding the vertical axis of prayer. In purely pragmatic terms, there may be little excuse for a negative judgment regarding the horizontal axis of group identity, since, horizontally speaking, group identity may be just as good as any other. Wary traditionalists or creative modernists, proud ethnics or universalist advocates of the melting-pot syndrome, cultural elitists or ardent populists—as long as they remain within the boundaries established by the theological critique of their own traditions, all of these may claim an equal right to exist, and by virtue of the fact that their members' shared artistic taste is reflected in their worship, they may all know equally the satisfaction of belonging to a group that matters.

But regarding the *vertical* axis, the possibility of recognizing God's presence in prayer, I am less certain of the chance of just any group succeeding. In the end they must all conjure with the pervasive influence of the *cultural backdrop*. Here and there are surely pockets of identity where people are immune from the dominant American denial of social distance and its call for the emergence of caring communities to take the place of the extended families and close-knit neighborhoods that once characterized the landscapes of our lives. But the overwhelming preponderance of worshipers cannot long escape the grim realities of a social life progressively more bereft of natural communities; and it is doubtful whether limited liability communities that traffic in *signs* but not in *symbols* can evoke the sure knowledge that God is among us.

With regard to the vertical axis, then, I cannot emphasize enough the need to develop our worship in the direction of symbolic communication that enhances the sense of community in which the presence of God is manifest, rather than the nineteenth-century sense of awe that projected God into the distant void. *We need spaces that do not separate laity from clergy; music that collapses social distance; accessible warm melodies and poetically touching texts.* Except on special occasions, it is not high drama that matters. In addition, we must avoid communicative messages (like sexist language) that exclude those about whom we say we care. We must rearrange seats so that people can see each other; encourage people to know who sits beside them; extend the liturgical action into the congregation or assembly; make Regulars aware of the presence of Watchers; and let the people themselves do the praying by singing, proclaiming, and acting out the script in the sure knowledge that it is *theirs*, not the guarded turf of professionals who are there to do it for them. We must discover the joy of knowing how it feels to be part of a closely knit fabric of people in touch with other people, an environment of absolute care and what we called total liability; for there it is that we find God.

Our failure to accomplish these ends is only partly explainable by our persistent refusal to adopt the right communication. Only partially can we lay our failure at "someone's" door: professionals charged with being ill-equipped, poorly trained, or pathologically immune to altering age-old habits; or "the people nowadays," who seem spiritually impregnable in a cultural fortress of rampant materialism. Scapegoating will not do. To be sure, those planning the liturgy, both professionals and laypeople, require a sense of worship as an art. They need to appreciate how worship works and to consider, in that regard, the music they use, the texts they read, the space they occupy, and the props they handle. But even if we were all *individually* to master the art of worship, claiming competence as well in all its various component arts, we would still have no guarantee that *together* our efforts would succeed. That is because people working together are a system. With

275

systems we began; and with systems we should end—for we have yet to look at the most persistent obstacle that stands in the way of worship: the fact that vested interests of all sorts conspire to keep systems intact, even dysfunctional systems, which may not be very effective at worship, but, true to the Law of Systems we postulated earlier, are surely quite effective at doing something else. The solution to our worship problems must go deeper than the art of worship alone. It must tackle the systemic nature of the church or synagogue in which the worship occurs by bringing to bear the joint participation of all its interfacing parts in an effort to make the system work for us, not against us. We call such systemic problem solving *systems intervention.*

Systems Intervention

Systems intervention is a common strategy for all helping agents called on to tackle a problem from the outside:

—a psychiatrist counsels an alcoholic, but also his or her family, trying to get at what too much drinking does "successfully," even as it destroys the fabric of family life. Alcohol may be inefficient as a family bonding mechanism, but even knowing that, the alcoholic needs to drink to excess, in part because it may very successfully prevent the family's coming to terms with other emotional issues that have been buried for years beneath the surface.

—a basketball coach wonders why his star center cannot execute plays with one particular guard feeding him the ball. Reasoning that it can't be a deficiency in the center's native ability, he inquires about this and that, and eventually discovers that both the center and the guard come from the same small town, where they were in competition all the way through school. The center was successfully refusing to compete again with his old high-school rival.

In these, as in all instances of a mysteriously chronic failure to perform adequately at the official task in question, we need to remember our corollary to the Law of Systems, namely, that all institutions have not one but two sets of defined goals. One is publicly proclaimed as official; the other is never even acknowledged—but when the two are in conflict, the unofficial one is the only one that counts.

When Freud first studied human nature, he shocked the world by revealing that individual men and women are at war with themselves in just this way. As individuals we too have conflicting agendas: not just the official goals and standards that we say motivate us, but the unofficial ones as well. Further study led him to see that we adopt complex rules of behavior ostensibly designed to accomplish our official goals, but which work instead in just the opposite way. Rather than make it more likely that we will succeed at our officially defined tasks, they serve as defense mechanisms to seal in all the neuroses that stand in our way! Think of the compulsive executive who has worked for a public company for over forty years now and has never thrown out a single piece of paper. As everyone in the office knows, he spends so much time filing that he never has a chance to consult anything that is already put away. He *says* he will some day write a great case study of the corporation where he works, and he wants to have all the paperwork ready at hand for his research. But he will never get around to the research; he will die still filing; and that is the point of the whole exercise, not the official point, but the unofficial one, the only one that counts, remember. He is afraid to start writing for fear of failure. So with the presumed good intention of making writing easier, he actually makes it impossible. He is his own worst enemy.

Institutions are like people. They just require a little more tacit collusion among their parts, that's all. They, too, become their own worst enemy, erecting a series of procedures designed to make things work efficiently, but which actually stand in the way of real job success. Their actual function is to protect the vested interests of unofficial goals that are never even acknowledged. The only way to get beyond them is to break down the collusion. And the only way to do that is to get the people doing the colluding to ask basic questions together about why they do what they do.

Plenty of examples of institutional collusion are found in the literature on corporate life. We tend to think of corporate giants as profitable maximizers of the human penchant for rational decision-making. It seems ludicrous to imagine that the Fortune 500 firms are riddled with inefficient bumblers on a par with our own family. But they are. Every once in a while, a mammoth miscalculation comes to our attention—an Edsel, say, which no one wants to buy, and we wonder, "How could Ford have produced that thing?" What we do not so readily note, however, are the daily little things that prevent full productivity, the offices that cannot function, the paperwork that gets done wrong every time, the bureaucratic bungling that comes our way only after being converted into higher prices passed along to the consumers.

Thomas Peters and Robert Waterman studied America's best-run companies to see what makes them excellent, and concluded (among other things) that the rational model of corporate management is a giant piece of fiction. They chronicle case after case of institutional defense mechanism in which rational decision-makers armed with postgraduate degrees work long hours designing more academically sound mathematical projections at the cost of losing the competitive edge in the real world; where overly rule-conscious managers seek efficiency in a smoothly running machine with a rule for everything, little realizing that the rules they invent to grease the machine are really slowing it down to a crawl.

Their investigations should lead us to think more nervously about the claims of churches and synagogues, too, for it is a truism by now that religious institutions have adopted corporate models for their own structure and operation. We have boards, committees, elections, and even that elusive thing called "company culture," the hard-to-define element that makes one church different from another. The woman who belonged to "Fort Baptist" knew what it was to affiliate with a religious corporation in which a senior pastor is elected as the Chief Executive Officer charged with selling the product, namely religion, to a larger and larger market share. It is not that I have any quarrel with the corporate model. When royal courts were in fashion, churches were like palaces, and bishops were like princes, after all. No, I am certainly not arguing that we abandon corporate religion; I am saying that if we are going to be corporations, then within the bounds of our ethics and principles, we should at least be good at it. We should be among the ones Peters and Waterman cite as worth emulating in their book *In Search of Excellence.*

How would your church or synagogue have fared in the study?

—Good corporations, they say, have a bias for action, any action, rather than for multiplying paperwork that pretends to be action, but really stifles it.

—Good corporations care deeply for the customer.

—Good corporations foster creative competition and value creative souls, whom the authors call "product champions."

The beginning of change is an objective estimate of how hard it will be to get change to occur. If your church or synagogue is filled with paperwork, but not activity; if you haven't seen ninety per cent of the parishioners or congregants in years, so that you haven't sought out with some regularity what they think of your "product"; if there is little competition among the professional staff and the board regulars to try out new ideas and do things differently; and if you find instead an innate conservatism that would squelch any product champion in a maze of committee red tape, then face it: your house of prayer is suffering from institutional defense mechanisms equally as deleterious as those Freud found in his neurotic patients. Nothing will change until the system comes to terms with itself.

That, then, is the first and all-important step: coming to terms with what we are. It is a charge that should not sound foreign to people engaged in religion! Should we not demand of ourselves, at the outset, a fair accounting of what we do wrong? If we do not ask that hard question, we will emerge from committee meetings on our worship with the "sound" decision that this or that scapegoated element in our midst is at fault, whereas the real culprit is the institution itself, which has yet to get as far as Pogo, who knew that he had met the enemy and "the enemy is us!"

Only people inside the church or synagogue in question can actually say what is going wrong with their own worship. They may be unconsciously protecting an old status quo rather than experimenting with novelty. They may be protecting their flank against a new incursion of members with new values or different ethnic sensitivities. They may have to revise an old, rational religious school model. They may have to face up to the fact that they were raised in an era and place that gave little credence to spiritual claims, even though official ideology said the opposite, so that as adults now they have difficulty confronting their own spirituality. In the discussion that focuses on these and other problems, much much more will surface, too. Not unlike a patient in therapy, the "worship care committee"—which is what I will call the representatives of the religious community who come together to ask the hard questions—will have to learn how to be open with each other in a freewheeling stream of consciousness that moves around and through many topics until the pieces fall into place, pointing to a sense of the truth about why the institution the committee represents has ended up the way it has. Like therapy, too, it will require mutual understanding and acceptance of the foibles that plague us all, insofar as we are all human. And in that trusting atmosphere, individual members of the committee will be moved to see how they, personally, may have joined the collusion effort for their own gain. One person is afraid of change in general; another thinks that a new way of worship threatens his strongly held values; a third would do things differently, if only she had been trained to; a fourth really doesn't care what the Watchers think, and if the truth be told, would rather not co-opt their help for fear that "help" leads to "empowerment."

All the systems are involved. The school may have to move the annual event of honoring its teachers out of the sanctuary and back into the classroom. The sisterhood may have to give up its *pro forma* sisterhood Sabbath—or do it differently, anyway. The rabbi or minister may have to move the pulpit from which she or he preaches down to the pew level for dialogue. The cantor may have to find new music, hire a flutist, or learn to teach congregational singing. (The board may have to vote the money to make it possible for the cantor to attend a summer institute where this latter skill is taught and, in the meantime, be supportive of all the other things that the cantor does well, as he or she pursues professional retooling!) The lighting may have to be changed, and the seating redesigned. And so on. Only the community engaged in honest self-evaluation will have the answers, and only slowly, after long and patient struggle, in a caring and supporting network of community members who have come together because they believe worship can work.

Ironically, just the effort to formulate such a group will go a long way toward solving the problem, if only because such a committee, which meets in the mutual spirit of spiritual self-discovery, best exemplifies the caring community of which we spoke earlier when we noted the need for a totally liable religious community to take the place of extended families and functioning neighborhoods.

I have rarely seen liturgical problems that are not really, at a deeper level still, communal problems. Solve the problem of the absence of community, and we go a long way toward solving the problem of the absence of prayer. I do not know if (as the old saying used to go), "the family that prays together stays together"; but I am convinced that the community of souls who are so accepting of each other that they want to stay together will probably want also to pray together. And then it will be true that their successful liturgical celebration of community—and of God in their midst—will further enhance their chances of staying together. For their worship will be just that—*theirs, born of their mutual self-discovery that they are a people of God, charged with a mission* to care for one another and, together, to care for a world. They will discover their communal bonds even as they sink roots deeply into their communal past, linking them to generations long gone by and generations yet to come; and through it all, they will find, in their own way, the presence of the voice that they call God, calling them to a sense of meaning in their lives that only the art of worship gives. In the charged atmosphere of discovery, age-old liturgical signs will become symbols; empty ritualizations will become rituals; and emerging crystal-clear and luminous in their clarity, in sanctuaries once best known as "bare ruined choirs," will be the Ritual Moments for which we yearn. At bottom, this quest to celebrate human meaning is a religious quest; and it is never too late for that quest to begin.

APPENDIX

FOR FURTHER READING

I am not sure exactly when and where the ideas in this book occurred to me. Largely the outgrowth of a decade or so of thinking and teaching about prayer, they seem, on retrospect, to have taken shape slowly over time, partly in response to reading other people's theories, but mostly as a form of personal dialogue within myself, in which I have steadfastly tried to argue that the spiritual impoverishment that marks public worship in our churches and synagogues need not be accepted as inevitable.

Still I owe a great deal to people who have thought through similar problems in other disciplines. I have cited some of them and referred to others. What follows is an annotated list of sources to whom I am beholden.

Of all the social sciences, anthropology has been my best teacher, so it is fitting that my Introduction opens with a citation from Colin M. Turnbull, *The Human Cycle* (New York: Simon and Schuster, 1983). The closing vignette comes from Clifford Geertz, *Islam Observed* (Chicago: University of Chicago Press, 1971).

The discussion in Chapter One is directly related to Abraham H. Maslow, *Religions, Values and Peak Experiences* (1964; reprinted with a new introduction, New York: Viking, 1970), and the brief but insightful discussions of time by Edward T. Hall in *The Silent Language* (New York: Doubleday Anchor, 1973) and *Beyond Culture* (New York: Doubleday Anchor, 1977). That there are many institutions whose rituals approximate in some way those we call religious is by now a truism, but I first came to the idea by reading Michael Novak, *The Joy of Sports* (New York: Basic Books, 1976). Recognition of the religious nature of civic and political ritual, such as the political conventions I describe, goes back to the literature on civic religion, which by now is considerable, but was initiated by Robert N. Bellah's 1967 *Daedalus* article, "Civil Religion in America." It is reprinted with his own afterthoughts and several other excellent essays in Russel E. Richey and Donald G. Jones, *American Civil Religion* (New York: Harper and Row,1974). Political ritual *per se* is richly documented by David I. Kertzer in *Ritual, Politics, and Power* (New Haven and London: Yale University Press, 1988). The emptiness of ritualization as opposed to the full satisfaction of true ritual is expressed by, among others, Erik Erikson (especially in *The Life Cycle Completed: A Review* [New York and London: W. W. Norton, 1982]), though not in exactly the way I mean, nor with the same taxonomy that I use.

The literature on symbols is vast and confused, what Edmund Leach calls "a terminological maze." Readers can gain a quick idea of the anarchy implicit in the literature by glancing at the note on page 10 of Leach's *Culture and Communication* (Cambridge: Cambridge University Press, 1976) and then at the article to which he refers us, J. W. Fernandez, "Symbolic Consensus in a Fang Reformative Cult," *American Anthropologist* 67 (1965): 902-29. Though I do not subscribe to C. G. Jung's general philosophy of archetypes and a collective unconscious, my perspective on symbols (in Chapter Two) is consistent with Jung's dichotomy between symbol and sign, which Jung himself explains in nontechnical terms in his popular *Man and His Symbols* (1964; reprinted, New York: Dell Publishing Co., 1968). The "handbook" to which I refer is by Robert Wetzler and Helen Huntington, *Seasons and Symbols: A Handbook on the Church Year* (Minneapolis: Augsburg Publishing House, 1962). There are others, too, of course: see Gertrude Grace Sill, *A Handbook of Symbols in Christian Art* (New York: Collier Books, 1975), and most recently the appendix to Hoyt L. Hickman, Don E. Saliers, Laurence Hull Stookey, and James F. White, *Handbook of the Christian Year* (Nashville: Abingdon Press, 1986).

Chapters Three through Five all deal with systems theory as applied to worship and can best be handled together here. I first discovered systems thinking by reading the articles in Arthur Koestler and J.R. Smythies, *The Alpbach Symposium: Beyond Reductionism* (1969; reprinted, New York: Macmillan, 1970), especially Paul A. Weiss's exciting discussion of a systemic conceptualization of a living organism (pp. 3-55). Arthur Koestler's more popular *Ghost in the Machine* (Chicago: Henry Regnery Company, 1967) and Ludwig von Bertalanffy's *General System Theory: Foundations, Development, Applications* (New York: George Braziller, Inc., 1975) provided a more general basis for me. Ideas like scapegoating and monitoring came from Albert E. Scheflen with Alice Scheflen, *Body Language and the Social Order: Communication as Behavioral Control* (Englewood Cliffs, New Jersey: Prentice-Hall, 1972). The double-bind inherent in the communication-metacommunication conflict I owe to Gregory Bateson, whose *Steps to an Ecology of Mind* (New York: Ballantine Books, 1972) deserves reading and rereading. In their *Inside the Family: Toward a Theory of Family Process* (1975; reprinted, New York: Harper and Row, 1976), David Kantor and William Lehr showed me what systems thinking could do to reshape the way we think about a problem, and I got the idea for some of my examples from their analyses of family systems. My discussion of relatively homogeneous ethnic or religious communities that we once knew comes from many sources, but is best presented in Maurice R. Stein, *The Eclipse of Community* (Princeton: Princeton University Press, 1960) where a summary of the Chicago school of urban anthropology, to which I refer, is given as well. The symbolic capacity of shared language in such communities is, again, a matter of wide discussion now, but best investigated by Basil Bernstein—see his set of essays available in *Class, Codes and Control* (1971; reprinted, New York: Schocken Books, 1975)—and then utilized creatively indeed by Mary Douglas in her *Natural Symbols* (New York: Random House, 1970) and, in popular format, by Edward T. Hall in *Beyond Culture* (see above).

The Interlude of Chapter Six pleads for the translation of theological ideas into a "neutral" vocabulary. I first came across the idea of a "translation grammar" in Paul M. Van Buren, *The Edges of Language* (New York: Macmillan, 1972). The notion of language communities with their own discourse systems is found in many places now, but a popular introduction exists in Peter Farb, *Word Play* (New York: Knopf, 1974). I borrowed the idea of "teenspeak" from (of all places) an article I came across in an airline magazine: Michael Anania, "Teenspeak," *Review* (April 1987): 44-9. Examples of specialized languages that I used are found in Nathan Silver, "Architect Talk"; Diane Johnson, "Doctor Talk"; David S. Levine, "My Client Has Discussed Your Proposal to Fill the Drainage Ditch with His Partners: Legal Language"; and Liam Hudson, "Language, Truth, and Psychology"—all assembled by Leonard Michaels and Christopher Ricks, in *The State of the Language* (Berkeley: University of California Press, 1980). I was reminded of the comprehensive literary world of the hobbits by R. A. Sharpe, *Contemporary Aesthetics: a Philosophical Analysis* (New York: St. Martin's Press, 1983), through his discussion of Prokofiev's ballet dealing with the nonexistent Lieutenant Kige (p. 83). The close relationship between aesthetic language and religious language is apparently an insight we owe to Wittgenstein himself (judging by G. E. Moore's account of Wittgenstein's lectures—see his article in *Mind*, 1955, referred to by Cyril Barrett in his introduction to *Wittgenstein: Lectures and Conversations on Aesthetics Psychology and Religious Belief* (Berkeley: University of California Press, n.d.). Mary Douglas describes the nature of limit-oriented holistic societies in *Purity and Danger* (London: Routledge and Kegan Paul, 1966). The role of Gothic art in telling truths is emphasized by Georges Duby, *The Age of the Cathedrals: Art and Society, 980-1420*, translated by Eleanor Levieux and Barbara Thompson (Chicago: University of Chicago Press, 1981), and Erwin Panofsky, *Gothic Architecture and Scholasticism* (New York: World Publishing Company, 1957). My idea for dividing cultural predilections into binary opposites is clearly derived from the work of Claude Lévi-Strauss—on whom, see later—whose thought is introduced very helpfully by Edmund Leach, *Claude Lévi-Strauss* (1970; reprinted, New York: Penguin Books, 1976).

Chapter Seven takes up the theme of worship as art. The model of art for human enterprises of all sorts is distinctly in vogue today. In religion, generally, it is found in Thomas R. Martland, *Religion as Art: An Interpretation* (Albany: State University of New York, 1981). But see also Thomas J. Peters and Robert H. Waterman, Jr., *In Search of Excellence: Lessons from America's Best-Run Companies* (New York: Harper and Row, 1982), p. 61 (esp.), from whom I borrowed citations of Watson and Gell-Mann, and who imply that business is itself an art. The forerunner for this theme is Robert Nisbet, first in his *The Sociological Imagination* (New York:

Basic Books, 1966), pp. 18-20, and then in *Sociology as an Art Form* (London, Oxford, and New York: Oxford University Press, 1976), whence I have drawn several examples. The role of art in overcoming entropy is discussed by many authors, but I mention here the intriguing essay by Rudolf Arnheim, *Entropy and Art: An Essay on Disorder and Order* (Berkeley, Los Angeles, and London: University of California Press, 1971). I drew my information on scientific discovery from Hans Reichenbach, *From Copernicus to Einstein* (1927; reprinted in English translation by Ralph B. Winn, 1942, and again, New York: Dover Publications, 1980). The example of Memorial Day was chosen on the basis of W. Lloyd Warner's classic description in *American Life: Dream and Reality* (Chicago: University of Chicago Press, 1953; reprinted in Richey and Jones, *American Civil Religion* [see above]). I use the word "elements" as the building blocks of art, following Susanne K. Langer, *Feeling and Form* (New York: Charles Scribner's Sons, 1953) and *Problems of Art* (New York: Charles Scribner's Sons, 1957). The geographers to whom I refer are Peter Gould and Rodney White, *Mental Maps* (United States of America, England, and Australia: Pelican Books, 1974). My examples from Israeli society come from Charles S. Liebman and Eliezer Don-Yehiya, *Civil Religion in Israel: Traditional Religion and Political Culture in the Jewish State* (Berkeley, Los Angeles and London: University of California Press, 1983). The Jewish scheme of sacred space comes from essays by Richard S. Sarason and Joseph Gutmann in Lawrence A. Hoffman, ed., *The Land of Israel: Jewish Perspectives* (Notre Dame: University of Notre Dame Press, 1986). R. A. Sharpe (see above) emphasizes "alternative world theory," as Langer does in her own way (see above) in her theory of art as "virtual reality," and from a sociological perspective, so do Peter L. Berger and Thomas Luckmann in *The Social Construction of Reality* (New York: Doubleday, 1966). Elizabeth Kübler-Ross, *On Death and Dying* (New York: Macmillan, 1969) is cited expressly in my text. Erikson's work on the life cycle is cited above, but particularly here see his *Young Man Luther: A Study in Psychoanalysis and History* (New York and London: W. W. Norton and Company, 1958).

The issues of faith raised in Chapter Eight begin with some consideration of faith development, a field pioneered by James Fowler. For a recent overview see his essay reprinted in Craig Dykstra and Sharon Parks, *Faith Development and Fowler* (Birmingham: Religious Education Press, 1986). Erikson's eight stages find a place here, too, particularly the first one, which he sums up best in the books already cited above; but see also his *Childhood and Society* (New York and London: W. W. Norton, 1950) and the essays reprinted in *Identity and the Life Cycle* (New York and London: W. W. Norton, 1980). The Bateson model of patterns is drawn from Gregory Bateson, *Mind and Nature: A Necessary Unity* (New York: Dutton, 1979). Victor Turner discusses rituals of resolution conflict and status reversal in his *The Ritual Process: Structure and Anti-Structure* (Chicago: Aldine Publishing Co., 1969) and *Dramas, Fields, and Metaphors: Symbolic Action in Human Society* (Ithaca and London: Cornell University Press, 1974). I draw on the former also for a description of *Communitas* (which Turner links explicitly to Martin Buber's *I and Thou*) as a model of contemporary spirituality—the vertical axis. The model is fully discussed along with Otto's more normative nineteenth-century paradigm and the early "mystical" strand in Judaism and Christianity, too, in Lawrence A. Hoffman, *Beyond the Text* (Bloomington: Indiana University Press, 1987). Readers knowledgable in classical sociological theory will find echoes of Durkheim's functionalism here. I owe a special debt (again) to Mary Douglas who is a master at linking culture to social structure. For an intriguing discussion of the rivalry between popular culture and elite culture to which I allude, see Herbert J. Gans, *Popular Culture and High Culture: An Analysis and Evaluation of Taste* (New York: Basic Books, 1974). I return also to Maurice R. Stein's *Eclipse of Community* (see above), coupled with the sociological concept of limited liability communities, which I drew from Gerald D. Suttles, *The Social Construction of Communities* (Chicago and London: University of Chicago Press, 1972). The example of "Fort Baptist" is real, cited by *A Summary of Qualitative Research of the Unchurched*, a 1978 research report by the Gallup organization and the Princeton Religious Research Center and published by Religion in American Life (815 Second Avenue, New York, NY 10017).

Chapter Nine takes up the ways in which alternative worlds are presented by artists and religions, and is a cross between alternative-world theory (on which, see above) and paradigm theory (see esp. Thomas S. Kuhn, *The Structure of Scientific Revolutions* [Chicago: University of Chicago, 1962] and Kuhn's postscript in the reprinted version of 1969) and some earlier related thinking of my own regarding religious and artistic traditions—using also some of the sources cited above, like Sharpe and Martland. Ritual as theater comes, in part, from Turner (see above) and Clifford Geertz, *Interpretation of Cultures* (New York: Basic Books, 1973) and *Local Knowledge* (New York: Basic Books, 1983), esp. pp. 26-28 in the latter, where Geertz discusses the model, which he locates in Turner's thought. The cultural theme of "the city" comes directly out of Nisbet (see above), and the Gold Coast and Bohemia contrast derives from the Chicago school of urban studies summed up in Stein (see above).

The matters of space explored in Chapter Ten come from a few sources only. My diagrams are modified versions of those given by J.G. Davies in his *New Westminster Dictionary of Liturgy and Worship* (Philadelphia: Westminster Press, 1986) and Louis Bouyer, *Liturgy and Architecture* (Notre Dame: University of Notre Dame Press, 1967). The various categorizations of space as 1) fixed, semi-fixed, and personally negotiable; 2) intimate, personal, social, and public; and 3) sociopetal or sociofugal all derive from Hall's *Hidden Dimension,* which summarizes earlier data (see above), and Robert Sommer, *Personal Space* (Englewood Cliffs, New Jersey: Prentice-Hall, 1969). Sommer's *Tight Spaces: Hard Architecture and How to Humanize It* (Englewood Cliffs: Prentice-Hall, 1974) is the source for "hard architecture" as a theme. The idea of cultural analogues came in a conversation with a colleague, Gerald Lardner, at the University of Notre Dame, and was reinforced by Thornton Wilder's vivid discussion of the box stage, which reminded me of worship settings I had visited. Wilder's "Preface" to *Three Plays* (New York: Harper and Row, 1957), from which I quote, is superb. The "network effect" is cited from Ross V. Speck and Carolyn L. Attneave, *Family Networks* (New York and Toronto: Random House, 1973).

Chapters Eleven and Twelve are a unit devoted to performative communication. Saussure's linguistic breakthrough is evident from his own course notes, assembled by Charles Bally and Albert Sechehaye in collaboration with Albert Riedlinger and translated into English by Wade Baskin as *Course in General Linguistics: Ferdinand de Saussure* (New York: Philosophical Library, 1959) and discussed ubiquitously, but see as a start Jonathan Culler, *Ferdinand de Saussure* (United States of America: Penguin Books, 1977); and chapter two of Terence Hawkes, *Structuralism and Semiotics* (Berkeley and Los Angeles: University of California Press, 1977). An introduction to Wittgenstein is found in Justus Hartnack, *Wittgenstein and Modern Philosophy* (1962; reprinted in a second edition, Notre Dame: University of Notre Dame Press, 1986). The best account of Wittgenstein in context, which, however, denies any break between his early and later philosophies, is Allan Janik and Stephen Toulmin, *Wittgenstein's Vienna* (New York: Simon and Schuster, 1973). The data on his life was taken from A. J. Ayer, *Wittgenstein* (Chicago: University of Chicago Press, 1985). An introductory treatment of language functions is Peter Donovan, *Religious Language* (New York: Hawthorn Books, 1976). An alternative philosophical treatment of prayer from the perspective of the role of language is D. Z. Phillips, *The Concept of Prayer* (1965; reprinted, New York: Seabury Press, 1981). J. L. Austin (*How to Do Things with Words* [Cambridge: Harvard University Press, 1962]) is the father of performative theory, and I have also cited John R. Searle, *Speech Acts: An Essay in the Philosophy of Language* (Cambridge: Cambridge University Press, 1969). I applied Saussure on semantics and syntactics—though with a modified taxonomy—to music, and drew the Levi-Strauss analysis from his *Naked Man* (1971; English translation published, New York: Harper and Row, 1981). An understanding of musical communities comes from Fabio Dasilva, Anthony Blasi, and David Dees, *The Sociology of Music* (Notre Dame: University of Notre Dame Press, 1984). The Copland citation comes from Aaron Copland, *What to Listen for in Music* (New York: McGraw-Hill, 1939).

Chapter Thirteen recapitulates the book's argument. Peters and Waterman (see above), are cited regularly as exemplifying functional vs. dysfunctional systems, and the idea of scaling value judgments along a spectrum from taste to art to ethics is something I encountered in Sharpe (see above).